Modern American Drama: Playwriting 2000–2009

DECADES OF MODERN AMERICAN DRAMA: PLAYWRITING FROM THE 1930s TO 2009

Modern American Drama: Playwriting in the 1930s
by Anne Fletcher

Modern American Drama: Playwriting in the 1940s
by Felicia Hardison Londré

Modern American Drama: Playwriting in the 1950s
by Susan C. W. Abbotson

Modern American Drama: Playwriting in the 1960s
by Mike Sell

Modern American Drama: Playwriting in the 1970s
by Mike Vanden Heuvel

Modern American Drama: Playwriting in the 1980s
by Sandra G. Shannon

Modern American Drama: Playwriting in the 1990s
by Cheryl Black and Sharon Friedman

Modern American Drama: Playwriting 2000–2009
by Julia Listengarten and Cindy Rosenthal

Modern American Drama: Playwriting 2000–2009

Voices, Documents, New Interpretations

Julia Listengarten and Cindy Rosenthal

Series Editors: Brenda Murphy and Julia Listengarten

methuen | drama

LONDON • NEW YORK • OXFORD • NEW DELHI • SYDNEY

METHUEN DRAMA
Bloomsbury Publishing Plc
50 Bedford Square, London, WC1B 3DP, UK
1385 Broadway, New York, NY 10018, USA
29 Earlsfort Terrace, Dublin 2, Ireland

BLOOMSBURY, METHUEN DRAMA and the Methuen Drama logo
are trademarks of Bloomsbury Publishing Plc

First published in Great Britain 2018
Paperback edition first published 2021

Copyright © Julia Listengarten, Cindy Rosenthal, and contributors, 2018

Julia Listengarten and Cindy Rosenthal have asserted their right under the Copyright,
Designs and Patents Act, 1988, to be identified as authors of this work.

For legal purposes the Acknowledgements on p. x constitute
an extension of this copyright page.

Cover design by Louise Dugdale
Cover image: Supporters of Barack Obama attend a campaign rally, February 28,
2008 in Fort Worth, Texas. Photo © Charles Ommanney/Getty Images

All rights reserved. No part of this publication may be reproduced or
transmitted in any form or by any means, electronic or mechanical,
including photocopying, recording, or any information storage or retrieval
system, without prior permission in writing from the publishers.

Bloomsbury Publishing Plc does not have any control over, or responsibility for,
any third-party websites referred to or in this book. All internet addresses given
in this book were correct at the time of going to press. The author and publisher
regret any inconvenience caused if addresses have changed or sites have
ceased to exist, but can accept no responsibility for any such changes.

A catalogue record for this book is available from the British Library.

A catalog record for this book is available from the Library of Congress.

ISBN: HB: 978-1-4725-7147-2
PB: 978-1-3502-1549-8
ePDF: 978-1-3500-2476-2
eBook: 978-1-3500-2475-5
Pack: 978-1-4725-7264-6

Series: Decades of Modern American Drama: Playwriting from the 1930s to 2009

Typeset by Fakenham Prepress Solutions, Fakenham, Norfolk NR21 8NN

To find out more about our authors and books visit
www.bloomsbury.com and sign up for our newsletters.

CONTENTS

List of Tables and Boxes ix
Acknowledgements x
Biographical Note and Notes on Contributors xi
General Preface Brenda Murphy and Julia Listengarten xiii

1 Introduction: Living in the 2000s *Julia Listengarten* 1
   Background 1
   Society 2
      War on Terror 2
      Economy 4
      Education 8
      Crime 9
      Identity politics 9
      Environment 11
   Politics 12
      Timeline of major political events 14
      Terrorist attacks around the world 16
   Everyday life 17
      Family life 17
      What things cost 17
      The gadgets we purchased 19
      How much we spent 19
      Housing 19
      Work 20
      Words that entered the vocabulary and were in common
         usage 21

Trends in smoking and drug abuse 21
Culture 22
   Film 23
   Music 25
   Art 27
   Books 28
   Sport 29
   Celebrity culture and fashion 30
Media 31
   Television and television journalism 31
   Radio and newspapers 32
   Social media 33
Technology and science 34
   Digital media 34
   Timeline of major technological developments 35
   Scientific discoveries 38

2 Theatre in the 2000s *Julia Listengarten* 41
   Background 41
   Theatre responds to 9/11 43
   Theatre collectives: Site-specific, interactive and immersive work 50
   Musical theatre: Broadway and beyond 57
   Theatre for young audiences 64
   Interdisciplinary and global trends on mainstream and experimental stages 68
   New writing 78
      Companies and ventures 78
      Plays and playwrights 82
   Conclusion 88

3 Charles Mee *Scott T. Cummings* 91
   Introduction 91
   Big Love 94

bobrauschenbergamerica 98
Wintertime 105
Conclusion 108

4 Lynn Nottage *Cindy Rosenthal* 113
   Introduction 113
   Intimate Apparel 116
   Fabulation, or the Re-Education of Undine 122
   Ruined 127
   Conclusion 134

5 Theresa Rebeck *Dorothy Chansky* 137
   Introduction 137
   Omnium Gatherum 143
   Mauritius 148
   The Understudy 152
   Conclusion 155

6 Sarah Ruhl *Wendy Arons* 161
   Introduction 161
   Eurydice 165
   The Clean House 171
   In the Next Room or the vibrator play 177
   Conclusion 183

Afterword *Julia Listengarten* 185

Documents 197
   Charles Mee: Interview with Cindy Rosenthal, 17 April 2015, New York City 197
   Lynn Nottage: Interview with Cindy Rosenthal, 19 June 2015 208
   Who is it for? by *Theresa Rebeck* 219

Theresa Rebeck: Interview with Cindy Rosenthal, 21 May
   2015, New York City 224
Sarah Ruhl: Interview with Cindy Rosenthal, 10 June 2015,
   New York City 232

Notes 243
Bibliography 273
Index 285

LIST OF TABLES AND BOXES

Tables

1.1 Unemployment rates by race/ethnicity in 2009 11
1.2 Consumer Price Index 18
1.3 Median and average sales prices of new homes 20

Boxes

1.1 War on Terror 4
1.2 Pew Charitable Trusts report 7
1.3 Demographics 8
1.4 Types of crime 9
1.5 Proposition 8 10
1.6 Neoconservatism 12
1.7 The Tea Party 13
1.8 Video games 23
1.9 Film industry response to 9/11 24
1.10 The Grammy Awards 26
1.11 Writers' response to 9/11 28
1.12 2004 Super Bowl 'wardrobe malfunction' 30
1.13 *Queer Eye for the Straight Guy* 31
1.14 Social networking 33
1.15 Development of the World Wide Web 34
1.16 Technological devices 38

ACKNOWLEDGEMENTS

We would like to thank our colleagues Wendy Arons, Dorothy Chansky and Scott T. Cummings for their excellent contributions to this book. We appreciate their enthusiasm for the project and value their scholarly input throughout the process. The chapters they have contributed provide important critical perspectives on the playwrights featured in this book. The playwrights, Chuck Mee, Lynn Nottage, Theresa Rebeck and Sarah Ruhl, graciously agreed to be interviewed for the book, and we thank them for their time and critical insight. We would also like to thank Theresa Rebeck for giving us permission to publish her essay in the book.

We are grateful to the series editor Brenda Murphy for her invaluable editorial feedback. Our editors at Bloomsbury Methuen Drama, Mark Dudgeon and Emily Hockley, helped us bring this project to life, and we are thankful for their guidance and generous advice. We would like to acknowledge support offered by our respective academic institutions – the University of Central Florida and Hofstra University. Our research assistants, Alex Hodson, Elizabeth Horn, Ann Kinnebrew, Mark Nichols and Tori Oakes, were instrumental in gathering background research and bibliographic materials. Their voices undoubtedly had an impact on the shaping of the book.

This project would not have been completed without the unconditional love, support and patience of our families. We dedicate this book to them.

BIOGRAPHICAL NOTE AND NOTES ON CONTRIBUTORS

Julia Listengarten is Professor of Theatre and Artistic Director at the University of Central Florida, USA. She has worked professionally as a director and dramaturg and her translation of *Christmas at the Ivanovs'* premiered Off-Broadway at Classic Stage Company (1997) and was included in *Theater of the Avant-Garde, 1890–1950* (2001). Her research interests include modern and contemporary American theatre, avant-garde theory and performance, Russian theatre, translation theory, and nationalism in theatre. She is the author of *Russian Tragifarce: Its Cultural and Political Roots* (2000) and co-editor of *Theater of the Avant-Garde: 1950–2000* (2011) and *Playing with Theory in Theatre Practice* (2012). She has also contributed to many academic journals and edited collections including *Women, Collective Creation, and Devised Performance* (2016), *National Theatres in a Changing Europe* (2008) and *A Companion to Twentieth-Century American Drama* (2004).

Cindy Rosenthal is Professor of Drama and Dance at Hofstra University, USA. She is a scholar, theatre director, dramaturg and performer. She has directed Off-Off-Broadway (Cynthia Sophiea's *Everyone Has Tears*, TBG Theatre, NYC, 2012) and has performed professionally Off-Broadway and in regional theatre. She is a founding member of the Equity ensemble at the Bread Loaf Theatre, Vermont. Rosenthal has written on political theatre, on the avant-garde and on women playwrights and directors in the *New York Times*, *Women and Performance*, *Theatre Survey* and *TDR*. She is co-editor with James Harding of *Restaging the Sixties: Radical Theatres and Their Legacies* (2006) and *The Rise of Performance Studies: Rethinking Richard Schechner's Broad Spectrum* (2011). With Hanon Reznikov, she co-edited *Living on the Street: Plays of the Living Theatre from 1989–92* (2008). Current work includes *Ellen Stewart Presents: Fifty Years of La Mama Experimental Theatre* (forthcoming 2017).

Wendy Arons is Professor of Drama at Carnegie Mellon University in Pittsburgh, USA. Her research interests include German theatre, eighteenth- and nineteenth-century theatre history, feminist theatre and performance and ecology. She is author of *Performance and Femininity in Eighteenth-Century German Women's Writing: The Impossible Act* (Palgrave Macmillan, 2006) and co-editor, with Theresa J. May, of *Readings in Performance and Ecology* (Palgrave Macmillan, 2012). She has published articles in *Theatre Survey*, *Theatre Topics*, *The German Quarterly*, *Communications from the International Brecht Society*, *1650–1850*, *Text and Presentation* and *Theatre Journal*, as well as chapters in a number of anthologies.

Dorothy Chansky is Professor in the School of Theatre and Dance at Texas Tech University, USA. She writes about American theatre, audiences and feminist theatre, and, most recently, about translation. Her most recent book is *Kitchen Sink Realisms: Domestic Labor, Dining, and Drama in American Theatre* (University of Iowa Press, 2015). She co-edited *Food and Theatre on the World Stage* (Routledge, 2015) with Ann Folino White. Her book *Composing Ourselves: The Little Theatre Movement and the American Audience* won a President's Book Award at Texas Tech in 2006. Her work has appeared in *Theatre Journal*, *TDR*, *Text and Performance Quarterly*, *Women and Performance*, the *Journal of American Drama and Theatre*, *Theatre History Studies* and the *Journal of Adaptation in Performance and Film*.

Scott T. Cummings is Professor of Playwriting and Dramatic Literature in the Theatre Department of Boston College, USA, where he served as Chair from 2010 to 2014. His directing work for Boston College includes four different programmes of fully produced one-acts by BC student playwrights, an original devised work called *Ashley's Purpose*, and plays by Shakespeare, Marivaux, Beckett, Fornes and Mee. He is the author of *Charles Mee, Anne Bogart and the SITI Company* (Cambridge University Press, 2006) and *Maria Irene Fornes* (Routledge, 2013) and the co-editor (with Erica Stevens Abbitt) of *The Theatre of Naomi Wallace: Embodied Dialogues* (Palgrave MacMillan, 2014).

GENERAL PREFACE

Decades of Modern American Drama: Playwriting from the 1930s to 2009 is a series of eight volumes about American theatre and drama, each focusing on a particular decade during the period between 1930 and 2010. It begins with the 1930s, the decade when Eugene O'Neill was awarded the Nobel Prize for Literature and American theatre came of age. This is followed by the decade of the country's most acclaimed theatre, when O'Neill, Tennessee Williams and Arthur Miller were writing their most distinguished work, and a theatrical idiom known as 'the American style' was seen in theatres throughout the world. Its place in the world repertoire established, American playwriting has taken many turns since 1950.

The aim of this series is to focus attention on individual playwrights or collaborative teams who together reflect the variety and range of American drama during the eighty-year period it covers. In each volume, contributing experts offer detailed critical essays on four playwrights or collaborators and the significant work they produced during the decade. The essays on playwrights are presented in a rich interpretive context, which provides a contemporary perspective on both the theatre and American life and culture during the decade. The careers of the playwrights before and after the decade are summarized as well, and a section of documents, including interviews, manuscripts, reviews, brief essays and other items, sheds further light on the playwrights and their plays.

The process of choosing such a limited number of playwrights to represent the American theatre of this period has been a difficult but revealing one. In selecting them, the series editors and volume authors have been guided by several principles: highlighting the most significant playwrights, in terms both historical and aesthetic, who contributed at least two interesting and important plays during the decade; providing a wide-ranging view of the decade's theatre, including both Broadway and alternative venues; examining many historical trends in playwriting and theatrical production during the decade; and reflecting the theatre's diversity in gender and ethnicity, both across the decade and across the period as a whole. In some decades, the choices are obvious. It is hard to argue with O'Neill, Williams, Miller and Wilder in the 1940s. Other decades required a good deal of thought and discussion. Readers will inevitably regret that favourite playwrights are left out. We can only respond that we regret it too, but we believe that the playwrights who are included reflect a representative sample of the best and most interesting American playwriting during the period.

While each of the books has the same fundamental elements – an overview of life and culture during the decade, an overview of the decade's theatre and drama, the four essays on the playwrights, a section of documents, an Afterword bringing the playwrights' careers up to date, and a Bibliography of works both on the individual playwrights and on the decade in general – there are differences among the books depending on each individual volume author's decisions about how to represent and treat the decade. The various formats chosen by the volume authors for the overview essays, the wide variety of playwrights, from the canonical to the contemporary avant-garde, and the varied perspectives of the contributors' essays make for very different individual volumes. Each of the volumes stands on its own as a history of theatre in the decade and a critical study of the four individual playwrights or collaborative teams included. Taken together, however, the eight volumes offer a broadly representative critical and historical treatment of 80 years of American theatre and drama that is both accessible to a student first encountering the subject and informative and provocative for a seasoned expert.

> Brenda Murphy (Board of Trustees Distinguished Professor
> Emeritus, University of Connecticut, USA)
> Julia Listengarten (Professor of Theatre at the University of
> Central Florida, USA)
> Series Editors

1

Introduction: Living in the 2000s

Julia Listengarten

Background

What else could possibly have gone wrong in the first years of the twenty-first century? The country lived through the devastating terrorist attacks of 11 September 2001; major corporate bankruptcies; the collapse of the car industry; the deep economic recession; mass shootings; political and sex scandals. The unemployment rate rose above 10 per cent for the first time since 1983. Surveillance culture grew and intelligence gathering proliferated. Climate change led to environmental catastrophes, such as Hurricane Katrina and its aftermath. While the fear of a massive Y2K computer meltdown did not materialize on midnight of 1 January 2000, other fears soon entered the lives of many Americans: the fear of snipers near Washington, DC, and anthrax attacks, the fear of global terrorism, the fear of losing one's home, the fear of losing a job, the fear of losing a loved one to the wars in Afghanistan and Iraq.

'The noughties', as the British sometimes refer to the decade, was a period of great calamities and inventions. Indeed, this decade of major economic and political upheavals also featured many groundbreaking technological discoveries, including the explosion of Internet-based culture. It was also a decade of great paradoxes: the period of conservative politics in the country coincided with a number of progressive changes toward social equality; globalism and the growth in social networking produced a sense of isolation – both national and personal – and anxiety over the loss of identity and originality. Was it 'the lost decade' of massive political and environmental disasters? The 'digital decade' of Facebook, Twitter and video games? The decade of the 'look-at-me generation', of reality TV and celebrity culture? This chapter explores the decade from these various perspectives and discusses key events and developments in the 2000s which include

- War on a global scale
- The Great Recession
- Changing perspectives on gender and sexual identity
- Racial politics and religious intolerance
- Environmental concerns
- The rise of neoconservatism and the Tea Party
- Evolving definitions of 'family'
- The emergence of digital and social media

Society

War on Terror

> It was, we were soon told, 'the day that changed everything', the 21st century's defining moment, the watershed by which we would forever divide world history: before, and after, 9/11.
>
> Jon Henley, *Guardian*, 9 September 2011

On 11 September 2001, nineteen Islamic fundamentalists hijacked four US airliners. Two planes were crashed into the World Trade Center in New York City, collapsing the Twin Towers; one was crashed into the Pentagon, seriously damaging the building; and one that was targeted at the White House or the US Capitol instead crashed in a cornfield in Shanksville, Pennsylvania, after passengers tried to stop the hijackers. The al-Qaeda organization, led by Osama bin Laden, was responsible. Nearly 3,000 people perished as a result of the 9/11 terrorist attacks. The long-term effects included significant physical and mental health issues. In June 2007, New York City commissioned the World Trade Center Medical Group to analyse the short-term health effects of 9/11 and project the long-term care needs of people exposed at ground zero. The report, issued in 2009, found that 15,688 people that year received publicly funded treatment for World Trade Center-related health conditions. Furthermore, over 40,000 first responders and workers were screened or monitored for disease.

In response to the 9/11 attacks, the US launched wars in Afghanistan and Iraq in 2001 and 2003, respectively, with the support of an international coalition. These would become the longest military conflicts in US history. In Iraq, US military fatalities exceeded 4,300 up to 2009. In Afghanistan, US combat deaths numbered 946 up to 2009.

The immediate and long-lasting effects of the wars on the US military personnel deployed in Afghanistan and Iraq included post-traumatic stress disorder (PTSD), traumatic brain injury (TBI), major limb amputations and self-inflicted wounds. In 2003, there were 977 cases of the PTSD diagnosis reported among the deployed personnel; by 2009, the number rose to 13,863. TBI cases reached 28,877 by 2009.[1]

As the country engaged in the War on Terror, various national security policies emerged, authorizing domestic surveillance as well as detention and interrogation programmes. The establishment of the Department of Homeland Security aimed to unify national security efforts. The National Security Agency (NSA) implemented the Terrorist Surveillance Program (TSP) to intercept al-Qaeda communications, although the programme was later implicated in engaging in widespread domestic surveillance. Blackwater Security Consulting, a private security company, was contracted by the Federal government to conduct risky and at times controversial military operations in the wake of 9/11. During the 16 September 2007 Blackwater operation in Iraq, seventeen Iraqis were killed and twenty-four wounded when Blackwater operators opened fire in a traffic circle in central Baghdad.

BOX 1.1: WAR ON TERROR

The War on Terror, a phrase first used by President Bush on 20 September 2001, is an ideological concept that emerged after the 11 September attacks to fight terrorism. It also refers to the series of international military and diplomatic campaigns aimed at putting an end to international terrorism, largely associated with radical Islamist groups such as al-Qaeda, Hezbollah and Hamas. The War on Terror campaigns were launched by the US, with support from NATO and other allies, in the aftermath of the 11 September terrorist attacks.

In addition to the Bush administration-led wars in Afghanistan and Iraq, the War on Terror also involved covert military operations and new security legislation, as well as efforts to block the financing of terrorist organizations. There was widespread criticism of 'War on Terror' as an approach to combating global terrorism and strengthening national security. Critics argued that, instead, this concept promoted an ideology of fear and mistrust, both domestically and internationally.

Economy

The decade's economy in the US was plagued by a series of crises leading to a major economic decline, also referred to as the Great Recession. The decade began with the dot-com bubble bursting and ended with the meltdown of the financial system caused by the crisis in subprime mortgages.

The development of the global economy prompted the outsourcing of US service and technology, which precipitated what Thomas Friedman called the 'flattening' of the world.[2] The rise of China and India as world financial powers presented a challenge to the US economy, as the global balance of power began to shift toward the East.

Dot-com bubble burst

The period of the dot-com bubble (also referred to as the Internet bubble or information technology bubble), which began roughly in 1997, achieved its climax on 10 March 2000, when the NASDAQ stock exchange soared to over 5,100.00 in intraday trading. The bubble was created by a combination of rising stock prices, market confidence in future profitability of dot-com companies and easily obtainable venture capital. In April 2000, inflation reports triggered the collapse of the bubble. As a result, a large number of information technology companies ran out of capital and filed for bankruptcy. Many companies were subsequently liquidated or acquired. In March 2000, the market value of NASDAQ companies peaked at $6.7 trillion; in October 2002, it reached its bottom at $1.6 trillion.[3]

Corporate and investment frauds

The decade was marked by a significant rise in fraud involving major corporate organizations and accounting firms. These scandals stemmed from improper accounting practices: inflated revenues, overstated sales, understated earnings, misused or misdirected funds.

2001: Enron, a top energy company, and Arthur Andersen, one of the top five public accounting firms, were involved in corporate fraud that resulted in the bankruptcy of Enron and dissolution of Arthur Andersen. Shareholders lost more than $60 billion.

2002: WorldCom, a major telecommunications company, was caught in fraudulent accounting operations to maintain the price of its stock. As a result, the company filed for bankruptcy. According to investigators, the company's total assets had been inflated by about $11 billion.

2002: Tyco, a manufacturer of electronic components and health care and safety equipment, also became engulfed in an accounting scandal when its CEO, Dennis Kozlowski, along with several other top executives, was exposed for selling shares of unauthorized stock for $450 million and smuggling these funds out of the country disguised as executives' bonuses and benefits.

2008: Bernard Madoff, owner of an investment advisory firm and former chairman of NASDAQ, admitted to running a huge Ponzi scheme, as a result of which his investors had been defrauded of $18 billion. Madoff's Ponzi scheme was one of the largest investment frauds in Wall Street history.

Subprime housing collapse and financial crisis

In the first half of the decade, the housing market was thriving, housing values kept inflating and the phenomenon known as subprime lending began to emerge. Subprime and alternative mortgages with very low or no down payments and very low initial rates became available for people without steady jobs or with tainted credit histories who would not have qualified for regular mortgages in the past. These mortgages were then packaged into mortgage-backed securities and sold to investors. As the interest rates rose, the mortgage payments became increasingly higher, and the inflated housing prices went down. These people were unable to make their mortgage payments and were eventually crushed by debt. As a result, home foreclosures rose and the value of the mortgage-backed securities fell. As of September 2008, 25 million subprime and other mortgages were outstanding, with an unpaid principal of over $4.5 trillion. This led to the collapse of major investment banks, whose portfolios of loans were worth nothing. Some of these institutions had also been involved in fraudulent accounting practices such as deceitful transactions (in the case of Lehman Brothers). In late 2008, the Bush administration stepped in to mitigate the financial crisis by creating the Troubled Assets Relief Program (TARP) to bail out failing financial institutions.

Economic downfall of 2008

As banks had no lending ability because of their loss of assets, consumers and businesses could no longer borrow money, which affected their spending and productivity growth. New houses did not sell. The amount of foreclosures became unprecedented. Unemployment rose and consumer spending went down.

By the time the Obama administration reached the White House in January of 2009, the economy was in a deep recession. The US national debt more than doubled (from $5,674,178,209,886.86 in 2000 to $11,909,829,003,511.75 in 2009) due in part to governmental efforts to mitigate the financial crisis. At the end of 2009, the US economy began to show some signs of recovery. A Pew Charitable Trusts report provides some relevant detail.[4]

BOX 1.2: PEW CHARITABLE TRUSTS REPORT

Income: US households lost on average $5,800 in income from September 2008 through to 2009.

Government spending: Federal spending, due to government interventions to alleviate the financial crisis (Troubled Assets Relief Program), amounted to $2,050 for each household.

Home values: The US lost $3.4 trillion in real estate wealth between July 2008 and March 2009, according to the Federal Reserve – $30,300 per household. The subprime mortgage crisis resulted in 500,000 more foreclosures than had been expected.

Stock values: The US lost $7.4 trillion in stock wealth from July 2008 to March 2009, according to the Federal Reserve – roughly $66,200 per household.

Jobs: 5.5 million more American jobs were lost during the financial crisis because of slower economic growth than had been predicted.

The economic crisis had major global repercussions. The US economy experienced significant decline in the growth of both exports and imports, which led to slowing production and employment cuts in the rest of the world.

> **BOX 1.3: DEMOGRAPHICS**
>
> In December 2009, the US population was 308.2 million. Non-Hispanic whites made up about two-thirds of the population.

Education

The unsatisfactory quality of American elementary and secondary education continued to be a hot topic in political debates. To effect major changes in public education, President Bush signed the No Child Left Behind Act into law in 2002. This reform focused on four principles: stronger accountability for results, increased flexibility and local control, expanded options for parents, and teaching methods that had been proven to work.

In an effort to improve elementary and secondary education, the Common Core State Standard Initiative was announced on 1 June 2009 to provide consistent and clear expectations of what students must learn.

Secondary education graduation rates increased. In 2009–10, 3,128,022 public school students nationwide received a high school diploma; this resulted in an Averaged Freshman Graduation Rate of 78.2 per cent.[5] In post-secondary education, between 2000 and 2008 the proportion of adults aged twenty-four and older with a bachelor's degree or higher increased from 24 per cent to 28 per cent. The proportion of adults with an associate degree rose from 6 per cent to 8 per cent, while the number of adults completing college education without receiving a degree remained 21 per cent.

Although educational achievement continued to increase among all racial and ethnic groups, there were still considerable gaps. In 2008, 31 per cent of non-Hispanic whites and 50 per cent of Asian Americans had completed college or graduate education, compared to only 13 per cent of Hispanics and 18 per cent of Blacks.[6]

Between 1999 and 2009, published tuition for four-year colleges increased by 39.8 per cent from the previous year; for two-year colleges, tuition increased by 3.1 per cent.

Crime

In 2002, the US incarceration rate reached the highest level in the world. The total number of prisoners continued to increase, from 6,437,400 in 2000 to 7,225,800 in 2009. While rates of violent crime declined (the homicide rate declined by nearly half, from 9.3 homicides per 100,000 residents in 1992 to 4.7 in 2011), crime involving federal offences and firearms slightly increased. In 2009, the number of people arrested on suspicion of federal offences reached 183,000, a significant rise from 140,000 in 2005. Firearm violence increased from 7.3 per cent of all violence in 2000 to 7.4 per cent in 2009; firearm homicides also increased from 1.7 per cent in 2000 to 2.7 per cent in 2009.[7]

Drug cases remained the most prevalent in terms of adjudication and sentencing. In 2009, five judicial districts along the US–Mexico border had more than 56 per cent of all federal arrests.

BOX 1.4: TYPES OF CRIME

New types of crime involved cybercrime and online bullying. Examples of cybercrime included hacking, theft of information in electronic form, email bombing, virus/worm attacks and Trojan attacks. The decade also experienced an increase in corporate fraud and a spike in mass shootings. The deadliest mass shooting occurred in April 2007, when a student at Virginia Tech killed thirty-two people and wounded fifteen others before shooting himself.

Identity politics

While the gender inequality gap continued to decrease, issues such as lower wages for women, a small percentage of women in leadership positions and a declining number of women in the labour force persisted. In 2010, women in the US on average received 81 per cent of the salary of their male counterparts, compared to about 62 per cent in 1979. In 2009, only 24 per cent of chief executive officers (CEOs) in the US were women, and their salaries were 74.5 per cent of what male CEOs earned.[8] While women's participation in US labour during the previous decades had increased, between 2000 and 2010 it dropped from 60 per cent of representation to 46.7 per cent.[9]

LGBTQ (lesbian, gay, bisexual, transgender and queer) rights evolved in varying degrees by state. Starting in 2000, some states began to recognize civil unions between same-sex couples. In 2004, Massachusetts became the first state to issue marriage licences to same-sex couples. By 2009, five states had passed same-sex marriage legislation.

Many states outlawed discrimination based on sexual orientation and gender identity. Hate crimes also became punishable by federal law under the Matthew Shepard and James Byrd Jr. Hate Crimes Prevention Act of 2009.

BOX 1.5: PROPOSITION 8

Proposition 8, or Prop 8, was a California ballot proposition and a state constitutional amendment that defined marriage as a relationship between a man and a woman. Created by opponents of same-sex marriage, it was passed in 2008 during state elections, overturning previous legalization of same-sex marriages by the state. A federal court then ruled Proposition 8 unconstitutional in 2010.

The decade experienced remarkable achievements in race relations ranging from culture to politics. Colin Powell became the first African American to serve as Secretary of State (2001); Halle Berry and Denzel Washington won the Academy Awards for Best Actress and Best Actor in the same year (2002); Condoleezza Rice became the first African American woman to serve as Secretary of State (2005); Barack Obama became the first African American to win the presidency (2008); Sonia Sotomayor became the first Hispanic Supreme Court Justice (2009). Despite these significant strides, racial and ethnic inequalities remained obdurate, especially in employment and income distribution, criminalization and immigration policies, and life expectancy.

Table 1.1 Unemployment rates by race/ethnicity in 2009

Asian-Americans	Whites	Hispanics	Blacks
7.5%	8.7%	12.4%	15.3%

The recession of 2008 hit African-American and Latina/Latinx communities particularly hard. The 4-percentage-point gap between unemployment rates for whites and Blacks in 2000 grew to nearly 7 percentage points by 2009. The unemployment gap between whites and Latina/Latinx increased significantly as well.[10] In the wake of the 9/11 terrorist attacks, racial profiling and religious intolerance surged. A *New York Times* article reported in 2006 that 'in the aftermath of Sept. 11, Arab Americans [had] a greater fear of racial profiling and immigration enforcement than of falling victim to hate crimes'.[11]

Environment

The alarming environmental changes raised concerns about the world's irresponsible consumption of natural resources, prompting research groups, business corporations and politicians to think of new ways to make our planet a greener, cleaner and ecologically safer place. The topic of climate change and its negative effects received much attention both domestically and globally, especially after the melting of the Antarctic ice sheet and the recession of Arctic glaciers that occurred significantly faster than experts had predicted. Melting ice, drought, early springs and disappearing polar bears, among other species, were some of the disconcerting effects of the decade's climate change. Climate change was also linked to devastating natural disasters such as the Southeast Asian tsunami in 2004 and Hurricane Katrina in 2005.

Developing renewable energy sources and clean energy technologies became one of the principal goals of major environmental research and investment programmes. According to a 2009 United Nations Environment Program report, in 2008, $155 billion was invested globally in renewable energy, including hydropower and biofuels, a fourfold increase since 2004. While the US continued to lag in its effort to embrace green initiatives, politicians and businesses paid more attention to environmental protection. During all three presidential elections in the period, environmental concerns became a significant element in presidential debates. To protect the country's key natural resources, the Obama administration launched America's Great Outdoors Initiative in 2010.

Other global environmental concerns included overpopulation, the water crisis, oil and coal ash spills, nuclear waste disposal, endangered species, pandemics and superbugs, all rooted in environmental causes.

Politics

A Republican held the White House for most of the decade. George W. Bush became the 43rd US president after the Supreme Court ruling in his 2000 election dispute with Democrat Al Gore and won re-election in 2004. Barack Obama, a Democratic senator from Illinois, won the 2008 election and became the first African American president in US history.

National security drove domestic and foreign policies after the 9/11 attacks. As a result of the Homeland Security Act in 2002, the Bush administration formed the US Department of Homeland Security as 'a concerted national effort to prevent terrorist attacks within the United States, reduce America's vulnerability to terrorism, and minimize the damage and recover from attacks that do occur'.[12] The US foreign policy after the 9/11 attacks that relied on a strategy of 'preemptive strikes' to protect the security of the country is often referred to as 'the Bush Doctrine'.[13]

BOX 1.6: NEOCONSERVATISM

Neoconservatives (at times referred to as neocons) rose to prominence during the Bush presidency and played a crucial role in promoting and planning the invasion of Iraq. Prominent neoconservatives in the administration included Vice President Dick Cheney, Donald Rumsfeld, Paul Wolfowitz, Richard Perle and Paul Bremer. Neoconservatism advocates promotion of American interests in international affairs and adopts strategies such as the use of military force.

The 2001 invasion of Afghanistan was followed by the 2003 Operation Iraqi Freedom. Its main mission, according to Bush, was 'to disarm Iraq of weapons of mass destruction, to end Saddam Hussein's support for terrorism, and to free the Iraqi people'.[14]

The wars in Afghanistan and Iraq became increasingly unpopular, especially after the dissemination of official findings that Iraq had no chemical or biological weapons of mass destruction before the invasion. The public discontent with the wars also stemmed from the spikes in violence in Afghanistan and Iraq, as well as the rising numbers of US military casualties. In the meantime, the US grappled with the challenges of globalization, such as terrorism, growing environmental concerns and financial and economic crises.

During the Bush administration, economic policies included the tax cuts of 2001 and 2003, the Economic Stimulus Act of 2008 to boost the economy and prevent the recession, and the Emergency Economic Stabilization Act of 2008, commonly referred to as a bailout of the US financial system.[15] In 2009, President Obama formed the Presidential Task Force on the Auto Industry to manage the financial bailout of car manufacturers Chrysler and General Motors. Following task force recommendations, which included fuel-efficient cars, the US government loaned $25 billion to the companies.

BOX 1.7: THE TEA PARTY

The Tea Party, which emerged as a grassroots political movement, consists of libertarian, populist and conservative activists. It sprang up in full force in early 2009 with multiple protests, including one at the US Capitol and National Mall, demanding reduction of government spending and taxes. (The Tea Party has also been called an 'AstroTurf' movement – a fake grassroots movement that actually was started and financed by elite groups.)

Timeline of major political events[16]

2000

George W. Bush won the US presidency after the Supreme Court ruling despite winning fewer popular votes than Al Gore.

Hillary Rodham Clinton won a United States Senate seat from New York, becoming the first First Lady to win public office.

2001

11 September: The terror attacks on the US orchestrated by Islamic fundamentalists caused nearly 3,000 deaths.

18 September: The first anthrax attacks by mail against targets among journalists and government officials were reported.

7 October: In response to the 11 September attacks, the US military, and its United Kingdom ally, began the first phase in the War on Terror by launching an offensive against the Taliban and al-Qaeda in Afghanistan. This war became the longest military conflict in US history.

26 October: Bush signed into law the USA PATRIOT Act. Its title stands for 'Uniting and Strengthening America by Providing Appropriate Tools Required to Intercept and Obstruct Terrorism'.

2002

21 May: The State Department declared that seven nations sponsored terrorism: Iran, Iraq, Cuba, Libya, North Korea, Sudan and Syria.

2003

March: The US invaded Iraq, coordinating military operations with British, Australian, Polish and Danish ground troops.

April: The US-led coalition seized control of Baghdad, driving Iraqi President Saddam Hussein from power. He was later arrested and executed on 30 December 2006.

June to November: Amnesty International and the Associated Press reported that the US military and the CIA abused detainees at Abu Ghraib prison in Iraq. In 2004, the American Civil Liberties Union released documents obtained under the Freedom of Information

Act that indicated that the US government authorized the use of torture ('enhanced interrogation techniques') against prisoners at Guantanamo Bay, Cuba, and in Afghanistan and Iraq.

2004

January: The CIA's top weapons adviser in Iraq, David Kay, admitted that the country possessed no active weapons of mass destruction or related production facilities before the war – refuting the US justification of the invasion. In September, Kay's successor as the CIA's chief weapons inspector, Charles Duelfer, testified before Congress that Hussein had no chemical or biological weapons and no capacity to make nuclear weapons.

2 November: Bush won re-election over Democratic Senator John Kerry from Massachusetts.

2005

29 August: Hurricane Katrina's storm surge overwhelmed levees in greater New Orleans, flooding 80 per cent of the city: the confirmed death toll was 1,836 and the total damage was estimated at $108 billion. Katrina, arguably the greatest natural disaster in US history, prompted heated public debates about the local, state and federal governments' lack of preparation and mismanagement of relief efforts.

2006

In the mid-term elections, the Democratic Party won control of both the US House of Representatives and the Senate. This overwhelming victory was attributed to growing public discontent over the Bush administration's Iraq policy.

2007

January: California Representative Nancy Pelosi became the first woman Speaker of the US House of Representatives.

January: Bush announced a 'surge' of additional troops into Iraq to stop attacks against coalition forces and civilians.

June: A terror plot to blow up jet fuel supply tanks and pipelines at JFK International Airport in New York was foiled.

2008

October: Bush signed into law the Emergency Economic Stabilization Act – a bailout of the US financial system. The $700 billion Troubled Assets Relief Program to purchase failing bank assets was the government's response to the subprime mortgage crisis.

November: Barack Obama overwhelmingly won the presidential election over John McCain. Obama became the 44th US president in January 2009.

2009

February: Obama signed into law the American Recovery and Reinvestment Act, an economic stimulus package.

April: Some 750 Tea Party protests emerged across the nation in response to government spending, such as the bailout of the banking and car industries that had begun during the Bush administration and expanded under Obama.

October: Joblessness climbed above 10 per cent, signalling that the recession had deepened.

December: Obama announced a 'surge' of 30,000 additional troops in Afghanistan to curb increased Taliban attacks.

Terrorist attacks around the world

2001, 11 September: 9/11 terrorist attacks, US (2,996 killed)
2002, October: Bali bombings, Indonesia (202 killed)
2002, October: Moscow theatre hostage crisis, Russia (130 killed)
2003, November: Istanbul bombings, Turkey (57 killed)
2004, March: Madrid train bombings, Spain (191 killed)
2004, September: Beslan school hostage crisis, Russia (334 killed)
2005, July: London bombings, UK (56 killed)
2007, August: Yazidi communities bombings, Iraq (796 killed)
2008, November: Mumbai attacks, India (164 killed)

Everyday life

Family life

The definition of family continued to expand, especially with the legalization of civil unions and same-sex marriages. Despite legal hurdles concerning adoption for same-sex partners, the percentage of gays and lesbians with adopted children increased. While only about 8 per cent of same-sex couples had an adopted child in 2000, this number rose to about 19 per cent in 2009.

Both marriage and divorce rates continued to decline. Whereas in 2000, the marriage rate was 8.2 per 1,000 individuals, in 2009 it dropped to 6.8. In 2000, the divorce rate was 4 per 1,000 people; in 2009 it decreased to 3.5.[17]

Pregnancy rates declined, reaching their lowest level in twelve years in 2009: 102.1 per 1,000 women aged fifteen to forty-four. Pregnancy rates for women younger than age thirty dropped; rates for women thirty and older increased. Rates for teenage pregnancy dropped, reaching a historically low level in 2009. Also, the abortion rate in 2009 was at its lowest level since 1976. Birth rates slightly rose in the middle of the decade but dropped again by 2009: from 2008 to 2009, the number of births declined by 3 per cent.[18]

Life expectancy continued to increase gradually. In 2009, life expectancy was 80.9 years for white women, 77.6 years for Black women, 76.4 years for white men and 71.1 years for Black men.[19]

What things cost

From 2000 to 2009, the Consumer Price Index (the government's inflation measure) as a whole rose by 24.5 per cent.

Table 1.2 Consumer Price Index

Product	1999 price	2009 price	Change
Slurpee, largest, 7-11	$0.99	$2.12	114.14%
Gallon of petrol	$1.30	$2.56	96.92%
Disneyland (one-day adult ticket)	$41.00	$72.00	75.61%
Average expanded basic cable (per month)	$31.22	$49.65	59.03%
Babysitting (per hour)	$7–$10	$10–$15	50.00%
Budweiser (six-pack of cans)	$4.01	$5.99	49.38%
Cinema ticket	$5.06	$7.18	41.90%
Aspirin (Bayer, 100-count)	$3.47	$4.81	38.62%
Sugar, 5 lb.	$2.13	$2.90	36.15%
Cheerios, one box	$3.89	$5.15	32.39%
Stamp, US, first class	$0.33	$0.44	33.33%
Cigarettes (Marlboro, per pack, California)	$4.65	$5.95	27.96%
Mobile phone bill (average)	$40.24	$49.57	23.19%
McDonald's Big Mac	$2.50	$2.99	19.60%
Coca-Cola, 1 litre	$1.14	$1.34	17.54%
Wedding, average cost	$18,900.00	$20,398.00	7.93%
Gallon of milk	$2.88	$3.05	5.90%
Coffee (Maxwell House, 34.5 oz.)	$9.99	$9.49	−5.01%
Average domestic airfare	$329.00	$301.00	−8.51%
Credit card average APR	15.07%	13.71%	−9.02%
Batteries (4 AA, Energizer)	$3.99	$3.49	−12.53%
iMac desktop computer	$1,499.00	$999.00	−33.36%

Online shopping grew rapidly, as products were being advertised via video ads on websites, contextual ads on search engines and text messages to mobile phones.[20]

The gadgets we purchased

iPhone, Amazon Kindle, iPod, Garmin GPS, Wii Remote, TiVo DVR, Slingbox, Blackberry, XBox, Sony PlayStation 3/Blu-Ray, Sonos Multi-room Music System, Flip Video Ultra, Jabra Bluetooth earpiece, USB flash drive.

How much we spent

According to the US Bureau of Labor Statistics,[21] in 2008 average annual expenditures per consumer unit (i.e. family) were as follows:

Average annual expenditures	$50,486
Food at home	$3,744
Food away from home	$2,698
Housing	$17,109
Petrol and motor oil	$2,715
Healthcare	$1,976
Apparel and services	$1,801
Personal care products and services	$616
Education	$1,046
Entertainment	$2,835
Alcoholic beverages	$444
Tobacco products	$317

Housing

In 2008, homeownership was at 66.6 per cent, a decline from 67.2 per cent in 2007. As a result of the housing bubble and subprime mortgage crisis, foreclosures reached a record high: during the third quarter of 2009, one in every 136 housing units received a foreclosure filing.[22]

Table 1.3 Median and average sales prices of new homes

Year	Median	Average
2000	$169,000	$207,000
2001	$175,200	$213,200
2002	$187,600	$228,700
2003	$195,100	$246,300
2004	$221,000	$274,500
2005	$240,900	$297,000
2006	$246,500	$305,900
2007	$247,900	$313,600
2008	$232,100	$292,600
2009	$216,700	$270,900

Work

Unemployment statistics

From January 2000 to December 2009, unemployment rose from 4.0 per cent to 9.9 per cent, with the big hike from 2008 to 2009 due to the recession. As of October 2009, nearly 16 million people in the United States were unemployed.

Average earnings

In 2000, median household income was $53,164. By 2004, it fell to $51,174, then recovered to an extent by 2007 before it fell to an even lower level by 2010: $49,445. By 2010 the (inflation-adjusted) household income level was 7 per cent below that in 2000.

Poverty

In 2008, a family with two adults and two children was considered poor if its income fell below $21,834. In 2008, the total poverty rate rose to 13 per cent, while the child poverty rate reached 19 per cent, marking the highest rates since 1997. For working-age adults, poverty increased by 1 per cent from 2007 to 2008.[23]

Words that entered the vocabulary and were in common usage

American Dialect Society's Words of the Year:

2000: **chad** (from the 2000 US presidential election controversy, in reference to fragments hanging from paper ballots during the manual recount of votes in Florida)
2001: **9/11**
2002: **weapons of mass destruction** (or WMD, in the Iraq War)
2003: **metrosexual** (an urban man concerned about his grooming and fashion)
2004: **red state, blue state, purple state** (from US elections)
2005: **truthiness** (coined by television comedian Stephen Colbert)
2006: **plutoed** (demoted or devalued, as was the former planet Pluto)
2007: **subprime** (a risky loan to someone with poor credit)
2008: **bailout** (a government rescue of a collapsing corporation)
2009: **tweet** (a short post sent via Twitter)
2010: **app** (application software)

The word of the decade was **google** (used as a verb).

Other popular words included **Y2K, dot-com, blog, texting, sustainable, embedded.**

New phrases included **climate change, financial tsunami, ground zero, war on terror, carbon footprint, cloud computing.**

Trends in smoking and drug abuse

Smoking declined as a result of stricter regulations on tobacco advertising and restrictions in public places. Anti-smoking tobacco policies led to the significant price increase for tobacco products, which also contributed to the decline in smoking. The decade experienced unprecedented deaths from drug overdoses. Since 1980, overdose death rates increased five times. By 2009, drug overdose deaths had outnumbered deaths resulting from motor vehicle crashes. Prescription drugs, especially opioid analgesics, were increasingly involved in overdose deaths. During this period, opioid-related overdose deaths exceeded overdose deaths involving all illicit drugs such as heroin and cocaine. Rates of emergency room visits because of pharmaceutical misuse or abuse escalated dramatically.[24]

Culture

Corporate entertainment and technology continued to affect the development of culture. With a huge jump in broadband Internet (there were 77.4 million broadband subscribers in the US in December 2008) and an increased use of wireless networks, blogs, portals, intranets and wikis became common electronic dissemination methods for professionals, amateurs and businesses.

Peer-to-peer technology such as Skype and file-sharing applications such as KaZaA and Limewire made cultural exchanges, communication and peer evaluation more effective. While the debate over the ethics of file-sharing continued, legal music download services such as iTunes and streaming services such as Spotify opened up new markets.

Netflix began to provide online digital streaming in 2007 while it continued to rent DVDs to its subscribers through an online service: by 2009, its DVD collection had grown to include 1,000,000 titles and its subscriber base had exceeded 10 million users. Hulu (2007) and Amazon Instant Video (2008, initially called Amazon Video on Demand) also entered the market, providing instant streaming of selected films and TV shows.

With the help of the latest technology, stand-up comedy achieved new popularity, reaching a wider audience across ages, races, genders and economic status. Comedians celebrated cultural idiosyncrasies and embraced technological innovations, employing various media. Performers such as Sarah Silverman, John

Leguizamo and Dave Chapelle won public acclaim by confronting and subverting gender stereotypes and ethnic/racial assumptions. Dane Cook became one of the first comedians to maximize the potential of Internet marketing (such as MySpace), reaching a large young audience. Dan Whitney offered blue-collar comedy. Other noteworthy comedians included Chris Rock and Aziz Ansari.

BOX 1.8: VIDEO GAMES

The video game industry's profits surpassed the profits of the film industry in 2004. With a constant advancement of video game consoles – PlayStation 2 (2000), Xbox 360 (2005) and PlayStation 3 (2006) – the quality of 3D graphics significantly improved. As video gaming increasingly became one of the cultural markers of the 2000s, criticism emerged about the games' violent content (as in *Grand Theft Auto* and *Super Columbine Massacre RPG*) and addictive effect.

Film

The decade's top-grossing movies included *Avatar* (2009), *The Dark Knight* (2008), *Shrek 2* (2004) and *The Lord of the Rings: The Return of the King* (2003). Major trends encompassed the proliferation of science fiction and fantasy, the impact of technology on popular culture and the celebration of a superhero. The decade produced a considerable number of film sequels such as *Pirates of the Caribbean* and *Shrek*, as well as movies based on novels such as *Harry Potter* and *The Da Vinci Code*, demonstrating a continued trend toward the mass commercialization of the film industry.

Notable highlights of the Academy Awards included:

2001: The 'Best Animated Feature Film' category was added; *Shrek* won the award.

The decade experienced a surge of African American winners in the categories of Best Actor/Actress and Best Supporting Actor/Actress. Between 2000 and 2009, seven awards were presented to African Americans: Denzel Washington (Best Actor, *Training Day*, 2001), Halle Berry (Best Actress, *Monster's Ball*, 2001), Jamie Foxx (Best Actor, *Ray*, 2004), Morgan Freeman (Best Supporting Actor, *Million Dollar Baby*, 2004), Forest Whitaker (Best Actor, *The Last King of Scotland*, 2006), Jennifer Hudson (Best Supporting Actress, *Dreamgirls*, 2006) and Mo'Nique (Best Supporting Actress, *Precious*, 2009).

2005: Ang Lee received the Best Director Oscar for *Brokeback Mountain*, a 'gay cowboy movie' about a sexual/romantic relationship between two men.

BOX 1.9: FILM INDUSTRY RESPONSE TO 9/11

The film industry's response to 9/11 included Spike Lee's *25th Hour* (2002), the television movie *DC 9/11: Time of Crisis* (2003), Oliver Stone's *World Trade Center* (2006) and Paul Greengrass's *United 93* (2006). Michael Moore's *Fahrenheit 9/11* (2004), a biting commentary on Bush administration politics in the aftermath of the 9/11 terrorist attacks, became the biggest-grossing documentary of all time. It won major film awards including the Palme d'Or at the 2004 Cannes Film Festival.

Other documentaries that raised social consciousness in the decade included Moore's *Bowling for Columbine* (2002), exploring the roots of gun violence in the US, and Al Gore and Davis Guggenheim's *An Inconvenient Truth* (2006), pointing to the dangers of global warming.

2009: *The Hurt Locker* received the Best Picture Oscar, and its director, Kathryn Bigelow, became the first woman to win Best Director. The film's plot centres on the lives of American soldiers during the Iraq War.

Other movies that won Best Picture from 2000 to 2009 were *Gladiator* (2000), *A Beautiful Mind* (2001), *Chicago* (2002), *The Lord of the Rings: The Return of the King* (2003), *Million Dollar*

Baby (2004), *Crash* (2005), *The Departed* (2006), *No Country for Old Men* (2007) and *Slumdog Millionaire* (2008). The decade also featured increased representation of foreign-born actors and directors among the Oscar winners: Benicio del Toro (Best Supporting Actor, *Traffic*, 2000), Roman Polanski (Best Director, *The Pianist*, 2002) and Javier Bardem (Best Supporting Actor, *No Country for Old Men*, 2007). Notable films depicting foreign settings included *Slumdog Millionaire*, 2008 (Best Picture and Best Director – Danny Boyle), and *The Pianist*, 2002 (Best Actor – Adrienne Brody, and Best Director – Polanski).

Music

The decade's technological advances made a significant impact on music's digital distribution, marketing and public access. Napster, a free online digital music-sharing website, operated from 1999 until 2001, closing because of copyright infringement (it later reopened as a paid membership website). With the downfall of Napster, the iPod (2001) and iTunes (2001) stepped in to appeal to the younger generation. Apple claimed that the iPod became the fastest-selling music player in history. Apple's iTunes Music Store (2003) sold individual songs in digital format for less than a dollar and became the biggest music market and most convenient way for music distribution. With the launch of YouTube (2005), music sharing entered a new era: homemade music videos went viral, bringing overnight popularity to artists. Live concerts, however, continued to draw big crowds of music fans. Music began to cross cultures, with the influence of rap, hip-hop and pop around the world.

The decade offered a variety of music genres; these genres included hip-hop (Eminem, Kanye West, Jay-Z), R&B (Alicia Keys, Beyoncé, Rihanna, Usher), Pop (Britney Spears; country style – Taylor Swift), electronic pop (Lady Gaga), pop (pop punk music – Blink 182; Emo music – Jimmy Eat World; garage rock – the Strokes, the White Stripes), jazz (Norah Jones) and others. The boy-band craze of the 1990s abated; Justin Timberlake (formerly of N'Sync) moved on to have a successful solo career as a singer and actor. The use of Auto-Tune technology (audio processor) and futuristic synthesizers changed the sound of pop music, popularized by the Black Eyed Peas with songs such as 'I Gotta Feeling'. The 'mashup' emerged as a musical form that juxtaposes several songs different in style. Children's pop music had a strong presence, with movies, TV shows and artists such as the Cheetah Girls, High School Musical, Hannah Montana and the Jonas Brothers.

> ## BOX 1.10: THE GRAMMY AWARDS
>
> The Grammy Award recipients for Best New Artist were Christina Aguilera (2000), Shelby Lynne (2001), Alicia Keys (2002), Norah Jones (2003), the rock metal band Evanescence (2004), the pop rock band Maroon 5 (2005), John Legend (2006) and Carrie Underwood (2007). The 2008 and 2009 awards went to the British singers Amy Winehouse and Adele.

Notable events in music include:

2001: A tribute concert for 9/11 aired on VH1 on 20 October, with performances by Paul McCartney, the Rolling Stones, Bon Jovi, the Who, Billy Joel and others.

After Eminem's album *The Marshall Mathers LP* drew backlash from the Gay and Lesbian Alliance Against Defamation, openly gay singer Elton John responded by performing with Eminem at the Grammy Awards in 2001. The message he sent was that he would 'rather tear down walls between people than build them up'.

2002: *American Idol* – an American singing competition series based on the British series *Pop Idol* – became one of the most popular television shows. It is also noteworthy for its interactive feature: winners were selected by viewers voting through telephone, Internet and text messaging. Kelly Clarkson won the first season.

2003: 'From the Big Apple to the Big Easy' was a collaborative music event involving Madison Square Garden and Radio City Music Hall to raise funds for the Hurricane Katrina relief efforts. Proceeds from the simultaneous benefit concerts reached $9 million;

performers included Elton Jones, Irma Thomas, Lenny Kravitz and Elvis Costello.

2009: Michael Jackson, the self-proclaimed 'King of Pop', died. His personal physician was found guilty of involuntary manslaughter for administering Jackson a massive dose of the anaesthetic propofol. After his death, Jackson became the bestselling albums artist of 2009.

Art

Technology permeated the decade's art scene. The trends included multimedia installations created with new technology, virtual art tours of museums and galleries and the use of social media to spark conversations around the issues of contemporary art. Art critic Jerry Saltz, for instance, used Facebook as a platform to bolster critical debates. Museums' efforts to become more accessible and target a new audience resulted in exhibitions displaying popular content: in 2000, the Guggenheim Museum in New York City held an exhibition of Giorgio Armani's fashion designs; in 2002, the Brooklyn Museum organized a tribute to *Star Wars*.[25]

Artworks also explored the decade's themes of self-conscious anxiety and isolation that emerged in response to globalization and the growing social interactivity. In addition to reflecting on issues of identity and self-reflections, contemporary art – often through site-specific installations – emphasized environmental concerns that persisted during the period. Furthermore, artists grappled with what it meant to be an artist during wartime. Dario Robleto's 'Caught in Man's Amnesia', for instance – 'a collection of bullets made of melted and cast unused bullet casings from every American war' – invited the viewer to contemplate 'the notions of war, peace, memory, and salvation'.[26]

The art world reflected the decade's economic bubble and its subsequent bursting: in 2006 and 2007, auctions sold artwork for outrageous prices; then in 2008, art sales sharply plummeted. During the economic bubble, the Neue Galerie in New York purchased a Klimt painting for $135 million (2006), and Damien Hirst's 'For the Love of God', a human skull covered in platinum and encrusted in diamonds, sold for $100 million (2007).

New and reconstructed museum spaces opened across the country. The reconfigured and enlarged Museum of Modern Art in New York City reopened in 2004. New York's New Museum for Contemporary Art opened at a new location in the Bowery in 2007. Prominent collectors built their own museums: for example, the Rubell Family Collection in Miami (opened in 1996) and the Broad Contemporary Art Museum in Los Angeles (opened in 2008).

In February 2003, the design competition to rebuild the World Trade Center was complete. Architect Daniel Libeskind won the award.

Books

The decade's bestselling novels were *The Da Vinci Code* (2003) by Dan Brown (about conspiracy in the Catholic Church), *The Kite Runner* (2003) by Khaled Hosseini (written by an Afghan writer and set in Afghanistan, it provides a global perspective to American readers), *Twilight* (2005) by Stephenie Meyer (the first in a series that won new popularity for the genre of vampire romance) and *Harry Potter and the Deathly Hallows* (2007) by J. K. Rowling (the final book in the *Harry Potter* series).

> **BOX 1.11: WRITERS' RESPONSE TO 9/11**
>
> Writers began to tackle the subject of 9/11 by delving into the emotional impact of the terrorist attacks. Some of the books in this category included William Gibson's *Pattern of Recognition* (2003), Jonathan Safran Foer's *Extremely Loud and Incredibly Close* (2005), Don DeLillo's *Falling Man* (2007) and Joseph O'Neill's *Netherland* (2008).

Among the Pulitzer Prize winners in the category of Fiction were *The Quick and the Dead* (2001) by Joy Williams, *Blonde* (2001) by Joyce Carol Oates, *The Corrections* (2002) by Jonathan

Franzen, *Evidence of Things Unseen* (2004) by Marriane Wiggins, *The March* (2006) by E. L. Doctorow, *After This* (2007) by Alice McDermott, *Tree of Smoke* (2008) by Denis Johnson, *All Souls* (2009) by Christine Schutt and *The Plague of Doves* (2009) by Louise Erdrich.

The decade experienced the trend of popularizing novels through other media such as film or musical theatre. Novels made into films included the *Harry Potter* series; the *Twilight* series; *Where the Wild Things Are*; *The Chronicles of Narnia*; *The Da Vinci Code*; Dr Seuss: *How the Grinch Stole Christmas*, *The Cat in the Hat* and *Horton Hears a Who!*; and *The Lord of the Rings* series.

Remakes or adaptations of classics included *Charlotte's Web*, *A Christmas Carol* and *Charlie and the Chocolate Factory*.

Novels made into musicals included *The Wild Party*, *Seussical the Musical*, *A Year with Frog and Toad*, *Wicked*, *The Color Purple*, *The Light in the Piazza* and *Little Women*.

Sport

Sports programmes and live events on television continued to draw a diverse viewership, although the audience that watched programmes that ranked in the top ten prime-time broadcasts was only at around 8 per cent between 2001 and 2008; in 2009, it jumped to 19.4 per cent.[27]

Trends in sport reflected the decade's general concerns and developments. After 9/11, security significantly intensified at major sporting events, with more sombre moments dedicated to the military and patriotism. Increased globalization entered the sports arena, with the National Football League beginning to play games at Wembley Stadium in London, starting in 2007, and Major League Baseball playing two spring training games in China in 2008. The explosion of the Internet affected sport, as Fantasy Football websites made Fantasy Football one of the most important marketing tools for the NFL, while Twitter allowed sports commentators to debate online.

Major League Baseball was put under the microscope when record-holders such as Barry Bonds and Mark McGwire were suspected of using performance-enhancing drugs. American football grew in popularity, for both the NFL and college teams.

In 2007, two African American head coaches faced each other in the Super Bowl for the first time: Lovie Smith of the Chicago Bears and Tony Dungy of the Indianapolis Colts.

BOX 1.12: 2004 SUPER BOWL 'WARDROBE MALFUNCTION'

In 2004, the Super Bowl halftime show, featuring Janet Jackson and Justin Timberlake, turned controversial when a 'wardrobe malfunction' exposed Jackson's breast (with a decorative nipple shield).

Celebrity culture and fashion

Because of the explosion of Internet culture, the lives of celebrities became increasingly more public. The public were obsessed with celebrities' relationships, pregnancies, diets, nervous breakdowns and addictions. The celebrities whose tribulations attracted most public attention were Anna Nicole Smith, Britney Spears, Paris Hilton and Lindsay Lohan. Couples and love triangles also garnered media interest: Jennifer Lopez and Ben Affleck ('Bennifer'); Tom Cruise and Katie Holmes; Cruise and ex-wife Nicole Kidman; Brad Pitt and Angelina Jolie ('Brangelina'); and Pitt and ex-wife Jennifer Aniston. The term 'celebrity worship syndrome' first appeared in 2003.

Just as music was not dominated by any one genre, fashion also was eclectic:

- Popular designers included Alexander McQueen and Vera Wang.
- Popular fashion styles included 'hobo chic', gender bending, Ugg boots, faded and torn denim, and vintage-inspired clothing.
- Popular stores included Old Navy, H&M and Target.

BOX 1.13: *QUEER EYE FOR THE STRAIGHT GUY*

Queer Eye for the Straight Guy, a reality TV makeover show, premiered in 2003. This represented the inclusion of openly gay personalities in popular culture and appropriated the stereotype that homosexual men have superior taste in both fashion and culture.

Media

The proliferation of digital and social media outlets as well as online (on-demand) access to music, television shows and films characterized the decade. The rise of digital media resulted in the steady decline of printed books, magazines and newspapers. E-readers and online blogs continued to increase in readership and popularity. Online news outlets attracted aspiring journalists and writers who embraced digital platforms; as a result, digital journalism began to emerge. The Internet and other forms of digital media became major sources of information.

Television and television journalism

The way we watch television was transformed by DVR, online streaming, digital cable and video on-demand. **DirectTV** experienced significant growth, providing its viewers with increased access to global culture. **TiVo**, a digital video recorder (DVR), allowed the user to pause and rewind live TV. It also offered features such as 'WishList' searches or 'Season Pass' schedules, which could record every new episode of a television series. The advent of TiVo affected advertising: as viewers could skip through commercials, more companies invested in product placement, or embedded marketing, especially in reality TV.

Reality TV became extremely popular. Among shows attracting large audiences were *Survivor* (receiving top ratings in 2001 and 2002) and *American Idol* (receiving top ratings in 2004 through to 2009). Reality television categories included competition shows (*Big Brother, Survivor*), singing/dance/talent competition shows (*Dancing with the Stars, American Idol*), fashion-themed series (*Project Runway, America's Next Top Model*), documentary or narrative-style shows (*The Hills, The Real Housewives*), game shows (*Deal or No Deal, Who Wants to Be a Millionaire*), cooking shows (*Top Chef, Chopped*) and makeover shows (*The Swan*, for instance, depicts women undergoing extensive plastic surgery).

Emmy Awards were instituted to reflect the large popularity of reality television: these included Outstanding Reality Program (2001), Outstanding Reality-Competition Program (2003) and Outstanding Host for a Reality or Reality-Competition Program (2008).

Television sitcoms and dramas that gained viewers' popularity included *Arrested Development, South Park* (adult animation), *The West Wing, The Sopranos, The Wire, Lost, The Office, Weeds, Mad Men, Dexter* and *Breaking Bad*.

The most popular television shows that provided commentary on current political events and affected public opinion were *The Daily Show*, a late-night comedy programme hosted by Jon Stewart; *Saturday Night Live*, a late-night live sketch comedy and variety show that started in the 1970s; and the *Colbert Report*, hosted by comedian Stephen Colbert. Other nightly news broadcasts included shows on the major broadcast networks ABC, CBS and NBC.

According to the Pew Research Center findings, the difference in how the public received election news in 2000, 2004 and 2008 was considerable. In 2000, television news dominated and the Internet was 'a relatively minor source for campaign news', but in 2004, the Internet gained almost equal footing with news outlets such as 'public television broadcasts, Sunday morning news programs and the weekly news magazines'. In 2008, the percentage of the population that received most of its campaign news from the Internet tripled from 2004 (from 10 per cent to 33 per cent).[28]

Radio and newspapers

Radio declined in popularity as more listeners used MP3 players and iPods to customize music while driving. To compete with digital media, many radio stations such as National Public Radio streamed their content over the Internet to allow online users to gain access to their programmes. New radio technologies included satellite radio and HD radio, providing a higher quality and wider reach broadcast programming than a standard radio broadcast.

Newspapers suffered a major blow with the development of the Internet, especially as free sites such as Craigslist replaced much of the need for classified advertising. As circulation of printed newspapers declined, the number of online newspapers (some were free), newspaper blogs and Twitter accounts, online newspaper archives and online magazines grew exponentially.

Social media

The social media explosion offered users new and effective ways to connect, interact, post comments, share ideas and multimedia content, stage 'flash mobs' and influence political events.

Kaplan and Haenlein, in their article 'Users of the World, Unite! The Challenges and Opportunities of Social Media', identify the decade's six different types of social media: collaborative projects, blogs, content communities, social networking sites, virtual game worlds and virtual social world. Social media technologies included Internet forums, wikis, blogs, podcasts, multimedia sharing, wall-postings, email and instant messaging, among others. A blending of technology and social interaction for the co-creation of value drove social media development.[29]

BOX 1.14: SOCIAL NETWORKING

Social networking accounted for 22 per cent of all time spent online in the US. Twitter processed more than one billion tweets in December 2009 and averaged almost 40 million tweets per day. Over 25 per cent of US Internet page views occurred at one of the top social networking sites in December 2009, up from 13.8 per cent a year before.[30]

As social media became more accessible, concerns grew about online bullying and the necessity of parental control. 'Unfriend' was the New Oxford American Dictionary word of 2009.

Technology and science

Digital media

Technological innovations during the first years of the century significantly transformed the ways in which we communicate, obtain information and present ourselves to the world. Inventions such as instant text messaging, Wikipedia, YouTube, Facebook and Twitter, among others, defined this decade as a digital age. The digital revolution both simplified and complicated our ability to process and analyse data. The instant availability of unlimited informational resources improved our daily activities, but also caused a great deal of confusion and frustration, as there was no longer a single voice of authority. Computers and gadgets began to rule our lives. Video games and social networking offered people the opportunity to create alternative realities and assume virtual identities.

BOX 1.15: DEVELOPMENT OF THE WORLD WIDE WEB

The development of the World Wide Web marked the decade. Web 2.0 – a new phase in web technology – allowed users to interact with web content, collaborate with each other in a social media environment and generate new content. The user-generated movement became publicly acknowledged when in 2006 *Time* magazine named 'You' its Person of the Year. As *Time* magazine's editor, Lev Grossman, explained, 'It's a story about community and collaboration on a scale never seen before. It's about the cosmic compendium of knowledge Wikipedia and the million-channel people's network YouTube and the online metropolis MySpace.'[31]

Information technology enabled people to interact with the world with unprecedented efficiency and maintain their virtual presence through social media. Technological developments were also intricately connected to many political controversies, such as the post-9/11 culture of surveillance as well as the leaking of documents, photographs and videos over the Internet.

Timeline of major technological developments

2000
GPS (**Global Positioning System**), the satellite-based system, originally developed by the Department of Defense, became available to civilian users.

Toyota Motor Corporation introduced the **Prius**, an affordable hybrid car, to the US market.

AT&T became the first US cellular company to offer **instant text messaging** for mobile phones.

Sony released **PlayStation 2**, followed by Microsoft's **Xbox** in 2001. These groundbreaking video game consoles sparked the development of the video gaming industry.

Trek Technology and IBM began to market the first **USB flash drives** with a storage capacity of 8 MB, exceeding the capacity of floppy disks by more than five times.

2001
Jimmy Wales and Larry Sanger, Internet entrepreneurs and project developers, launched **Wikipedia**, a free-access, online, user-edited encyclopaedia. Despite debates over the accuracy of its content, Wikipedia remained the Internet's most extensive and popular reference site. The launch of Wikipedia signified a new era of user-generated content.

Apple introduced the **iPod**, which instantly became the bestselling digital music player and a cultural icon, transforming the music industry forever. With the click of a mouse, consumers could buy and download music albums, rendering CD and record stores obsolete. Apple continued to update the model, expanding it to Shuffles, Nanos and finally the iPod Touch. While the original iPod could only hold 1,000 songs, the iPod classic model in 2009 had capacity for up to 40,000 songs.

2002

Replacing a two-way pager that became available in 1999, **BlackBerry** introduced a generation of mobile devices – the BlackBerry smart phone – allowing its users to send text messages, communicate via email, access the Internet, take photographs, make phone calls, and so on. It first won popularity among corporate executives but gradually became a mainstream gadget.

Friendster was launched. Based on the 'Circle of Friends' technique for networking people in virtual communities, Friendster triggered the social networking revolution. It was the top online social networking service until 2004.

2003

Chris De Wolfe and Tom Anderson introduced **MySpace**, an online social networking service that quickly outgrew **Friendster** and, between 2005 and 2008, became the largest networking site in the world.

Second Life, a user-centred online 3D virtual world, sparked the public's obsession with creating virtual environments populated by avatars, the users' virtual representation of themselves.

2004

Mark Zuckerberg, with his classmates and fellow students at Harvard University, launched **Facebook** – an online social networking service that eventually exceeded **MySpace** in popularity and became a major force driving the decade's social networking. This advanced social networking service allowed users to engage in a variety of online activities such as posting status updates and photos, sharing videos, exchanging messages and receiving notifications.

2005

The launching of the video-sharing website **YouTube** gave an average person unprecedented power over social media. Any person could now record and share personal stories and performances, as well as broadcast social and political controversies. With the help of an inexpensive hand-held camera or a smart phone, anyone could become a virtual sensation.

2006

The online social networking service **Twitter** was launched to promote brief, instant and frequent communication. The service enables users to send and receive 140-character messages called tweets. Twitter brought brevity to social networking and increased the social and political impact of social media. Furthermore, to better facilitate student interactions in large lecture classes, Twitter was used as a learning tool in educational settings. As users were able to follow other users (not necessarily mutual friends), Twitter turned into a valuable information platform – but also a way to compromise one's reputation.

Nintendo launched **Wii** and **Wii Sports**, revolutionizing video gaming. Wii targeted a broader demographic by facilitating 3D participation in a video game: a person could play tennis or engage in a cardiovascular exercise while operating the controller.

2007

Apple released the touchscreen **iPhone**, whose consumer-friendly design as well as sizable memory and processing power made a significant impact on the smart phone industry. Mobile applications in smart phones – whether they are iPhones, BlackBerries, Android-powered phones or Palm devices – allowed people to perform a variety of tasks, such as playing a video game or accessing the Internet.

Amazon introduced the **Kindle**, the first generation of e-book readers that enabled users to shop for, download, browse and read e-books and other digital media via Wi-Fi.

2008

The **Retail DNA Test** became available to the public, giving people access to their genetic profiles.

Tesla Motors released the **Tesla Roadster**, the first highway-capable battery-powered car.

2009

The **solar shingle**, a residential roof shingle in the form of a solar panel, became available on the market.

BOX 1.16: TECHNOLOGICAL DEVICES

Technologies and devices that were introduced in the 1990s but proliferated in the 2000s include Google Web Search, digital cameras, TiVo digital video recorders and DVDs. Toward the end of the decade, technological devices became smaller, more sophisticated and intuitive for users.

Scientific discoveries

The human genome project

An international scientific research project that explored the sequencing of human DNA to identify and map all human genes was completed in 2003. The project, which the US funded, is considered the world's largest collaborative biological project. The project's discoveries benefit multiple fields, including medicine, forensic sciences, agriculture and anthropology.

Stem cell research

Stem cell research continued despite restrictions that President George W. Bush imposed in 2001 on federal funding of research on human embryonic cells. Scientists achieved significant breakthroughs in research that uses adult stem cells. In 2009, President Barack Obama issued an executive order on 'Removing Barriers on Responsible Scientific Research Involving Human Stem Cells'. The decade's stem cell research resulted in great success in treating spinal injuries and reversing blindness.

NASA research

In NASA research, major breakthroughs included the advent of orbital space tourism in 2001, with the first space tourist, American Dennis Tito, self-sponsoring his week-long stay in the International Space Station. In 2004, the Mars Exploration Rover Mission – an ongoing robotic space mission that includes two rovers – reached the surface of the planet Mars and communicated detailed data and images back to Earth. The mission found evidence of past water on the Martian surface. The Voyager I spacecraft entered the heliosheath, the outermost layer of the heliosphere, marking its first departure from the solar system. In 2005, with the discovery of Eris, an object in the Kuiper belt (an area beyond the solar system) larger than Pluto, Pluto was demoted to a 'dwarf planet'. It had been considered a planet for 76 years. In 2009, the first Earth-like planet with a solid structure was discovered outside the solar system. Scientists also detected water ice on the Moon.

Medical research

The decade's significant advances included the standardization of Highly Active Anti-Retroviral Therapy, or combination therapy, for treating HIV/AIDS, as well as therapies for cancer treatment. The Food and Drug Administration approved 244 new drugs.

2

Theatre in the 2000s

Julia Listengarten

Background

Mapping a landscape for the future of American theatre at the beginning of the twenty-first century, Ben Cameron – the executive director of Theatre Communications Group (TCG)[1] at the time – identified challenges for theatre managers, artists and writers to address during the coming decade. He underlined the importance of serving broad communities by diversifying the audience base and identified theatre's needs to create performance spaces to present experimental new work, to reassess the impact of technology on viewers and to commit to broader representation of traditionally marginalized groups. Asserting that 'our audience increasingly operates from a visual, associative framework of perception', Cameron urged practitioners to consider the implications of the increasingly developing Internet and image-driven culture for theatre, 'long a teller of linear, narrative stories'. He acknowledged that American theatre had begun to tackle generational issues and had made significant strides in addressing racial concerns, but also said that 'issues of gender, sexual orientation, and physical ability still tend[ed] to remain, unfortunately, on the peripheries of discussion'.[2]

As the country experienced devastating terrorist attacks, disastrous wars and financial meltdowns, as well as the incredible growth of digital and social media, Cameron's call to re-examine the direction of American theatre resonated throughout the first decade of the 2000s. Theatre companies and practitioners looked for new ways to rethink financial and marketing strategies, increase activism locally and nationally, foster new artistic partnerships, collaborate with non-stage media and cultivate new audiences. These efforts continued into the next decade as theatre professionals, during roundtable discussions or through surveys that TCG facilitated in 2010 and 2011, pondered strategies to bring artists, institutions and communities together.[3]

This chapter aims to explore American theatre's response to the unstable political, economic and cultural climate of the 2000s. While the following discussion addresses major developments on Broadway, Off-Broadway and in regional and experimental theatres, particular attention is paid to significant themes and trends that emerged from increased globalization, international conflicts, economic recession and national isolation. Some involved contention with identity and politics, expanded representation of marginalized voices, and moral and political relativism. Others concerned new methods of engagement with the audience, increased interdisciplinary and multicultural exchanges, and the effects of technological advancements on stage. Notably, the majority of these discussions and developments occurred across various types of theatre, often blurring the distinctions between commercial and not-for-profit organizations and encompassing traditional venues such as Broadway and regional theatres, as well as ensemble-based collectives committed to experimental work. In order to offer a wide-ranging perspective on American theatre during the decade, the chapter includes a discussion of new plays as well as a recognition of the growing importance of non-scripted, devised work created through groups' collaborative processes. The goal of this study is to capture many facets of American theatre from 2000 to 2009: its dialogue with popular culture, questions about cultural assumptions of identity, integration of different art forms, and response to national and global concerns.

Theatre responds to 9/11

The 9/11 terrorist attacks resulted in thousands of lives lost, immense physical and financial devastation and fear of global terrorism, which drastically changed American society and had a tremendous impact on US culture. Downtown Manhattan theatre organizations near the World Trade Center were damaged and lost their homes. Theatre institutions in New York and around the nation faced financial disaster. Despite the initial shock that American theatres experienced with the rest of the country, many theatre communities stepped forward to give the public opportunities to unite and reflect. 'Dark into Light, Light into Darkness: Atlanta Artists Respond', at Atlanta's Alliance Theatre Company, featured readings from classic plays and famous American speeches, including excerpts from William Shakespeare, John Steinbeck and Martin Luther King Jr. The text prepared by dramaturg Megan Monaghan for this occasion was subsequently performed in Philadelphia, Iowa City, Austin and Seattle. Additionally, theatre communities in New York City and elsewhere helped by organizing relief efforts and community dialogues. Starting on 22 October 2001, the Worth Street Theater Company held a free variety show every Monday evening, primarily intended for Ground Zero rescue crews. Titled *The TriBeCa Playhouse Stage-Door Canteen*,[4] the show included performances by Broadway celebrities such as Adam Pasqual and Kristin Chenoweth. Donations collected at each performance benefited the Twin Towers Fund.

Theatres made sensitive choices by cancelling or postponing productions whose subject matter could be a painful reminder of the tragedy. Five Broadway plays were cancelled in the week of 9/11: the *Rocky Horror Picture Show*; *If You Ever Leave Me, I'm Going with You*; *Stones in His Pockets*; *A Thousand Clowns*; and *Blast!* The McCarter Theatre in Princeton, New Jersey, cancelled a production of Richard Nelson's *The Vienna Notes* – a political tale about a self-absorbed politician and his callous, ineffective response to a terrorist attack – explaining that 'the context in which we would receive the play has changed drastically, and it would be insensitive of us to present the play at this moment in our history'.[5] The Broadway revival of Stephen Sondheim's *Assassins* at the Roundabout Theatre Company was postponed until the spring of 2004. *Zulu Time*, a 'techno-cabaret' performance piece that Canadian theatre-maker Robert Lepage conceived to recreate unsettling experiences of air travel, was removed from the bill of the Quebec-New York 2001 multi-arts festival.

One of the first shows that dealt with the 9/11 devastation, Reno's *A Rebel Without a Pause*, opened in late October 2001 at La MaMa in the East Village. Reno, a comic monologist and feminist performer who lived a few blocks from the towers and experienced the unravelling of the tragedy first-hand, offered her own gut-wrenching memories of the day and contemplated her initial reactions filled with bewilderment and incomprehension. This both cathartic and witty performance was intensely personal but also included a 'cheerfully scathing critique' of President Bush and his administration.[6] Filmmaker Nancy Savoca filmed Reno's performance on 18 December 2001; the movie opened in May 2003. As film critic Stephen Holden observed, 'There are no sacred cows in Reno's cynical and absurdist take on terrorism and politics. Even Rudolph W. Giuliani is not exempt from comic scorn.'[7]

Just a few blocks from Ground Zero, the Flea Theater in downtown Manhattan responded twelve weeks after 9/11 with the staging of Anne Nelson's *The Guys*. Prompted by Jim Simpson, the Flea Theater artistic director, Nelson – a first-time playwright – wrote a two-person play from her experience of helping a New York fire captain compose eulogies for firefighters. The production, starring Sigourney Weaver and Bill Murray, was subsequently staged in other American cities and abroad. In August 2002, Susan Sarandon and Tim Robbins took the play to the Edinburgh Festival, where they offered three sold-out performances. Commenting on the play's merit and the stars' excellent performances, critic Michael Billington also noted the script's 'congratulatory and politically incurious' nature.[8] In 2002, the play was adapted into a film, and in 2006, it returned to the Flea Theater for a commemorative run on the fifth anniversary of 9/11.

Although Christopher Shinn's *Where Do We Live* never references 9/11 directly, this play traces the catastrophe's impact on young New Yorkers living on Manhattan's Lower East Side. *Where Do We Live* was produced in May 2002 at the Royal Court Theatre in London before making its way back to New York for the American premiere in 2004 at Off-Broadway's Vineyard Theatre. In David Rimmer's *New York*, which opened in New

York in April 2002 at Lotus for the Disaster Psychiatry Outreach, characters engaged in personal contemplations of the tragedy as they individually reflect on their own harrowing experiences in a psychiatrist office soon after 9/11. *The Bomb,* a controversial piece performed by the International WOW Company in March 2002 at the Flamboyán Theater on the Lower East Side, 'wove together material dealing with the Second World War, the atomic age, and 9/11 to create a powerful meditation on modern violence and terror', scholar Marvin Carlson observed.[9] Pointing to the significance of this work in the aftermath of 9/11, *New York Times* critic Lawrence Van Gelder wrote that *The Bomb* 'raised questions not just about the role of the United States in creating nuclear bombs but also about responsibility, good and evil, and mankind's seemingly ineluctable propensity for waging war and wreaking mass destruction'.[10]

As the country struggled with anxiety over national security and the global implications of terror, theatre addressed concerns about the role of Western democracies in world politics but also pointed to the importance of personal responsibility and the tragic consequences of silence and denial. A few theatre works written or created before the attacks resonated in a post-9/11 world by challenging the audience to weigh difficult questions of blame, complicity and agency. Tony Kushner's *Homebody/Kabul* (1999), which captures the cultural divide between the West and Afghanistan, premiered on 25 December 2001, at the New York Theatre Workshop. Subsequently, the Theatre Workshop presented the first American production of Caryl Churchill's *Far Away* (2000); its opening, on 11 November 2002, perhaps intentionally followed the first anniversary of 9/11. Referring to these works as 'the powerful achievements of the deepest kind of political theater', critic Alisa Solomon wrote in the *Village Voice* that '*Far Away* – like *Homebody/Kabul* – is prophetic not so much in predicting catastrophe, but in exposing the devastation human beings have already wrought but failed to take responsibility for.'[11] Multiple productions of Greek tragedies, specifically *Medea* (Milwaukee's Chamber Theatre, the Pittsburgh Public Theater, the Will Geer Theatricum Botanicum in Topanga, California, Theatre de la Jeune Lune in Minneapolis and Classical Theater of Harlem in New York), compelled audiences to re-examine guilt, violence, retribution and suffering.

As the first anniversary of 9/11 approached and Americans began to grapple with the new post-9/11 reality, more intentional responses – sometimes subtle and indirect but more often explicit and full of heartfelt commentary – emerged in playwriting and performance. Craig Wright's *Recent Tragic Events* (which premiered in September 2002 at the Woolly Mammoth Theatre Company in Washington, DC, and was produced in September 2003 by Playwrights Horizons, an Off-Broadway company) concerned a blind date on 12 September 2001; it was called the first 9/11 comedy. Neil LaBute's *The Mercy Seat*, which opened in December 2002 at New York's Acorn Theatre and starred Weaver and Liev Schreiber, is also set on the day after the tragedy and taps into darker, morally ambiguous responses that a disaster of this magnitude may have triggered. The main character, Ben, worked at the World Trade Center but happened to be away with his mistress during the attacks. Thinking that his family might believe he died, he is consumed by an egotistical urge and contemplates eloping with his mistress and starting a new life. Schreiber, who portrayed Ben in the New York production, admired LaBute's willingness to address 'complicated and disturbing feelings around loss and grief and terror ... in their ugly and naked glory'.[12]

Anthems: Culture Clash in the District, commissioned and produced in August 2002 by Arena Stage in Washington, DC, offers a different perspective on post-9/11 America, in which racial and ethnic hatred dramatically increased. Richard Montoya, one of the co-founders of the Chicano troupe Culture Clash – known for biting satire of cultural stereotyping and sophisticated humour – began his research for the piece while flying to Washington, DC, six days after the attacks. He remembered how challenging it became for him, a person of colour, to negotiate the nation's airports a few days after the terrorist attacks. As he contemplated society's understanding and perception of terrorism, he invited the audience to step away from the immediate post-9/11 shock, look deeper into the harsh realities that various communities faced from past terror and reflect on the country's increasing sense of alienation and fear of the 'other'. 'Sometimes the face of terror comes in forty-one bullets in a vestibule, sometimes the face of terror wears a white sheet over its face ... sometimes terror kills transgenders in southeast D.C.' and 'sometimes the face of terror looks like Timothy McVeigh',[13] he said, referring to the 1999 New

York police killing of Amadou Diallo, the Ku Klux Klan, a wave of hate crime in Washington and the 1995 Oklahoma City bomber. A year later, a number of other plays that premiered in the fall and winter of 2002 offered moving, intimate meditations and personal reflections on 9/11. Jonathan Bell's *Portraits*, seven monologues in part inspired by real people and their stories of 9/11, was first produced in September 2002 at the Ridgefield Playhouse in Connecticut before moving to New York in 2003. The film version of Israel Horovitz's *3 Weeks After Paradize* aired on 11 September 2002, on the Bravo cable TV network. Written two months after the attacks, the one-person play – Horovitz's response 'from the heart and mind of a father worried about his children and the world they will inherit'[14] – quickly won national and international attention. Also on 11 September 2002, members of the New York theatre community organized a three-day marathon, 'Brave New World – American Theatre Responds to 9/11', the first united artistic response to the tragedy. The event took place at Manhattan's Town Hall where many theatre artists and playwrights embraced their artistic and social responsibility to contribute to the country's healing process. More than 100 artists, recognized and emerging performers and writers, presented short plays, multimedia shows and music to remember the victims, reflect on the impact of the attacks on individuals and society and help the country heal. New works featured during the event included Edwin Sanchez's *Pops*, about a young Hispanic man coming to terms with the death of his father, a bus boy at the Windows on the World restaurant in the World Trade Center; Jonathan Marc Sherman's *Ribbon in the Sky*, a series of concurrent monologues of male and female twins who were born during construction of the Twin Towers; and Stephen Flaherty and Lynn Ahrens's *A Song for LaChanze*, a tribute to the singer, whose husband was killed on 9/11.[15] Among short works at the event was LaBute's *Land of the Dead*, in which a woman has an abortion on the day her husband died in the attacks.

On the first anniversary of 9/11, critic Christopher Rawson offered his insight into the complexity and enormity of theatre's task in addressing the current physical and emotional devastation: '9/11 is no single traumatic event but a complex mix of reactions, issues and fears, running from personal loss to cultural sensitivity, from heightened security to altered funding.'[16] This task was the focus of eleven playwrights whose reflections about 'putting 9/11 on stage' were published in the September 2002 issue of *American Theatre* magazine. Playwrights such as Herman Daniel Farrell III (in *Justice*) and Montoya (in *Anthems: Culture Clash in the District*) spoke of their search for a balance between art and activism. Others, such as Brian Jucha and Caridad Svich, discussed their decision to employ technology to 'make sense out of [the] incomprehensible'.[17] Working with Houston's Infernal Bridegroom Productions, Jucha used transcripts of air traffic controllers' communication with pilots of the 9/11 planes to create a performance text for his interdisciplinary dance-theatre piece *We Have Some Planes*. Svich based her collaborative project *Return to the Upright Position* on a series of responses to 9/11 by a dozen theatre artists who communicated them across cyberspace. Some writers shared their personal feelings and the ways they expressed them – ferociously through grief and outrage or quietly in a more delicate, elegiac manner. Honour Kane, the author of *autodelete:// beginning dump of physical memory//*, remembered:

> I watched helplessly as my neighbors to the south began to leap from the windows of those burning towers ... A woman clawed her way upward as she plunged, trying so desperately to climb the sky. For months I couldn't write. The horrors of that day were too human. It was the day narrative was lost. But my memory of that climbing woman kept haunting me. Finally, after time, I found a way through my work to see her safely home, send her onwards, upwards and amend her brutal end.[18]

Other artists, the Lebanese American Najee George Mondalek and the Iranian Gita Khashabi, considered how their works (*Me No Terrorist* and *Chadoor*, respectively), which were written before 9/11, became transformed by the attacks and inadvertently offered new political meaning.

As the decade progressed and the emotional pain along with the feelings of shock and disbelief gradually subsided, new plays and production work began to interrogate the social implications and political reverberations of the 2001 terrorist attacks. In *Omnium Gatherum*, written by Theresa Rebeck and Alexandra Gersten-Vassilaros and first presented at the 2003 Humana Festival at Actors Theatre of Louisville, Kentucky, a small group of intellectuals at a dinner party engages in a passionate dialogue about the ramifications of 9/11.[19] Eve Ensler's *The Treatment*, presented by the Culture Project as a part of its Impact Festival in 2006 in New York City, is set during an American soldier's post-war therapy session with a military psychiatrist. Peter Sellars's 2006 production of *Children of Herakles*, an unfinished and rarely performed Greek tragedy about war refugees, evoked terrifying parallels with the post-9/11 immigration crisis. Sellars contended, 'The events after September 11 have made the refugee situation all the more horrifying ... Yet if you question any of this, you're perceived as being not patriotic.'[20] The Living Theatre's revival of Kenneth Brown's *The Brig*, directed by Judith Malina in 2007, responded indirectly to CIA covert operations during the wars with Iraq and Afghanistan, specifically resonating with the authorized abuse and torture of prisoners at Abu Ghraib, Guantánamo and secret prisons throughout the world.

Assessing theatre's response to 9/11 ten years after the tragedy, critic Mark Kennedy wrote that 'no single work has emerged as a definitive theatrical statement',[21] which, he argued, is a puzzling phenomenon in light of the theatre canon that developed in response to other significant moments in history, such as the Vietnam War and the counterculture (the musical *Hair*), the era of McCarthyism (Arthur Miller's *The Crucible*) and the AIDS crisis (Kushner's *Angels in America*), among others. British director Rupert Goold suggested that after 9/11, an artist might find it 'intimidating and hubristic' to attempt to 'go to the heart of this tragedy'.[22] Instead, he opted for a collaborative approach when choosing a theatrical work to commemorate the 10th anniversary of 9/11. Goold directed *Decade*, an immersive piece written by a team of American and British playwrights, including Shinn, John Logan and Lynn Nottage; it was performed by Headlong Theatre in an unused building along the River Thames in London. The presentation of this work coincided with a series of new 9/11 plays written around the 10th anniversary, such as Susan Charlotte's *The Shoemaker* (Acorn Theatre), Richard Nelson's *Sweet and Sad* (New York Public Theater) and Jonas Hassen Khemiri's *Invasion!* (Flea Theater). Although Goold's undertaking hardly evolved into a singularly powerful work of theatre about 9/11, it captured the feeling that many experienced on that unforgettable Tuesday morning: 'fragmented, contradictory ... disturbing and deeply human'.[23]

Theatre collectives: Site-specific, interactive and immersive work

As the decade featured major advances that made digital and social media more interactive for audiences, theatre embraced the opportunity to rethink ways of connecting to its audience and involving spectators in theatre-making. Creating immersive environments or facilitating active exploration of a specific site, theatre collectives reached out to new viewers, built communities and reflected on how we relate to the world and remember our history.

Theatre collectives discussed in this section may have distinct characteristics, including immersive, environmental, multidisciplinary, devising, site-specific, technological, community-based, but what they all have in common is the emphasis on collective creation and the process of interaction with the audience. While ensembles such as the Living Theatre, Mabou Mines and the Wooster Group had previously made a mark in American theatre, many more recently emerged collectives expressed a renewed, passionate commitment to offering innovative forms of audience engagement and exploring the concept of spectator as a co-creator of the performance. Among these groups were the Antenna Theater in Sausalito, California; Sojourn Theatre, a site-specific group that performs around the nation; and Tectonic Theater Project in New York. Other intensely collaborative and movement based theatre groups included Lookingglass Theatre Company in Chicago; SITI Company in Saratoga Springs, New York; and the Rude Mechanicals, an innovative and multidisciplinary theatre collective from Austin, Texas, to name a few.

The artistic philosophy of the Antenna Theater is rooted in the technological principles of an antenna: to receive, to transform and to transmit back. According to the theatre website, 'The name Antenna was chosen because we were not only interested in creating theater but finding a way to have an active collaboration with our audience – thus Antenna.'[24] Founded in 1980 by Chris Hardman, a co-founder of the experimental performing arts company Snake, this group continued to probe various forms of immersive theatre during the 2000s and inspired audiences to co-author their own interactive experiences. 'The Antenna experience can take the shape of a carnival, an immersive maze, a performance piece, a radio program, a guided mystery tour, a sideshow, or a giant walk-through sculpture. Antenna uses them all to put the audience member, or "audient," into the middle of the action.'[25] Antenna invited audiences to experience a walk-through dreamscape of Samuel Taylor Coleridge's poem 'Kubla Khan' that involved digital audio effects and infinite mirrors (*Euphorium*, 2000) and took spectators on a 90-minute bus ride through San Francisco to relive the hippie revolution of the summer of 1967 'through a mix of oral histories, rock 'n roll, live action, 3D and video projections'[26] (*Magic Bus*, 2010). In a site-specific piece called *Big Brother* (2006), the company experimented with MP3 player technology; groups in the audience received soundtracks with varying instructions and thus encountered different segments of the story, which was inspired by George Orwell's *1984*. Although some of these explorations continued earlier experiments with various technologies, Antenna's focus on activating spectatorship and transforming the audience into co-creators of their own experiences reflected the cultural trend of the decade to construct virtual realties and generate alternative public spaces through social media and video gaming.

The Sojourn Theatre, founded in 1999, consists of fifteen performers from eight cities who are committed to creating a civic dialogue. In partnership with city and state governments, social service agencies and multidisciplinary arts centres, the company devised socially engaged performances around the country. Working with elements of 'conscious spectacle', the company also focused on 'community research that moved beyond interviews into the territory of workshops, installations and public encounters'.[27] In designing spaces for energizing civic discourse, it contemplated 'how the action of theatre making can be best applied to the process of civic decision making'.[28] *Witness Our Schools* (2004), a project about public education in Oregon, was conceived to illuminate critical issues about schools, represent a number of voices in education debates and promote productive interactions between citizens and community leaders. The production, based on 500 interviews conducted over two and a half years, was performed in more than twenty communities in Oregon. *Built* (2007), a site-specific project developed in a large concrete warehouse in the South Front District in Portland, Oregon, explored the shifting landscapes and rapidly increasing populations of cities, asking, 'Where will we live?' The project, 'an event full of alternative occupations of space, physically, navigationally and through encounters of information', invited 'small audience groups [to traverse] the space with performer tour guides who may share a moment of awe at the new skyline, lambast affordability, and then invite you to cram into a shower stall for a real discussion of density'.[29] Its goal, according to Michael Rohd, the founding director of the company, was to achieve a productive balance between 'spectacle and exchange' and help the audience become 'witnesses and participants' and 'occupy places of imagination and reflection'.[30]

Tectonic Theater Project fully embraced aspects of devised performance and verbatim theatre in its celebrated production of *The Laramie Project* in 2000. Shortly after the brutal murder of Matthew Shepard, a gay student at the University of Wyoming, the artistic director Moisés Kaufman and ten company members travelled to Laramie to interview community members about the killing. The interviews became the basis for an extensive collaborative exploration/workshop during which company members devised the text, often switching or blurring their artistic roles. Employing the devising technique called 'moment work', the participants were encouraged to envision each moment in the story by approaching it from multiple perspectives – writer, actor, designer, dramaturg or director, for example. Contemplating the importance of theatre's civic responsibility but also the artists' ability to reflect on the process of their theatre-making, Kaufman wrote that the company's 'interest was to continue to have a dialogue on both how the theatre speaks and how it is created'.[31] Although this play is framed somewhat traditionally and does not necessarily invite audience interruptions or any other active audience participation, its form is rooted in civic discourse and community engagement; the story turns into a forum, an opportunity for Laramie to look beneath the surface, speak the truth and re-examine its values. *The Laramie Project* opened in February 2000 at the Ricketson Theatre in Denver before moving to Union Square Theatre in New York; in November 2002, the company performed in Laramie.

For the tenth anniversary of Shepard's murder, Tectonic Theater revisited the project by travelling to Laramie to reconnect with the community and to discover whether the community's values and attitudes had changed. In Kaufman's words, *The Laramie Project:*

10 Years Later, which had initially been conceived as a short sequel, turned into a full-length play that 'deals with history – how it's created, written, recorded and told. It deals with how communities (as well as individuals) construct their own narratives, and how these narratives change as a result of traumatic events. It poses questions about identity, both individual and collective, and about ownership – about responsibility and accountability.'[32] The opening of this production on 12 October 2009 turned into a national event that included 150 theatres, 1,000 performers and over 50,000 audience members. A live webcast from Lincoln Center's Alice Tully Hall introduced the performance, with local actors – some professionals, some university students, some community members – taking the stage at each venue. Afterward, audiences were invited to engage in a virtual dialogue: to tweet their responses and participate in a moderated question-and-answer session via the webcast. Through the use of webcast technology to frame the event, Tectonic Theater Project aimed to facilitate a different kind of collective theatre engagement and interactivity from the one that could be achieved for and within a local community. 'When we present the work in this manner on a national scale, are we able to affect the impact that theatre can have on a national dialogue?' Kaufman wondered. 'If in fact we created a national audience that was "together" even though they were geographically separated, how do we maintain and foster this kind of collectivity?'[33]

A growing number of theatre ensembles that emerged in the late 1990s and early 2000s evidenced a trend among young theatre professionals to search for alternative methods of creating transformative and innovative art outside the commercial pressures of traditional theatre organizations. Forging artistic paths sometimes beyond 'show business', these generative artists looked for a unique language to develop artistic and social communities. Most ensembles shared the same mission of developing a new audience, but they fostered different communities. One example is the Vampire Cowboys in New York, whose 'geek theatre' productions were primarily intended for fans of geek culture – video gamers, comic-book collectors, costumed role players and lovers of science fiction and fantasy. Another example is the Imaginists Theatre Collective, based in Santa Rosa, California, whose audience included Spanish-speaking migrant workers. Dedicated to 'art that welcomes everyone, including people whose stories often go unrepresented on stage and whose first language may not be English',[34] the Imaginists devised bilingual performances to reach out to California's Spanish-speaking population and to unite diverse communities. Focusing its mission on audience development, the collective engaged in building community partnerships by working in close collaboration with various not-for-profit organizations that assist day labourers and migrant workers. *Divide* (2007) and *Extranjeros en Su Propia Tierra/Strangers in Their Own Land* (2008) were bilingual community-based pieces conceived and performed by the group's bilingual ensemble. In 2009, with *El Show Arte Es Medicina/The Art Is Medicine Show*, the collective introduced its new aesthetic – a bilingual free-to-the-public touring model that involves 'cool looking bicycles and portable sets'. The playfulness and simplicity of this concept coincided with the seriousness of the issues the Imaginists examined – the economic downfall and immigration crisis. The use of eco-friendly bikes with flatbeds, saddlebags and trailers, specifically designed to enable travelling bilingual shows to carry mobile stages, puppets and other props, evolved into the group's signature style whose major challenge was 'to attract non-theatregoers and non-English-speaking audiences'.[35]

Addressing issues of identity related to race, gender, class, sexuality and nationality, theatre collectives employed comedy, especially satire, to lampoon cultural stereotypes and social anxieties. Some of these represented marginalized groups and voices, such as the Nibras Theatre Collective, an Arab American troupe, and Culture Clash, a Chicano troupe that incorporated self-deprecating jokes about being 'the other' in a post-9/11 world of escalated fear and surveillance. And while some of their performances were more scripted than others and hardly invited active audience participation, the process of theatre-making that these collectives espoused was intensely collaborative and included previously underrepresented voices and silenced stories.

Groups that confronted the surveillance culture, among them the Surveillance Camera Players and Improv Everywhere, staged street performances that enlisted the audience in challenging the policing of public space and human interaction. Exposing the proliferation of surveillance cameras by performing directly in front of them, the Surveillance Camera Players walked around New York's Rockefeller Plaza, holding posters – 'The Surveillance Camera

Players Present', 'It's OK Officer', 'Just Going to Work', 'On My Way Home', 'Getting Something to Eat' and 'Going Shopping' – right up to the cameras. Bill Brown, founder of the Surveillance Camera Players, suggested that 'the cameras turn public spaces into theatrical space by their [very] presence'.[36] Improv Everywhere, in turn, became popular by performing street 'missions' in which actors became 'undercover agents'. In an improvised performance piece called *Frozen Grand Central*, over 200 Improv Everywhere agents froze in place for five minutes in New York's Grand Central Station to stir public attention and, ultimately, confusion. 'Missions' were then uploaded on YouTube and became Internet sensations. Even though Improv Everywhere's founder, Charlie Todd, said the street provocations were designed to celebrate the magical and unexplainable in art rather than to incite a political protest, he admitted there was an important political aspect: to reclaim public places for artistic expression. 'The most exciting thing to me is to interact with people who don't realize they are part of a performance. I also like the idea of demonstrating that theatre/comedy/art can happen anywhere – not just within a frame,' he said.[37]

The use of technology to design interactive spaces in which the audience is a principal performer also guided aesthetic choices of emerging theatre collectives in the 2000s. Spectators were turned into passengers aboard a flight (*Charlie Victor Romeo*, created by a New York theatre group called Collective: Unconscious) or became live entertainers (*Loud Mouth*, created by the group Toxic Audio in Orlando, Florida); the pieces received the Drama Desk Award for Unique Theatrical Experience in 2000 and 2003, respectively. In *The MP3 Experiment* that Improv Everywhere staged a number of times, anyone could become 'an agent' in a 'mission' that intersected mediated culture and public space. One of the bloggers who participated in this mission described the instructions: 'We followed the Web site's instructions: (1) Wear a blue, red, yellow or green T-shirt with a white T-shirt underneath. (2) Download the MP3 Experiment audio file and load it onto our iPods – but do not listen to it. (3) Go to Roosevelt Island. At precisely 4 p.m., press Play.'[38] The next instructions told audience members to start square dancing, to wave to an 'omnipotent voice' coming from their iPods, to engage a non-participant by walking in a straight line behind the person, to fall on the ground for a short nap, to play games, to tell secrets, to take off headphones, and so on. Whether it was a flash mob or political rally within a seemingly apolitical context, the convergence of technology and audience interaction in a public space resulted in a collaborative peformance event – albeit mediated through the Internet and digital audio players. Through the employment of live webcasts, MP3 players, iPods, headphones and surveillance cameras, theatre collectives embraced new technological advancements. The goal was to transcend the boundaries between heavily mediated culture and live theatre and imagine new possibilities for theatre audiences to interact with and collectively create within intentionally designed environments or in open public spaces.

The Builders Association, an offshoot of the Wooster Group that was founded in 1993 in New York, also employs technology to investigate the effects of a hyper-mediated culture on humanity. Though the group's cross-media-based aesthetic, integrating live action with filmed material, video projection and animation, might have resembled mediated performances by the Wooster Group, Richard Foreman and the Ontological-Hysteric Theater, or George Coates and Performance Works in San Francisco, the Builders Association differed in its commitment 'to construct dramatic encounters that encompass real-life stories and illuminate our present-day disquietude with new digital means and media of transmission'.[39] Marianne Weems, the artistic director, explained, 'We've developed an unusual vocabulary that uses technology to talk about technology, and how it affects us as human beings ... I try to combine entertainment with critical thinking – to invite the viewer to investigate the invisible networks that surround us.' She pointed to the surreal qualities of the group's performances that were based on real-life stories taken 'from the modern-day landscape around us' and were thus evocative of 'our chaotic, global context'.[40] Questioning the culture of surveillance and data collection in *Super Vision* (2005) or meditating on the effects of digital culture on people's sense of location and dislocation in *Continuous City* (2007), the Builders Association engaged in the dialogue about negotiating real and virtual spaces and explored the decade's shift toward the digital and post-human.[41]

Musical theatre: Broadway and beyond

Broadway continued to be associated with the American musical, but faced with heavy competition from the Internet-driven culture, it looked to withstand economic pressures, maintain regular patrons and attract a younger generation. Accordingly, trends favoured revivals of well-known shows, adaptations of film or popular literature, jukebox musicals and Disney stage adaptations. Looking at the decade in American musical theatre from a broader perspective, critics noted a few major shifts, however, including increased global influence of the American musical; synergy of musical theatre, film and television; the disappearance of a traditional book musical with an original score; the development of institutions and organizations dedicated to creating new musicals;[42] and technological advances in production and marketing.[43] Economic instability dictated two other critical shifts: small- or smaller-cast musicals, among them *The 25th Annual Putnam County Spelling Bee* (2005), *The Light in the Piazza* (2005), the *Sweeney Todd* revival (2005) and *Next to Normal* (2009), and a move away from individual producers toward corporate sponsors.

Despite the country's economic downturn and the increase in the average ticket price (from $55.75 in 2000–1 to $85.56 in 2009–10), Broadway attendance remained at about 12 million people yearly. Audiences flocked to see revivals of favourite shows and enjoy stage adaptations of popular movies, bringing children to see reimaginings of much-loved Disney films. Revivals, three to six shows per season, included *Oklahoma!* (2002), *Into the Woods* (2002), *Man of La Mancha* (2002), *La Cage aux Folles* (2004), *South Pacific* (2008) and *Hair* (2009). But it was the interest in adapting films into musicals, however, that became one of the major driving forces on Broadway (especially in the first half of the decade). *The Full Monty* (2000), *The Producers* (2001) and *Monty Python's Spamalot* (2005) were among the most successful stage adaptions of popular films. Directed by Jack O'Brien, *The Full Monty* (with book by Terrence McNally and music and lyrics by David Yazbek) was adapted from the 1997 British movie about unemployed steelworkers who become striptease dancers. Mel Brooks, turning his own 1968 film *Producers* into a huge Broadway hit, worked with the production team of the musical (directed and choreographed by Susan Stroman) to offer a satirical reading of show business, presenting the audience with 'a bright, endlessly evocative dreamscape that skewers and celebrates the looks of great musicals from *Gypsy* to *Follies*'.[44] *Monty Python's Spamalot*, directed by Mike Nichols, was based on the 1975 British film *Monty Python and the Holy Grail* and attracted younger spectators, predominantly men, by 'dutifully [recreating] many of the beloved gags, stunts, and set-pieces Python fans expected, such as killer rabbits, flying cows, squeals of "Ni," flatulence, and fractured French'.[45] *Thoroughly Modern Millie* (2002), based on the 1967 movie that starred Julie Andrews, enticed Broadway with gentle charm and old-fashioned appeal. *Hairspray* (2002), an adaptation of John Waters's 1988 romantic comedy, was one of many musicals in the decade that celebrated the empowerment of women and, as Richard Norton observed, 'attracted a huge new demographic to Broadway musical comedy'.[46]

Broadway also reconceptualized popular stories from literature and television. Written as a prequel to *The Wizard of Oz*, *Wicked* (2003) offered an alternate, significantly darker version of the classic tale. With music and lyrics by Stephen Schwartz and direction by Joe Mantello, it focused on the troubled relationship between Glinda and Elphaba, who becomes the Wicked Witch, and underscored the story's political motifs. *Avenue Q* (2003), which opened at the Vineyard Theatre before transferring to Broadway, was conceived as an adult spoof of the children's television show *Sesame Street*. Notable for its use of hand puppets as characters, the show poked fun at the sanctity of childhood and lightheartedly yet firmly subverted cultural myths and narratives. Peppered with references to racism, pornography and sexuality, songs and dialogue in *Avenue Q* reminded the audience of the profound 'contrasts between the world according to children's television and the reality of adult life'.[47] Appealing to a younger demographic, *Avenue Q* successfully captured the sensibility of the generation affected by television culture. (As a side note, the television comedy *High School Musical*, which emerged in 2006, and then the TV series *Glee*, appearing in 2009, also fostered the interest of a younger generation in musical theatre.)

The surge of the jukebox musical, which employs popular songs in its score, stemmed from producers' interest in avoiding risky artistic choices and continuing to attract a built-in audience – fans and admirers of well-known artists and their 'hits'. Indeed, the number of jukebox musicals in the 2000s was unprecedented. The jukebox hits of the decade included *Mama Mia!* (2001), based on songs by the Swedish group ABBA, and *Jersey Boys* (2005), a 'shrink-wrapped biography of the pop group the Four Seasons'.[48] Commenting on the importance of grounding a musical in compelling storytelling, *New York Times* critic Ben Brantley wrote of *Jersey Boys* that 'the show's straightforward biographical approach is a relief after the hagiography of *Lennon* [about the former Beatles star John Lennon] and the clunky fantasy story lines ... of *Good Vibrations* [presenting the Beach Boys' music] and *All Shook Up* [featuring Elvis Presley's songs]'.[49]

Disney shows in the decade included *Tarzan* (2006), *Mary Poppins* (2006) and *The Little Mermaid* (2008). They provided much-needed escape and hope during an economically challenging time and impressed audiences with technical ingenuity, such as aerial virtuosity and multiple illusions. Disney advanced its brand of family entertainment on stage after establishing its presence on Broadway in the 1990s and achieving a smashing commercial success with *The Lion King* in 1996. While Disney shows that opened in the 2000s did not match the commercial success of *The Lion King*, directed by Julie Taymor, *Mary Poppins* also generated favourable critical reception and was performed on Broadway for over four years. An adaptation of the 1964 Disney film and stories by P. L. Travers, the production was a joint venture between Disney Theatrical Productions and British producer Cameron Mackintosh. Opening in 2004 in London under the direction of Richard Eyre and Matthew Bourne, the show moved to Broadway in a slightly augmented, more colourful version. A 'perfectly engineered piece of musical theater', the production featured imaginative dance numbers, elaborate stage effects and instances of magical stagecraft, such as Poppins removing multiple large items from her suitcase and conjuring a bed out of thin air, and 'the Banks' kitchen collapsing in chaos, only to be reassembled with a flick of Mary's wrist'.[50] Jim Steinmeyer, a leading illusion designer who had previously designed effects for the stage production of *Beauty and the Beast* and helped design special effects for Disney theme parks, created magical effects for this show.

As American theatre took part in debates about race, gender and sexuality, especially in relation to identity – personal, collective or national – musical theatre, too, paid attention to diversity in style and representation. Commenting on a 'decline in the dominance of the well-crafted book musical with an original score composed for the theatre', Richard Norton noted 'the concomitant emergence of pop music, rock, and rhythm and blues as the dominant language of musical theatre'.[51] In his list of musicals, which incidentally all relied on existing tunes and rhythms, he referred to '*Fela!*'s Afrobeat, *Come Fly Away*'s Sinatra sound, *Million Dollar Quartet*'s glimpse of early rock 'n' roll, or *American Idiot*'s contemporary punk rock sound from the band Green Day'.[52]

Perhaps even more important, along with Broadway's wider acceptance of formerly marginal music, the American musical began to grapple with difficult topics involving children, sexuality, racial and ethnic tensions and mental illness. *Spring Awakening* (2006) presented the audience with previously taboo issues of child sexuality, teenage abortion and suicide. An adaptation of a late nineteenth-century German play by Frank Wedekind that confronts tragic consequences from prejudice, narrow-mindedness and hypocrisy, the production (with music by Duncan Sheik and lyrics/book by Steven Sater) was developed at the Off-Broadway Atlantic Theater Company before moving to Broadway. Staged in a Brechtian style, with selected audience members sitting on the stage, and featuring rock music sung into performers' handheld microphones, this musical masterfully explored the tortured lives and complicated emotions of teens experiencing the thrills and pains of sexual awakening in a stifling, small and provincial town. In his enthusiastic review of the production, Charles Isherwood praised its bold and innocent approach to sex: '*Spring Awakening* makes sex strange again, no mean feat in our mechanically prurient age, in which celebrity sex videos are traded on the Internet like baseball cards.'[53]

Two other noteworthy productions showed that American musical theatre in the 2000s embraced a variety of styles and a diversity of topics. Hip-hop became the basis for the music in the production of *In the Heights* (2008; with music and lyrics by Lin-Manuel Miranda and book by emerging playwright Quiara Alegría Hudes), which presented complexities in the life of the Dominican community in New York City's Washington Heights. Rock powered the six-person musical *Next to Normal* (2009; with book and lyrics by Brian Yorkey and music by Tom Kitt), which portrayed a suburban family crippled by the mother's mental illness. *Next to Normal* was awarded the Pulitzer Prize for Drama in 2010, an honour that had been given to only a handful of musicals including *South Pacific* (1950), *Fiorello!* (1960), *A Chorus Line* (1976), *Sunday in the Park with George* (1985) and *Rent* (1996).

In addition to expanding its subject matter and aesthetic, the American musical demonstrated a strong propensity for satire and self-parody, perhaps first apparent in *The Producers*, in which, in Ben Brantley's words, 'shrill stereotypes [were] transformed into outsize comic archetypes, recalling the prelapsarian days of ethnic and sexual humor before political correctness'.[54] Following in this vein, *Urinetown* (2001) – 'a mock Brecht-Weill-Blitzstein musical comedy'[55] that opened nine days after the 11 September attacks – ventured into the perilous territory of satirical theatre, making fun of local and national political systems as well as conventions of musical comedy, leftist agit-prop and film noir. With book, lyrics and music by Broadway newcomers Greg Kotis and Mark Hollmann, *Urinetown*, which first appeared at the New York International Fringe Festival, is a political satire that exposes the corporate power denying access to public restrooms for the good people of Urinetown. *Avenue Q*, *The 25th Annual Putnam County Spelling Bee* and *Monty Python's Spamalot* also employed satire against theatrical convention, political correctness, cultural stereotypes and dominant social narratives.

Musical theatre's employment of satire that balances political directness and ambiguity might have been Broadway's indirect response to the decade's political controversies and economic turmoil fomented by the wars in Iraq and Afghanistan, the ubiquitous 'War on Terror' and multiple corporate frauds. Indeed, the evil of *Urinetown*'s megacorporation, whose absurd name 'Urine Good Company' resembles Eugene Ionesco's anti-plays such as *The Bald Soprano* (1950) or *Rhinoceros* (1959), perhaps forewarned the audience of the dangerous implications of corporate power. As many corporate scandals such as Enron and Tyco took place during the run of the show, *Urinetown* continued to remind the audience of the devastating impact corporate manipulation may have on ordinary folks. *Billy Elliot, the Musical* (2008), directed by Stephen Daldry with a score by composer Elton Jones and lyricist/librettist Lee Hall, which was originally created in London and was based on the 2000 film about the struggles of a working-class community in north-east England, also resonated with audiences worried about the economic crisis. The story of an eleven-year-old boy from an impoverished coal miner's family who gives up boxing to pursue dance celebrated human perseverance and artistic aspirations. '*Billy Elliot* is a hard-times musical,' Brantley wrote. 'And as the culture of the Great Depression made clear, in times of economic darkness there can be blessed relief in dreams of tripping the light.'[56]

Another major development in musical theatre was the emergence of a generation of composers who learned their craft outside Broadway's commercial venues and collaborated with innovative theatre artists such as George C. Wolfe, Craig Lucas, Tina Landau and Kushner. This group was recognized for 'writing scores that have an unprecedented harmonic sophistication, stylistic eclecticism and seriousness of content'.[57] As Broadway outsiders, they might have enjoyed greater freedom in breaking conventions and introducing atonality and melodic asymmetry to the American musical. Among these composers were Michael John LaChiusa, Adam Guettel, Ricky Ian Gordon and Jeanine Tesori, whose work spanned various music genres, including opera and incidental music for television and theatre productions. Although LaChiusa's *Marie Christine* (1999; book by LaChiusa) and *The Wild Party* (2000; book with George C. Wolfe) enjoyed Broadway success, his other theatre and opera credits included *Lovers and Friends (Chautauqua Variations)* (2001) at the Lyric Opera of Chicago, *See What I Wanna See* (2005) at the New York Public Theater and *Bernarda Alba* (2006), a one-act musical based on Federico García Lorca's play *The House of Bernarda Alba*, which premiered at Lincoln Center's Mitzi E. Newhouse Theater. Guettel, a grandson of Richard Rodgers, was a classically trained vocalist who performed at the Metropolitan Opera and New York City Opera as a boy soprano soloist. Influenced by Modernist and contemporary composers such as Igor Stravinsky, Maurice Ravel, Benjamin Britten and Samuel Barber, Guettel made a key contribution to musical theatre of the 2000s with the highly acclaimed romantic comedy *Light in the Piazza* (2005; with book by Craig Lucas), which won Tony Awards for Best Score and Best Orchestration and was praised for being 'nearly operatic in its scope and complexity'.[58]

The decade also featured a growing number of resident theatres dedicated to commissioning and producing musicals, among them TheatreWorks in Palo Alto, California, North Shore Music Theatre in Beverly, Massachusetts, and American Conservatory Theatre in San Francisco.[59] Lincoln Center Theater, in particular, played a crucial role in developing new musical theatre work, evidenced by *The Light in the Piazza* and *Bernarda Alba*. Furthermore, a handful of musicals that became Broadway hits were first workshopped or produced by not-for-profit theatres, including the Public Theater (*Caroline, or Change*), the Vineyard Theatre (*Avenue Q*), Second Stage Theatre (*The 25th Annual Putnam County Spelling Bee* and *Next to Normal*) and La Jolla Playhouse (*Jersey Boys*). The cross-pollination of musical and non-musical theatre forms flowered in music-centred productions such as *Jonah's Dream* (2005) at the Connecticut Repertory Theatre, *Lady Madeline* (2006) at Chicago's Steppenwolf Theatre Company and *Most Wanted* (2008) at La Jolla Playhouse. According to critic Mark Blankenship, these three shows represented 'an emerging genre that increasingly integrates music into a stage project without creating what's commonly understood as musical theatre'.[60]

The productive reciprocity between Broadway and Off-Broadway, as well as collaborations across genres, media and commercial and not-for-profit venues, also influenced non-musical theatre trends. Pointing to 'the growth of interdisciplinary exploration and audience expectation of multisensory experience' at the beginning of the twenty-first century, Cameron stressed the growing importance of sound in theatre, through 'the emergence of the sound designer, the notion of theatre scoring, [and] the integral presence of music in "straight" plays'.[61] He specifically encouraged theatre practitioners to move beyond the antagonism between 'musical' and 'non-musical' camps and to see each other 'as collaborators in a continuum, using music in differing degrees but with common power and purpose'. Cameron also said, 'Whether we're listening to the otherworldly underscoring of Tina Landau's *Space*, the hip-hop rhythms of *Stomp* or motifs that literally form the text of William Finn's *New Brain*, we must recognize music as a key element of the theatre of the future.'[62] While there were significant strides in transcending the existing and perceived boundaries between 'musical' and 'non-musical' theatre forms, Cameron's appeal continued to resound through to the end of the decade.

Theatre for young audiences

In 2003, the Children's Theatre Company of Minneapolis received the Regional Theatre Tony Award for sustained artistic excellence – the first time in American theatre history that a children's theatre was honoured with such a prestigious award. The national recognition of professional children's theatre marked a major shift in Theatre for Young Audiences (TYA)[63] that began at the end of the twentieth century, when several theatre companies originally spearheaded by Junior League volunteers grew into major professional companies, including Lexington Children's Theatre and StageOne Family Theatre in Louisville (both in Kentucky), Nashville Children's Theatre and the Rose Theater in Omaha, Nebraska.

Professional children's theatre companies and TYA programming grew rapidly in the 2000s, thanks in part to the recognition that children would benefit considerably from artistic, educational and social enrichment. Regional theatre expansion at the beginning of the century yielded major renovations of children's theatre spaces, including the Denver Center for the Performing Arts; the Children's Theatre of Charlotte, North Carolina; the Coterie Theatre in Kansas City, Missouri; Childsplay, a component of the Tempe Arts Center in Arizona; and Imagination Stage in Bethesda, Maryland. Membership organizations such as TYA/USA and the American Alliance for Theatre and Education (AATE) also grew. In 2000, TYA/USA partnered with the Kennedy Center to hold New Visions 2000: One Theatre World, which drew over 400 participants and featured Cameron as keynote speaker.[64] Moreover, with various initiatives in community engagement through an 'applied theatre' approach,[65] the commissioning of new children's plays and musicals and the development of master's-degree and doctoral programmes in TYA at leading universities, the trajectory of the field began to change. With the quality of their work improving and their social representation expanding, TYA companies and artists became increasingly recognized as part of the larger professional theatre world.[66]

During the decade, a number of playwrights and children's theatre companies incorporated distinct cultural voices and addressed communities that were often ignored or underrepresented on stage

– thus shifting the TYA field toward a conscious representation of diversity on stage. Young practitioners who had recently entered the field examined difficult issues facing youth, including poverty, violence, drugs, homophobia and racial prejudice. Children's plays began to tackle topics such as growing up with disabilities or confronting barriers of culture and language, naming and protecting one's identity or voice, and preserving cultural heritage in a multicultural society. Laurie Brooks's *The Wrestling Season* (2001), commissioned and originally produced by the Coterie Theatre under the artistic direction of Jeff Church, explores the brutal impact of peer pressure on teens who are in the process of discovering their identity and sexuality. Chicano playwright José Cruz González reaches out to Latina/o audiences by examining Latinx cultural themes and by bringing more diverse Latina/o representations into the theatre. While remaining culturally specific, his works also ponder broader social issues of identity and social justice, as well as the powers of imagination and love in helping people survive and heal. His play The Highest Heaven (2002), for instance, created in collaboration with Childsplay and artistic director David Saar, concerns the unlikely friendship between a twelve-year-old Mexican boy and a homeless African American man during the Great Depression. New commissioned children's musicals, too, ventured into the territory of previously underrepresented topics. The musical *Nobody's Perfect* (2007), for example, based on the book by Marlee Matlin and Doug Cooney and produced in collaboration with the Kennedy Center Theater for Young Audiences, explores the challenges of friendship experienced by a young deaf girl.

As part of the TYA trend toward diversity and inclusion, some initiatives focused on original and devised works with and by young people in the LGBTQ community. These organizations include About Face Youth Theatre in Chicago, True Colors in Boston, QSpeak Theatre in Phoenix, Pride Players under The Rose Theater in Omaha, and Proud Theatre in Madison, Wisconsin. Targeting at risk young people from various socioeconomic, racial and ethnic backgrounds, these theatre groups were conceived to create a safe environment for queer youth to express their voices and affect change. In a conversation with other leaders of queer youth theatre, Paula Gilovich of About Face Youth Theatre pointed to the crucial social impact of her organization within and across communities; specifically, she discussed its commitment to 'increase the safety, empowerment, and leadership capacity [of LGBTQ individuals and their allies] in order to catalyze youth-led civic dialogue and action within schools and communities'.[67] Focusing on collaborations with youth to develop and perform their own stories, she also stressed the importance of creating productions with professional theatre artists – thus modelling the process on professional theatre companies and promoting 'a cross generational artistic dialogue'.[68]

Theatre for the Very Young (TVY) also emerged as a new trend in the TYA field, whereby theatre practitioners sought to expand the young audience base and foster theatre education and child development for very young children. Inspired by international theatre experiments, a growing number of children's theatre companies began to create performance experiences for children aged four and younger. Imagination Stage, Children's Theatre Company of Minneapolis and Seattle Children's Theatre[69] were among the companies that connected to very young children 'on their eye level' by devising and producing non-verbal, non-linear, predominantly sensory performances that included interactive and immersive theatre components.[70] Shifting away from language-based productions to abstraction and sensory creations, theatre-makers such as Janet Sanford (Imagination Stage), Elissa Adams (Children's Theatre Company) and Linda Hartzell (Seattle Children's Theatre) inadvertently adopted aspects of post-dramatic theatre[71] for the very young. Playful, exploratory and driven by image, sound and movement, TVY performances aimed to create intimacy and encourage participation that enabled babies and toddlers to feel safe and imagine. Some companies worked with international groups to commission and co-produce new works for very young audiences. The Children's Theatre Company production of *A Special Trade* (2007), which featured over fifteen puppets, and the shadow puppet circus performance *Circoluna* (2009) were developed in partnership with the Swedish company Dockteatern Tittut.

As children's theatre companies worked to connect with more diverse audiences and to present a diversity of stories on stage, new community outreach initiatives and collaborations with partnering organizations were established. As a result, more programmes and producers tailored plays for children with special needs. Casting, too, underwent a transformation. Imagination Stage commissioned

Minneapolis playwright Kevin Kling to create *Perfectly Persephone: Little Greek Myth* (2005), a production in which three of the seven adult actors had physical or cognitive disabilities, including brittle bone disease and Down syndrome. Spectators included children with special needs who could identify with the empowering experience these performers provided. Children who were deaf or had other hearing difficulties were served by the Deaf Theatre Program at Seattle Children's Theatre, which worked with schools to help the children develop communication skills and discover their own identities within the deaf community and beyond. This effort was one example of the growing partnerships uniting theatre companies and schools that promoted arts integration practices as a productive approach to education and self-discovery. The emergence of sensory-friendly performances – shows in which sound and light effects were adjusted to ease the experience for viewers with sensory processing disorders – was another important undertaking of TYA practitioners during the 2000s.

The facilitation of new performance possibilities for young people and the emergence of innovative forms of expression in children's theatre – such as devising and visual storytelling – were indicative of the decade's attempts to grapple with the complexity of identity politics, increased media interactivity, and global cultural influences. Media and technology, too, began to be incorporated in children's performance-making, with digital storytelling becoming an integral way for children to tell their stories and share their experiences. Furthermore, museum curators, recognizing the need to connect with young audiences through interactive and immersive experiences, began to bring a variety of performances into their spaces. The Public Library of Charlotte and Mecklenberg County and Children's Theatre of Charlotte joined forces in 2005 to create ImaginOn – a 102,000-square-foot joint facility and collaborative venture – in order to engage the community through a wide range of storytelling activities. This collaboration between a public library and a children's theatre aimed at creating an innovative performance space that integrates creativity and education and fosters an original approach to learning, theatremaking and personal storytelling. With such partnerships, as well as a broader choice of themes and understanding of diversity, Theatre for Young Audiences manifested itself as a progressive part of American theatre of the 2000s.

Interdisciplinary and global trends on mainstream and experimental stages

In April 2009, *American Theatre* convened a discussion with 25 theatre artists about the field in the next twenty-five years. Entitled 'AT25: An Eye on the Future', it provided an array of perspectives envisioned by contemporary theatre-makers who pointed to the necessity of 'a sustained commitment to empowering the audience'[72] (Diane Paulus, artistic director of the American Repertory Theater), blurring public and private spaces in theatre-making (Steven Ginsburg, co-artistic director of HeartBeat Ensemble), nurturing a diversified national theatre community (David D. Mitchell, managing and interim artistic director of Run of the Mill Theater) and identifying ways to integrate technology and re-evaluate theatre's relationship with pop culture (Matt Saunders, scenic designer and associate artistic director of New Paradise Laboratories). Philip Bither, senior curator for performing arts at the Walker Art Center in Minneapolis, addressed inter-, cross- and multidisciplinary performance possibilities that theatre of the next generation would explore. As he contemplated the future of theatre in which multidisciplinary approaches and collaborative partnerships become standard, he suggested that 'complex media forms, visual art, new sonic and sensory designs, object theatre, creative movement, extended vocal techniques, new visual and ritual forms, simplicity and minimalism, physicality and high design, will all push theatre forward'. 'What's viewed as "experimental" today,' he envisioned, 'will become commonplace.'[73] Written at the end of the decade, this statement pointed to a myriad of unexplored performance possibilities but also hinted at significant endeavours spanning artistic disciplines in the 2000s that foregrounded this vision for the future in American theatre.

Over the last century, avant-garde artists experimented by integrating multiple art forms and collaborating across disciplinary borders, leading to a new understanding of artistic collaboration. These experiments challenged traditional models of communicating and sought to engage viewers by affecting their senses and disrupting their expectations. In the recent history of American theatre, cutting-edge collectives and artists such as Mabou Mines, the Wooster Group, Meredith Monk and Ping Chong worked to develop a theatrical language that integrated visual arts, music, puppetry and multimedia. Although this experimentation occurred mostly on the fringes of theatrical culture in the twentieth century, the inter- or multidisciplinary trend in the 2000s moved to the forefront of theatre, while continuing to remain the marker of avant-garde theatre. This redefining of 'theatre' and expansion of performance possibilities contributed to the process of eroding borders between mainstream and experimental stages, Broadway and not-for-profit theatre companies, highbrow and lowbrow cultures.

Forced to compete with the burgeoning Internet culture, American theatre of the 2000s reflected the contemporary sensibility defined by fragmentation, collage and multi-linear kaleidoscopic perspectives by mixing media and offering hybrid forms. Disrupting multiple hierarchies, institutional as well as artistic, theatre reacted to what the award-winning *New York Times* columnist Thomas Friedman described in his book *The World Is Flat* as a technology-fuelled level playing field of global culture. The 'flattening' of the world, in which 'all the knowledge centres on the planet [were now connected] into a single global network',[74] stimulated interconnections in theatre, on business and aesthetic levels. Regarding business, in this period of financial pressures and significantly reduced support from the National Endowment for the Arts,[75] not-for-profit theatres sought grants and endowments from private corporations and foundations in addition to local and state agencies. Grant initiatives included the New Generations Program, which the Doris Duke Charitable Foundation, the Andrew W. Mellon Foundation and TCG designed in 2000, as well as the Innovation Lab for the Performing Arts, launched in 2008 with $1.5 million from the Duke Charitable Foundation. Some foundations such as the Pew Charitable Trusts and the Lila Wallace-Reader's Digest Fund began to require theatre organizations to provide long-term fiscal planning and programming to combat recurring deficits and gain financial independence. The decade also featured increased partnerships between commercial and non-profit business models, manifested in the establishment of not-for-profit theatres on Broadway, such as the Lincoln Center Theater, the Roundabout Theatre Company, the Public Theater and the Manhattan Theatre Club. Such partnerships perhaps instigated a shift toward more commercially oriented work.[76]

Aesthetically, commercially driven entertainment theatre rejuvenated itself because of technological advancements, artistic experimentation and new marketing strategies that employed video clips and/or high-quality photographs of shows for Internet and television advertising. Cirque du Soleil performances, with their dazzling music, dance and elaborate scenic spectacles, established Las Vegas as an important site of theatrical culture that combined commercial entertainment with the most advanced artistic experimentation. Broadway, too, expanded the boundaries of the traditional musical by incorporating elements of dance-theatre, puppetry and multimedia into the form.

Improvisational dance served as a basis for storytelling in the musical *Contact* (2000), choreographed and directed by Susan Stroman. With dance, set to music ranging from Tchaikovsky to the Beach Boys, and storylines developed by dramatist John Weidman, seemingly disconnected narratives from different time periods were fused under the theme of love and attraction. *Movin' Out* (2002), 'the choreographer Twyla Tharp's shimmering portrait of an American generation set to Mr. [Billy] Joel's music',[77] likewise stretched into a category of dance-theatre. Brantley wrote that 'each principal performer seems to have his or her own special dialogue with the songs [and] the dances become shaded personality sketches'.[78] Puppetry – from singing hand puppets in *Avenue Q*, which was originally an Off-Broadway production, to an elaborate, 25-foot dragon puppet operated by four puppeteers in *Shrek the Musical* (2008) – further contributed to a vocabulary for the Broadway musical that integrated different art forms. Multimedia found a home on Broadway in *Next to Normal* (2009), which captured the characters' shattered reality through projected images – fractured projections of a house or a human face – heightening the show's sense of fragmentation, chaos and emotional pain. Broadway fully embraced the art of video projections in *Spider-Man: Turn off the Dark*, produced on the cusp of a new decade in 2011. Controversial because of its dangerous acrobatics, cast members' broken legs and protracted litigation between the show's original director, Julie Taymor, and the Broadway producers, *Spider-Man* featured massive multi-panel video projections that brought the Manhattan skyline into the theatre space, a thrilling 3D effect.

Regional theatre companies, too, took interest in interdisciplinary explorations. A number of them, such as Trinity Repertory

Company in Providence, Rhode Island, the American Repertory Theater in Cambridge, Massachusetts, and Steppenwolf promoted hybrid artistic forms that brought together puppetry, music, dance and multimedia. Playwright Paula Vogel and puppeteer Basil Twist developed a one-act play, *The Long Christmas Ride Home*, which involved Bunraku-style puppets for the 2003 production at the Trinity Repertory Company, directed by Oskar Eustis. Pointing to the unique collaborative effort between humans and puppets in the production process, Vogel acknowledged that prior to this experience most of her artistic team had never worked with puppets; she joked that 'in a very fun way, the puppets taught *us* how to write the play, how to produce the play, how to stage the play, and how to act and say the lines. It's been very intense for me to listen to these puppets'.[79] The playwright's involvement in this interdisciplinary dialogue was also indicative of the increased impact of puppetry on the playwriting process. In fact, the decade was distinguished by a number of artistic collaborations that challenged playwrights to reimagine the role of puppetry in the theatre. Among these productions were Erik Ehn's loose adaptions of Mary Shelley's *Frankenstein* at the Theatre of Yugen in San Francisco and *Santa Claus* with the Cornerstone Theater Company in Los Angeles, which incorporated shadow puppets, toy theatre and doll-style puppets.

Experimentation involving puppetry became one of the major characteristics of American theatre in the 2000s. Perhaps heightened by Broadway's production of *The Lion King*, interest in puppetry spread across genres, categories and forms of theatre and performance. It captured the century's fascination with non-human performance but also reflected our idealistic longing, in the age of digital revolution and fragmented culture, for capturing the childlike wonder, the direct and personal connection and the simplicity that a puppet evokes. As the artistry and sophistication of puppet-making advanced considerably, puppets travelled beyond theatres for young audiences and engaged adult audiences on Broadway, Off-Broadway and in regional theatres, as well as in productions of opera and ballet. Taymor and Twist's global aesthetic and innovative approach to puppetry inspired a generation of American theatre artists who began to re-envision the relationship between human performers and puppets and successfully integrated puppet-eering in stage productions across genres. Taymor's staging of

Mozart's *Magic Flute* in 2004 at the Metropolitan Opera introduced audiences to Bunraku and Indonesian puppet theatre. Commenting on the variety of theatrical forms and cultural traditions artfully fused together in Taymor's *Magic Flute*, *New Yorker* critic Alex Ross wrote that 'the Met stage has never been so alive with movement, so charged with color, so brilliant to the eye. The outward effect is of a shimmering cultural kaleidoscope, with all manner of mystical and folk traditions blending together.'[80] Twist – combining puppetry, dance and music – traversed dance, opera, Broadway musical theatre and regional and experimental stage productions. Moreover, he applied technological innovations to puppet design, offering a unique vocabulary of underwater puppetry.[81] A third-generation puppeteer, he created a puppet version of the Stravinsky-Fokine ballet *Petrushka*, first performed in 2001, collaborated with Mabou Mines on the production of *Red Beads* (2005), which offered a fusion of theatre, dance and aerial performance with puppetry and music, and directed and designed the opera *Hansel and Gretel* (2006), based on the fairy tale, for the Houston Grand Opera and the Atlanta Opera.

As puppetry broke ground in visual storytelling, a generation of composers who were also sound designers emerged to advance aural storytelling, marking an important shift in the creation of new musical forms in theatre. Specifically, composers such as Andre Pluess, Scott Killian and Mark Bennett made significant strides in integrating music in non-musical stage projects, thereby reconceptualizing the role of music and aurality in theatre. Reflecting on *Lady Madeline*, a 'musical re-imagining' of Edgar Allan Poe's 'The Fall of the House of Usher' at the Steppenwolf Theatre, Pluess said that he and collaborator Ben Sussman were drawn to the project – a 'musical but not "a musical"' – because it invited an innovative approach to synthesizing musical and non-musical theatre. The impetus was to generate 'a rich sonic atmosphere' that would become integral to storytelling.[82] Whether they signalled a rethinking of existing genres in music theatre or pointed to a new hybrid form of music-theatre, as critic Blankenship suggested, *Lady Madeline* and other music-theatre productions during the decade helped to redefine the role of sound dramaturgy in crafting a story.

Dance-theatre evolved by assimilating elements of pop culture such as circus or hip-hop and integrating aesthetics of performance art. Choreographer Martha Clarke directed a dance-inspired production of *A Midsummer Night's Dream* in 2004 at the American Repertory Theater, in which 'the fairies were played by three dancers who performed on wires, creating an ethereal complement to the crude, barren set'.[83] In addition to aerial performance, other art forms inspired Clarke's dance-theatre, as she explained: 'I use photography and painters and occasionally films for visual inspiration. The set [in *Midsummer*] came partly from the rough sparseness of Anselm Kiefer and the surrealist photographer Robert ParkeHarrison. The costumes evolved from Picasso's Rose Period and Goya's Caprichos.'[84] Known for her original works that combined dance, theatre and opera, Clarke belongs to the avant-garde generation of Robert Wilson and Pina Bausch, who began to synthesize art forms in the 1960s and 1970s. With their explorations continuing into the twenty-first century, these artists, like their methodologies, won recognition beyond their immediate avant-garde circles and inspired younger generations of artists.

As hip-hop became more mainstream, choreographers including Rennie Harris and the New York City duo Anita Garcia (a.k.a. Rockafella) and Gabriel Dionisio (a.k.a. Kwikstep) investigated the possibility of reimagining dance-theatre through the lens of hip-hop culture. The dance-theatre company Puremovement, which Harris founded in 1992, embraced the language of hip-hop dance in productions such as *Rome and Jewels* (2000), a dance-theatre piece based on Shakespeare's *Romeo and Juliet*, and *100 Naked Locks* (2006), a deconstruction of the hip-hop dance movement. Rockafella and Kwikstep created Full Circle Productions to explore various forms of hip-hop expression and urban street culture through a dynamic and gritty dance-theatre style. *Soular Power'd*, paying 'homage to rapping, DJ-ing, graffiti art, street boxing, urban poetry, and ... a plethora of dance forms',[85] was performed in 2002 at the New Victory Theater, making a successful Off-Broadway debut for the company.

In addition to the growth of hip-hop dance-theatre during the 2000s, experimental theatre culture flourished with image-based, often non-scripted avant-garde works that bridged different artistic media. In fact, theatre ensembles that sprouted during the 2000s became immersed in interdisciplinary explorations with a specific focus on creating visual and aural dramaturgy. The Brooklyn collective *mad dog* staged dance-theatre works that were 'sexy meditations on the physicality of urban bodies in motion'.[86]

Influenced by John Cage's chance theory as well as the art of Dutch avant-garde painter Piet Mondrian, the collective searched 'for what theatre can communicate in a pure way – a theatre without language'.[87] Performing in galleries and vacant office spaces, *mad dog* experimented with the physical embodiment of found environments, synthesizing movement, colour, shape and sound. Other experimental theatre groups developing an interdisciplinary aesthetic were Theatre Movement Bazaar, committed to work that 'merge[s] elements of dance, text, cinema, and media from diverse sources into a complex performance';[88] the Pig Iron Theatre Company, dedicated to ensemble-devised works; the Redmoon Theater, which integrated physical movement, masks and puppetry in outdoor ritualistic ceremonies; and Flaneur Productions, which performed in unexpected spaces – including a tent of cardboard boxes.[89] Some ensemble-based theatres entirely devised their work; some relied on literary texts as a foundation; some abandoned the spoken word and experimented with the visuality and aurality of performance. Performance artists such as Chicano performance activist Guillermo Gómez-Peña also worked with multiple media that included experimental radio, video, photography and installation art (*The Living Museum of Fetishized Identities*, 1999–2002, and the *Mapa/Corpo* series, 2004–7). However their methods or approaches varied, these artists and companies were united in their commitment to explore new performance-making, cross disciplinary borders in unexpected ways and create cutting-edge, hybrid work for contemporary audiences.

In many ways, the development of interdisciplinary perspectives in the late twentieth and early twenty-first centuries was integrally connected to the growing global cultural trends and the influence of global culture on American theatre. Although the concept of 'the new global culture' has been criticized for promoting 'corporate multiculturalism'[90] and privileging dominant narratives, international crossovers in the arts shaped theatre in the United States, leading to a wide range of pioneering work. Among the most important international influences were two British productions: *War Horse*, London's National Theatre's epic work involving life-size horse puppets, and *Sleep No More*, an immersive theatrical experience originally developed by the collective Punchdrunk, known for its site-specific and interactive work. Collaboratively created with the South African Handspring Puppet Company,

War Horse premiered in 2007 at the South Bank, then made its successful Broadway debut in 2011 at the Vivian Beaumont Theater as a co-production of the National Theatre and Lincoln Center. *Sleep No More*, based on the 2003 London performance at the Beafoy Building, was recreated in 2009 at the American Repertory Theater in the space of the Old Lincoln School, before arriving in 2011 to remodelled Manhattan warehouses that were turned into the fictional McKittrick Hotel. These theatrical works made a considerable contribution to the developing forms of puppetry and interactive performance in American theatre.

A number of British directors contributed to an intercultural exchange through their work produced in the United States: John Doyle received critical acclaim for his innovative directing of the Broadway revivals of *Sweeney Todd* (2005) and *Company* (2006); Simon McBurney, a founder and artistic director of the London-based Théâtre de Complicité, directed *The Resistible Rise of Arturo Ui* and *All My Sons* (2008), both in New York; and Les Waters, who served as an associate artistic director of the Berkeley Repertory Theatre, championed the work of emerging playwrights, including Sarah Ruhl. The collaboration between Anne Bogart and Japanese director Tadashi Suzuki offered another model for productive artistic exchange. Bogart and Suzuki joined forces to create a dialogue between the Suzuki Method and Viewpoints Training. Founded in 1992, their SITI Company carried its mission into the twenty-first century, striving 'to redefine and revitalize contemporary theater in the United States through an emphasis on international cultural exchange and collaboration'.[91] Other international collaborations included the Denver Theatre Center production of *Tantalus* (2000), a ten-and-a-half-hour revisioning of Greek myths staged by British director Peter Hall, and Peter Sellars's production of Euripides's *Children of Herackles* (2002), which played at international festivals in addition to the American Repertory Theater in 2003. Sellars stressed the importance of creating shared cultural spaces that included a diversity of voices. His production of *Children of Herackles* featuring an international ensemble of performers from Romania, the Czech Republic, Indonesia and the United States became one of these shared spaces: an artistic and ideological platform for 'raising questions about the possibility of honor, human rights and retribution in contemporary political life'.[92]

With the support of the Theatre Communications Group, several international residency and partnership programmes received substantial funding to facilitate inter- and multicultural exchange. Among them was the International Theatre Partnership Program (1999–2000) that fostered collaborations between five American theatres – Borderlands Theater (Tucson, Arizona), Dell'Arte Players Company (Blue Lake, California), GALA Hispanic Theatre (Washington, DC), Repertorio Espanol (New York) and San Diego Repertory Theatre – and theatre artists from Mexico, Brazil and Argentina. Other international initiatives under TCG sponsorship included the New Generations Program, which provided support for international fellowships, and the ACTivate Change: Bridging Cultural Exchange and Creativity Pre-Conference, which TCG/ITI-US (the US Center of the International Theatre Institute) held in 2009 in Washington, DC, 'a historic gathering [that] united 115 international artists, representatives from theatres, government agencies, labor unions and cultural ministries'.[93]

A few performing arts centres, summer programmes and laboratories offered emerging artists the opportunity to share creative space intended for interdisciplinary and multicultural experiments. The Eugene O'Neill Center in Connecticut, the Atlantic Center for the Arts in New Smyrna, Florida, and the Watermill Center in Water Mill, New York, provided places and inspiration for artistic initiatives that stimulate collaboration and forge the exchange of practices and resources. Rooted in an interdisciplinary approach to art-making that goes beyond performing arts disciplines, the Watermill Center was founded by Robert Wilson, a visual artist as well as a theatre director, in 2006. 'A community of global artists', Watermill focused on 'integrating performing arts practice with resources from the humanities, research from the sciences, and inspiration from the visual arts'.[94]

Interdisciplinary connections and global influences were features of international festivals that proliferated in the first decade of the century. The Brooklyn Academy of Music's annual Next Wave Festival continued to introduce American audiences to the most provocative performing arts projects created across the globe. Similarly, the Lincoln Center Festival held in the summer in New York City offered innovative performances in dance, music, puppetry and theatre, fostering interdisciplinary perspectives among different arts and audiences, in addition to an awareness of international trends. The New York International Fringe Festival, founded in 1997, presented emerging avant-garde work, often inter- and multidisciplinary in nature. The Under the Radar Festival, 'a festival tracking new theater around the world',[95] is of particular importance for the development of experimental and multicultural theatre. Created in 2005 by the former artistic director of P.S. 122,[96] Mark Russell, the festival introduced new visions, techniques and perspectives in theatre and performance art and instantly became a fertile ground for artistic innovation. Initially hosted by St Ann's Warehouse in Brooklyn, Under the Radar moved to the Public Theater in downtown Manhattan, where each January it celebrated the work of experimental individual artists and collectives from the United States and abroad that were deeply engaged in generating an original vocabulary that encompassed performance art, object theatre, puppetry, dance, spoken word, visual art, film and multimedia. Invited performers and collectives were often established avant-garde names, such as Bogart and the SITI Company, Ping Chong and Mabou Mines's Lee Breuer and Ruth Maleczech, as well as new ensembles and developing artists such as TEAM (Theatre of the Emerging American Movement) and Brooklyn-based hip-hop artist Lemon Andersen. The festival also featured hundreds of international collectives, including the United Kingdom artists Tim Etchells and Tim Crouch, the Moscow New Generation Theatre and the Belarus Free Theatre. Excitement about the work presented by Under the Radar triggered the growth of similar festivals: Performance Space 122's COIL Festival, the Incubator Arts Project's Other Forces, the Devised Theater Initiative at the Public Theater, and Radar L.A. – a Pacific Rim version of Under the Radar. Russell was committed not only to promoting international exchange but also to exposing a wider range of spectators to avant-garde culture. Commenting on his impetus to spark a relationship between experimental theatre collectives and regional theatre companies, Russell pointed to the untapped resources of regional theatres and asked, 'Why were these intriguing ensembles not intersecting with these slow-moving institutions? Can we take some of this energy and raise all boats?'[97]

As the decade neared its close, the connection between ensemble-based theatre groups – both from the United States and other countries – and institutional theatres grew stronger, perhaps because of the efforts of the Under the Radar Festival and similar theatre organizations. Artistic endeavours that challenge the distinction between traditional text-based work and non-traditional, non-scripted theatre included collaborations between the Actors Theatre of Louisville and the Philadelphia ensemble New Paradise Laboratories, La Jolla Playhouse and the Pig Iron Theatre Company, and the Oregon Shakespeare Festival and Culture Clash. To quote critic Steven Leigh Morris, 'International possibilities aside, ensembles are generating vitality on the home front ... altering the scope of theatre's seasons as well as the artistry they aim to nurture.'[98]

New writing

Companies and ventures

After the catastrophe of 9/11, the wars in Afghanistan and Iraq and increased political and economic polarization, theatre artists found greater need to re-examine issues of identity and diversity, especially in relation to power, moral relativism and cultural fragmentation. In playwriting, specifically, established as well as emerging writers sought to reflect on social anxieties of the time, which were an outgrowth of post-9/11 isolation and alienation. As playwrights tackled multiple tensions around the relativity of truth and the constructed nature of identity, they experimented with a variety of styles beyond traditional, linear storytelling – reflecting the modern world's associative, fragmented way of sending and receiving messages. The decade also saw a slight growth in interest on the part of producing theatre organizations and new play development initiatives in commissioning and staging new works that expanded the representation of previously silenced voices and perspectives.

Playwrights Horizons particularly stood out among American theatres that expressed a commitment to developing and producing new work during the decade. Presenting itself as 'a writer's theater dedicated to the support and development of contemporary American playwrights, composers and lyricists, and to the production of their new work', Playwrights Horizons was the only company in New York whose mission uniquely centred on fostering new writing. The list of significant new works that Playwrights Horizons produced in the first decade of the 2000s included Doug Wright's *I Am My Own Wife* (2004 Tony Award, Best Play); Doug Wright, Scott Frankel and Michael Korie's *Grey Gardens* (three 2007 Tony Awards); Craig Lucas's *Small Tragedy* (2004 Obie Award, Best American Play); Lynn Nottage's *Fabulation, or the Re-Education of Underline* (2005 Obie Award for Playwriting); and Annie Baker's *Circle Mirror Transformation* (2009). In 2008, the theatre received a special Drama Desk Award for 'ongoing support to generations of theater artists and undiminished commitment to producing new work'.[99] By 2009, Playwrights Horizons completed a major multi-phase renovation that began in 2001 and included a new theatre complex, as well as the remodelling of 440 Studios in downtown Manhattan, which considerably expanded the theatre's rehearsal space and provided further opportunities for developing plays and forging new artistic collaborations.

A few other New York-based and regional theatres, among them the New York Public Theater, the Vineyard Theatre, La MaMa, Woolly Mammoth in Washington, DC, Steppenwolf Theatre in Chicago and American Conservatory Theater in San Francisco, offered various initiatives for emerging playwrights. To encourage new work that would attract a younger, diversified audience, the New York Public Theater, under the artistic direction of Oskar Eustis, launched in 2007 the 'Emerging Writers Group' of young playwrights who, in addition to a two-year fellowship and stipend, would receive at least one reading at the theatre. The Vineyard Theatre, also recognized for producing exciting new theatre such as *Avenue Q* and Jenny Schwartz's 'arrestingly odd'[100] drama *God's Ear* (2008), offered the Paula Vogel Playwriting Award, which started in 2008 to provide financial and creative support to develop a new work over the course of one season. Another recent example of a newly established theatre project that focused on 'producing the work of new artists and building new audiences' was LCT3 – Lincoln Center Theater's programming initiative.[101] This programme was housed at the Claire Tow Theater, the two-storey, 23,000-square-foot space built on the roof of the Vivian Beaumont Theater; the Claire Tow Theater opened in June 2012.

The National Playwrights and National Musical Theatre Conferences at the Eugene O'Neill Theater Center continued to lead emerging playwrights and composers through development to production. Both *Avenue Q* and *In the Heights* were presented at the National Music Theatre Conference in 2002 and 2005, respectively. Nottage was a Writer in Residence at the O'Neill Center in the summer of 2006 while developing *Ruined*, a critically acclaimed play that won the Pulitzer Prize for Drama in 2009. Other plays developed at the O'Neill Center included Julia Cho's *Durango* (2006), Adam Bock's *The Receptionist* (2007), Rebecca Gilman's *The Crowd You're In With* (2007) and Jason Grote's *1001* (2007). Works developed at the O'Neill continued their production life at many New York and regional theatres – the Manhattan Theatre Club, the Cherry Lane Theatre, the Women's Project Theater, Steppenwolf Theatre Company, the Mark Taper Forum, Berkeley Rep, Yale Rep, Goodman Theatre, the Magic Theatre, Woolly Mammoth Theatre Company and Actors Theatre of Louisville's Humana Festival of New American Plays, to name a few.[102]

A few scattered efforts encouraged new plays by women writers and other minority groups. The Women's Project Theater, founded in 1978, remained loyal to its mission to develop and produce 'the work of female theater artists at every stage in their careers'.[103] One of its key initiatives, the Antigone Project, presented adaptations of *Antigone* by Tanya Barfield, Karen Hartman, Chiori Miyagawa, Nottage and Caridad Svich in the 2004–5 season. Another significant event, Chicago's Ignition Festival, which first opened in 2008 under the leadership of Victory Gardens Theater, attracted nearly 800 spectators and became a major platform for playwrights of colour younger than age 40. Sandy Shinners, associate artistic director of the Victory Gardens Theater who spearheaded this biennial event, specifically pointed to the festival's challenge 'to nurture new work by playwrights of color through the development process to mainstage productions'. She stressed the necessity 'to maintain the relationships we are building with these writers, and jump-start more productions around the country'.[104]

Despite the venues, awards and programmes that became available for new writing during the 2000s, concern grew among young playwrights about the substantial growth of overdeveloped and unproduced plays. To address this issue, the National New Play Network (NNPN), 'the country's alliance of nonprofit theaters that champions the development, production, and continued life of new plays',[105] began in 2002 to offer the National Showcase of New Plays – a three-day festival presenting unproduced plays in a staged reading format to members' artistic directors and literary managers. Of the plays presented at this festival, more than 80 per cent received their first production in the next three years.[106] Another initiative to counter 'the trend of endless readings and new play development programs'[107] came from playwrights themselves: 13P (Thirteen Playwrights, Inc.) was launched in 2002 by mid-career playwrights – Sheila Callaghan, Erin Courtney, Madeleine George, Rob Handel, Ann Marie Healy, Julia Jarcho, Young Jean Lee, Winter Miller, Sarah Ruhl, Kate E. Ryan, Lucy Thurber, Anne Washburn and Gary Winter – with the goal to fundraise and promote their work in order to produce one play by each member playwright.

Still, by 2009, a survey of the dialogue between playwrights and artistic directors across the country, presented in Todd London's book *Outrageous Fortune: The Life and Times of the New American Play*, found 'the relationship between playwrights and producing not-for-profit theatres is collaboration in crisis. The two groups studied are deeply divided in how they view each other, the audience and the successes and obstacles of the field of new play production.'[108] The study was conducted over a period of seven years and involved 250 playwrights and close to 100 not-for-profit theatres that regularly produced new work. In most playwrights' opinions, artistic directors' choices in selecting new work for production were primarily driven by theatre economics – a preoccupation with increasing ticket sales despite theatres' not-for-profit missions. Therefore, most plays they chose called for small casts or presented less controversial themes presumably favoured by the audience; theatres also privileged critically recognized playwrights over emerging young voices. Theatre leaders, in turn, expressed frustration over the lack of private and government funding and the playwrights' unwillingness to understand 'the cold realities of the business'.[109]

Also in the later years of the decade, the underrepresentation of women writers on American stages received heightened attention from playwrights and feminist scholars. Playwright Marsha Norman questioned American theatres' unfaltering resistance to producing plays written by women. Writing in 2009, she observed:

> This past season, theatres around the country did six plays by men for every one by a woman, and a lot of theatres did

no work by women at all, and haven't for years. And as the writing has disappeared, so have roles for actresses and jobs for costume designers and directors. It doesn't take an economist to draw a conclusion here. Either women can't write, or there is some serious resistance to producing the work of women on the American stage.[110]

This problem was even more frustrating, Norman argued, because 'in the last 10 years, according to *American Theatre*'s lists of the top 10 most-produced plays at TCG theatres, 30 percent of the top 2 on the lists were written by women. That's nearly double the percentage at which plays by women are produced overall.'[111] Scholars Penny Farfan and Lesley Ferris also confronted 'the lack of parity for women playwrights'. Their 2013 publication, *Contemporary Women Playwrights into the Twenty-First Century*, a collection of critical essays, was intended to 'support, promote, and advance the work of women playwrights'[112] in the United States and around the world.

Plays and playwrights

Although there is hardly a uniform subject matter that dominated new writing during the period, international conflicts, increased globalization and the national isolation that overshadowed the decade compelled American playwrights to tackle complicated questions of personal and social belonging and responsibility, especially around issues of sexuality, gender, race and politics. Since the work of the four playwrights featured in this book is examined in detail in the following chapters, this section will discuss briefly the contributions of other writers, paying primary attention to the larger dialogue about social responsibility and the necessity for personal empowerment and agency in contemporary society.

Tensions around gender identity and sexual orientation came into focus in American playwriting of the 2000s. In the one-man show *I Am My Own Wife* (2003), Doug Wright tells the extraordinary story of Charlotte von Mahlsdorf, an antiques collector from East Berlin who, living openly as a cross-dresser most of her life, survived both the Nazi regime and the Stasi, the East German secret police. 'In an age where politicians still routinely decry homosexuality on the evening news and "fag" remains the most stinging of all playground epithets, Charlotte's dogged insistence on her sexuality could prove downright curative; an antidote for a community too often besieged by public condemnation and internalized self-loathing,' Wright wrote in 2003, reflecting on his interest in writing a play about this remarkable person.[113] Richard Greenberg set *Take Me Out*, winner of the 2003 Tony and Drama Desk Awards, in a baseball team's locker room and examined the ramifications of being an openly gay athlete in a culture permeated by sexual and racial prejudice. Edward Albee, in *The Goat, or Who Is Sylvia* (2002 Tony and Drama Desk Awards), reinvigorated the discussion about the boundaries of personal and social tolerance as it relates to sexual orientation and moral responsibility.

As the representation of gender perspectives came to the forefront of American culture in the 2000s, playwrights continued to investigate gender dynamics in personal relationships as well as social structures. Rebecca Gilman's *Boy Gets Girl*, which premiered in 2000 at the Goodman Theatre in Chicago, is a story of a successful independent New York woman who loses her identity as she tries to escape from a menacing relationship with a man she met on a blind date. David Auburn's *Proof* (2001), a multiple-award-winning play, taps into gender stereotypes affecting women's potential for high achievements in science. Judith Thompson, a Canadian whose work received an enthusiastic response in the United States and was staged by several American theatres, including Playwrights Horizons, contemplates the implications of sexist attitudes in the military and society in her docudrama *Palace of the End* (2008). Among other topics, this play investigates the experience of women soldiers at war through the perspective of American Army Reservist Lynndie England, who was court-martialled for abusing prisoners at Abu Ghraib. Ensler's *Unnecessary Targets* (2001) and Nottage's *Ruined* (2009) tell the harrowing stories of women who were sexually abused and tortured in war zones.

Race and ethnicity found their way into the works of many playwrights of the decade, including Suzan-Lori Parks, Nilo Cruz, Svich and Cho. These writers viewed identity as a complicated, evolving concept that embraces transcultural sensibilities and a multiplicity of identities. Scholar Debby Thomson said Parks's plays 'are ... performing an archeology of race, and especially of

African American female identity as a subject position'.[114] Her 'Red Letter Plays', *In the Blood* and *Fucking A* (the former was originally produced in 1999 at the New York Public Theater; the latter premiered in 2000 at the experimental company Diverse Works/Infernal Bridgegroom Productions in Houston, Texas), treat identity as a problematic, fluid construct for race and gender. In *Anna in the Tropics*, Cruz, the first Latino playwright to receive the Pulitzer Prize for Drama in 2003, explores the culture of Cuban immigrants working in a sugar factory in Tampa, Florida. Noting that he was drawn to the celebration of Latin culture rather than the portrayal of its victimization, he pointed to his own Latin sensibility, which influenced the musical, poetic language of his plays as well as their cultural contexts. Svich, who was born in the United States to parents from Cuban, Argentine, Spanish and Croatian backgrounds, examines the 'sense of dislocation' through her work, including *The House of Spirits* (2009), an adaptation of Isabel Allende's celebrated novel tracing three generations of women in a Latin American country. As a writer negotiating many different cultures that she both inherited and discovered, Svich addresses 'explorations of wanderlust, dispossession, biculturalism, bilingualism, construction of identity'.[115]

Cho, in *99 Histories* (2002), focuses on intergenerational conflict in relation to her characters' personal memories and their grasp of cultural identity. Like other Asian American women playwrights such as Diana Son (in *Satellites*, 2006) and Young Jean Lee (in *Songs of the Dragons Flying to Heaven*, 2006), Cho resists fixed cultural assumptions in creating her characters, displaying a complex understanding of identity as multidimensional and evolving.

As the country went through the process of collective mourning after 9/11, playwrights, too, felt compelled to address the difficult subject of dying or coping with the death of a loved one. In *Rabbit Hole*, a play by David Lindsay-Abaire that won a Pulitzer Prize in 2007, a couple learns how to live with the loss of their four-year-old son in an car accident. Capturing an overwhelming sense of devastation and isolation that the characters struggle with, the play poignantly examines the dangerous impact of death on marriage, family, professional life and one's sense of self. *August: Osage County* (2008 Pulitzer Prize, Tony and Drama Desk Awards), Tracy Letts's black comedy about a highly dysfunctional family that reunites after the father goes missing, also explores the devastating implications of loss – real and imagined. Mary Zimmerman's *Metamorphoses* (2002 Drama Desk Award), a series of vignettes based on Ovid's classic poem, is a poetic contemplation on death and the transformative power of love. Developed at Northwestern University and the Lookingglass Theatre, the production moved to Off-Broadway's Second Stage Theatre, where it opened in October 2001. Although the play was not created in direct response to 9/11, its New York production was cathartic for the audience. Ben Brantley wrote in the *New York Times*:

> It was then less than a month after the terrorist attacks of Sept. 11, and the show's ritualistic portrayal of love, death and transformation somehow seemed to flow directly from the collective unconscious of a stunned city. *Metamorphoses* became a sold-out hit, and every night you could hear the sounds of men and women openly crying.[116]

Whether directly or indirectly, American drama also participated in the national dialogue about the representation of truth and freedom of speech. In *Copenhagen* by Michael Frayn and *Doubt* by John Patrick Shanley, characters seek truth, only to encounter ambiguity and conflicting points of view. *Copenhagen* (2000 Tony and Drama Desk Awards) poses the impossibility of reconstructing the past by relying on characters' memories. In *Doubt* (2005 Pulitzer, Tony and Drama Desk Awards), set in a 1960s Catholic school, a traditionalist nun accuses a progressive priest of sexually abusing the first African American boy to become a student there. Although her suspicion is never proved, the nun's accusations prompt the priest to leave the parish. (This play coincided with increased attention to cases of Catholic priests' sexual abuse of boys.) Shinn's *Now or Later* (2008), which premiered at the Royal Court in London, explores the tensions surrounding expressions of personal truth and freedom of speech, in this case in relation to political correctness and censorship. Alluding to the rioting and death threats around the world after a Danish newspaper published cartoons of the Prophet Mohammed in 2005, the play 'focuses on the ramifications of America's confrontations with the Islamic world', warning of the threat to free public expression 'posed by the fear of fundamentalist violence'.[117]

Theatre experienced a complicated relationship with media, embracing new methods of publicizing and marketing, but also critiquing media for generating and propagating cultural stereotypes and fetishes. Responding to America's infatuation with physical appearances promoted through media, particularly social media outlets, playwrights questioned the American fixation on physical beauty and glamorization of celebrity culture. LaBute's plays, including *The Shape of Things* (2001), *fat pig* (2004) and *Reasons to Be Pretty* (2009), confront 'our obsession with the surface of things, the shape of them'.[118] Christopher Innes asserts that these plays 'explicitly embody (in a literal and physical sense) the contemporary American obsession with advertising-determined physical ideals. What can be called or seen as beauty – and what should it matter in our estimate of ourselves, or others?'[119] Lisa Kron takes up questions of wellness and spiritual health in her autobiographical *Well*, which had a successful run in 2004 at the New York Public Theater and then debuted on Broadway in 2006. A renowned stand-up memoirist and a former member of the lesbian theatre collective the Five Lesbian Brothers, Kron suggests that wellness, regardless of the cultural obsession with physical appearance, is a state of mind rooted in our ability to embrace the confusing and the messy and to accept the complicated, uncomfortable and painful.

Other solo performance artists such as Anna Deavere Smith, Deb Margolin, Robbie McCauley and Peggy Shaw addressed illness, pain and aging. Smith's *Let Me Down Easy*, which premiered in 2008 at Second Stage Theatre, is a 'collection of testimonials about life, death and the care of the ailing body'.[120] Among the characters that Smith embodies in her show are athletes who push their physical ability beyond its human limits; writer and activist Ensler, who 'deplores the cultural pressure on women to simulate agelessness';[121] and a physician at a New Orleans public hospital who shares heartbreaking stories about his patients in the aftermath of Hurricane Katrina. Unlike the documentary character of *Let Me Down*, which Smith created from multiple interviews that she conducted (a methodology that she employed in her other acclaimed solo works), the performances offered by Margolin in *O Yes I Will (I will remember the spirit and texture of this conversation)* (2007), Shaw in *Must: The Inside Story* (2008) and McCauley in *Sugar* (2011) were confessions about the artists' own struggles with illness and pain. Feminist scholar Elin Diamond wrote:

> Eloquently, wittily, Margolin, McCauley, and Shaw beckon us into their states of emergency ... Shame at their pain isolates us and yet queerly, beautifully, it also activates our interest, our uncontrollable relation to their bodily lives, not in spite of cancer, diabetes, and stroke, but because of them, and because of what we know of them in our own lives.[122]

Many playwrights in the first decade of the 2000s wrote for film and television, provoking discussion about maintaining the uniqueness of theatre or further blurring the boundaries between theatre and screen. In 2008, the Humana Festival of New American Plays, Actors Theatre of Louisville and *American Theatre* convened a conversation with playwrights Gina Gionfriddo, Rolin Jones and Adam Rapp, who wrote for TV shows such as *Law and Order*, *Weeds* and *The L Word*, respectively. Addressing 'the culture and aesthetics of crossing media',[123] they pointed to a landscape changed by the television networks such as HBO, Showtime and FX that offered an economical alternative to expensive theatre-going. The accessibility of good television shows, in their opinion, prompted playwrights to rethink their approaches to storytelling in theatre and recognize the significance of visual storytelling techniques, often through integrating technology and digital media. In addition, they identified the implications of television and new media for their theatre writing, especially economy in the plot and compression of dialogue. Rapp observed that 'the compression of scenes ... is really important in television and film. The mood is more important than dialogue ... Learning how to compress has made me a better editor and a better first-draft writer. My theatre scripts are a little leaner now.'[124]

Although playwrights benefited from media-inspired shifts in writing style, they expressed resistance to heavily mediated culture. A younger generation of women writers stood out, directly responding, in different ways, to the shifting cultural environment and multiple pressures that theatre experienced in a media-dominated global landscape. Gionfriddo (*After Ashley*, 2004) sharply ridiculed the intrusive, damaging role of media after the murder of a woman. Baker (*Circle Mirror Transformation*, 2009) captured the quiet naturalness and precision of conversations among people in a creative drama class in a small Vermont town. Svich (*Iphigenia Crash Land Falls on the Neon Shell That Was Once Her Heart*, 2004) barraged the audience with videotaped and live-streamed images. Commenting on the intersections of media, technology and the representation of a female body in Svich's play, critic Lillian Manzor wrote that 'Iphigenia ... a rave fable ... performs the mediated culture of simulacra of global capitalism, where the body, especially the female body, is objectified to the point that the boundaries between the "real" and the mediated are blurred.'[125]

Conclusion

Writing about a recent past offers many advantages – but also many challenges. A plethora of information, in print and on the Internet, about events of the 2000s and their aftermath was available to inform our attempt to contribute to and, in some cases, to establish discourse on American theatre in the decade. As Cindy Rosenthal and I became aware of a multitude of histories and memories of the period, we decided to take a broad, necessarily subjective, view. It might be too early to step back and view the period with perspective, however. Our choices of plays, productions and trends unavoidably exclude some histories, even though we privilege a multiplicity of voices. We must acknowledge that for all our effort, we might have omitted significant events and discoveries.

Regardless of an individual perspective and aesthetic preference, regardless of whether an audience member enjoyed Broadway musicals or embraced experimental theatre experiences, what seems certain in looking at the decade is that theatre consciously engaged in multiple dialogues about political and social concerns. Indeed, in addition to the particular events, trends and artistic interactions that the chapter has addressed, this engagement can be seen in theatre communities' moves to protest against the Iraq and Afghanistan wars, raise awareness about environmental devastation, especially after the Katrina disaster, and draw attention to human rights violations. Theaters Against War (THAW), which was formed in late 2002 and included over 250 member theatres, primarily in New York City, facilitated a series of performances, readings and demonstrations that opposed the US-led wars.[126] Post-Katrina plays and performances such as José Torres-Tama's multimedia solo piece *The Cone of Uncertainty* (2005) and John Biguenet's metaphoric drama *Rising Water* (2007) grapple with 'the nature of home, memory, loss, environmental decay and destruction, the city's insider-versus-outsider dynamic, racism, and economic and social justice'.[127] Theatre artists and playwrights continued to wrestle with environmental (in)justice, ecological degradation and sustainability, expanding the dialogue about the environment beyond American borders to address international crises. This dialogue, which included eco-plays by E. M. Lewis (*Song of Extinction*, 2009) and Kia Corthron (*A Cool Dip in a Barren Saharan Crick*, 2010), re-examined ecological meanings and perspectives, reconceptualized 'community' to incorporate 'the nonhuman and/or land as characters or agents' and reimagined 'intersections between nature and culture'.[128]

Writing about the Culture Project's revival of *The Exonerated* in 2012, *New York Times* critic Ken Jaworowski remarked that 'ten years after its New York premiere', this documentary play based on personal accounts of people unjustly sentenced to death 'still has the power to unsettle'.[129] This power of theatre to unsettle, to affect viscerally, to instigate political debate and to form an immediate bond between theatre-makers and the audience reverberated throughout the decade in and across different settings – Broadway and experimental stages, regional theatres and site-specific performances, playwriting and devised work, traditionally staged productions and cross-media theatrical events. As theatre artists searched for new ways to express themselves and for new models to finance their expressions, American theatre remained a dynamic social and cultural force in the 2000s.

3

Charles Mee

Scott T. Cummings

Introduction

> I like to take a Greek play, smash it to ruins, and then, atop the ruins, write a new play. The new play will often take some of the character names of the Greek piece and some of the story – even some of the ruined structure. But it will be set in today's world. I feel no need to be faithful in any way to the 'original.' Indeed, I often wonder if what I start with can really be considered an original anyway.
>
> Charles Mee[1]

At the start of the twenty-first century, Charles Mee emerged on the national theatre scene as an important and singular playwright whose radical aesthetic challenged conventional thinking about authorship and originality. His work stems from the conviction that cultural production on both an individual and societal level is a perpetual and palimpsestic process of reusing and recombining the materials, techniques and ideas of the past in new and different ways. His plays make this process overt and explicit. Inspired by visual artists from Max Ernst and Kurt Schwitters to Joseph Cornell and Robert Rauschenberg, Mee has championed the use of collage practices as a playwriting strategy. Not only are most of his scripts built on the shattered scaffolding of a classical play, mainly the Greeks but also Shakespeare, Molière, Racine, Gorky and Brecht, they are filled with passages that are taken verbatim from a wide range of sources, from political theorist Hannah Arendt and cultural critic Elaine Scarry to Internet chat rooms and grocery store tabloids.

Mee's cut-and-paste dramaturgy results in plays that are extravagant, disjointed and wild in their theatricality. But they are not dada plays or chance operations in the spirit of John Cage. They are shaped by Mee's idiosyncratic sensibility, animated by big thematic questions about what it means to be a human being, and populated by characters driven more by primal passions than personal psychology. They demand a sure-handed director who can orchestrate language, movement, music and spectacle in a coherent fashion that does not smooth over the rough edges or rationalize the abrupt leaps of fancy that characterize the texts. In this regard, Mee has benefited from his association with some of the most creative American stage directors of his time, among them Martha Clarke, Robert Woodruff, Anne Bogart, Tina Landau, Les Waters, David Schweizer and Daniel Fish.

Mee's plays also appeal to upstart theatre ensembles and ambitious young directors who welcome his invitation to 'pillage the plays as I have pillaged the structures and contents of the plays of Euripides and Brecht and stuff out of Soap Opera Digest and the evening news and the internet'.[2] To facilitate this, since the mid-1990s – that is, before the emergence of the Internet as we know it – Mee has posted his plays at no cost on his website titled 'the (re)making project'. While the texts are free as source material for a new work, the site reminds visitors that performance rights are required to produce the scripts as he composed them. Since 1998, those scripts and the playbills for Mee productions have included a note acknowledging the financial support of Richard B. Fisher and Jeanne Donovan Fisher, philanthropists with a love of the arts who became Mee's personal patrons. Their generous annual subsidy, unparalleled in American theatre, made it possible for Mee to quit his day job as an editor of health newsletters and concentrate on his playwriting full-time. He has been writing at a prodigious rate ever since.[3]

Mee first began to write plays in the 1950s as an undergraduate at Harvard. When he graduated in 1960, he moved to Greenwich

Village and got involved in Off-Off-Broadway theatre, writing one-act plays seen at various downtown venues and working as an editor at *TDR* (when it was still the *Tulane Drama Review*). Life, work and the politics of the late 1960s led him away from theatre for two decades. He went from being a fact-checker to editor-in-chief at *Horizon*, a highbrow, hardbound magazine of the arts published by American Heritage. He got involved in opposition to the Vietnam War and the presidency of Richard Nixon. And he began writing books about history for a general readership, many of them – such as *Meeting at Potsdam* (1975), *The End of Order: Versailles 1919* (1980), *The Marshall Plan: The Launching of the Pax Americana* (1984) and *Playing God: Seven Fateful Moments When Great Men Met to Change the World* (1993) – about international diplomacy and the liminal moment between war and peace.

In 1985, Mee was introduced by Joseph Papp to the choreographer Martha Clarke when she was in the process of creating *Vienna: Lusthaus*, a dance theatre piece inspired by the art of fin-de-siècle Vienna. Mee joined the project and contributed a series of monologues – some based on his own dreams and some taken from the writings of Freud and Wittgenstein – that offset Clarke's erotic movement sequences and the vivid imagery provided by the designers.[4] The success of this production effectively marked the beginning of Mee's career as a playwright, and as it toured the US and eventually abroad, his other scripts gained more and more attention, leading to readings, workshops and productions at several downtown theatres. Two of these plays from the late 1980s – *Bedtime Stories* and *The Rules*[5] – call for the producer and director to add a 'performance piece' (unscripted by Mee) between scenes of the play, an early sign of his Postmodern penchant for disrupting the continuity of his spoken texts with outbursts of spectacle, often determined by the director and performers. In this and other ways, Mee's work is insistently open to interpretation and interpolation. He exercises minimal control over the production of his plays. He prefers to stay away from rehearsals, even for the first production of a new script, unless explicitly asked to attend by the director, observing (with characteristic wit), 'I'm not a person who thinks there's a definitive version of anything – of civilization, of a history book, or of a production of a play. Plus, I've always thought the playwrights who get the best productions are the dead playwrights, so I thought it might be best to behave like one.'[6]

In the 1990s, Mee began to remake Greek tragedy from his contemporary point of view. He created versions of *Orestes*, *The Bacchae*, *Agamemnon* and *The Trojan Women*, each filled with karaoke numbers, variety acts, dance breaks, fight sequences, performance events and physical outbursts. This was also the decade in which Mee initiated collaborations with three cutting-edge directors – Woodruff, Bogart and Landau – who were central to the early stage of his career. Within a span of two years (1991–3), all three of them staged productions of Mee's *Orestes 2.0*, a savage and dystopian play that transposed the action from the palace at Argos to the psychiatric ward of a military hospital, which is somehow also the lawn of 'a palatial white Newport-style or Palm Beach-style beach house'.[7] Matt Wilder, an early champion of Mee's work, described his take on Euripides as 'an outcry that seems to encapsulate all the atrocity and folly of the contemporary predicament. Its assemblage of found texts high and low produces less an eighties-style "postmodern" collision or commentary than a schizzy meltdown of all boundaries. It mates fear and pity with scarring Artaudian cruelty with the crippling panic attack caused by picking up a newspaper.'[8]

Over the course of the decade, the apocalyptic tragedy of Mee's *Orestes 2.0* gave way bit by bit to plays that contained elements of comedy, such as the genre's interest in exploring normative social values and the vagaries of love, romance and relations between men and women. In the first decade of the new century, this led Mee to turn from the Greeks to Shakespeare and other sources for inspiration, but not until after he wrote one more variation on the Greeks: *Big Love*. It has proven to be his most popular and frequently produced play.

Big Love

Big Love premiered in March 2000 at the Actors Theatre of Louisville, the first of six Mee plays to debut at its annual Humana Festival of New American Plays between 2000 and 2015. This original production, directed by Waters, was also presented at Long Wharf Theatre in New Haven, Berkeley Repertory Theatre and Chicago's Goodman Theatre, and at the prestigious Next

Wave Festival at the Brooklyn Academy of Music. More productions followed at other noteworthy US regional theatres, including Seattle Repertory Theatre, Rude Mechanicals in Austin, Woolly Mammoth Theatre Company in Washington, DC, Dallas Theater Center, Wilma Theater in Philadelphia, as well as at the Abbey Theatre in Dublin. The play is hardly conventional, but its strong, simple narrative, appealing characters and romantic themes have helped to make it Mee's most widely seen play, with productions at dozens of colleges and universities around the US and even a handful of secondary schools. In effect, the play put Mee on the map of nationally recognized playwrights.[9]

Big Love is based on *The Suppliants*, once thought to be the oldest extant Greek tragedy, and on what is known from surviving fragments from the second and third plays in Aeschylus's Danaid trilogy. The trilogy tells the story of fifty sisters, the daughters of Danaos and descendants of the Argive priestess Io, who flee Egypt and a forced marriage to fifty cousins in order to seek asylum in their ancestral homeland in Greece. Pelasgos, king of Argos, receives them, but when the would-be grooms arrive in pursuit and the Egyptian army lays siege to the city, the sisters have no choice, it seems, but to submit. Instead, they take a solemn oath and conspire to save themselves on their wedding night by murdering their husbands in their beds. All of them do exactly that, except for Hypermestra who claims to love her assigned mate and is put on trial for her betrayal. Based on fragmentary evidence, scholars have concluded that Aphrodite, the Goddess of Love, intercedes as the deus ex machina and resolves matters in Hypermestra's favour. Just as Aeschylus's *Oresteia* depicts the mythic origins of a Greek system of justice based on the rule of law and trial by jury, the Danaid trilogy is thought to dramatize the mythic origins of the institution of marriage based to some extent on love and a degree of mutual consent.

Mee telescopes the trilogy's narrative into a single play and shifts the setting to the terrace of a luxurious seaside villa in present-day Italy. For a Mee play, the plot is uncharacteristically clear and complete. The reluctant brides – reduced to three sisters named Lydia, Thyona and Olympia – arrive from Greece and appeal for sanctuary from the villa's wealthy and politically connected owner, Piero. The aggravated grooms – Nikos, Constantine and Oed, Greek by birth but American in attitude and citizenship – arrive in pursuit and demand the return of the women. Piero invites them in to see if some kind of compromise can be reached. That effort fails, so the wedding goes forward right there on the terrace until, in mid-ceremony, violence erupts and the brides turn on their husbands, leaving all of them dead but one. Lydia is immediately put on trial for violating her oath and sparing her husband Nikos. With Piero's mother Bella acting as judge and jury, Lydia is acquitted because, in the end, as Bella says, 'Love trumps all. Love is the highest law.'

On the model of Greek tragedy, the play alternates between these dramatic episodes and what amounts to choral interludes. There is no separate chorus per se, but the narrative pauses regularly as characters come forward – mainly the brides and the grooms but also Bella and her gay grandson Guiliano – to comment on their situation, express ardent feelings or share an anecdote about love and romance. These monologues include or alternate with music and movement that add flamboyant spectacle to the performance. For example, shortly after the brides arrive, they sing Leslie Gore's 1960s top-40 hit 'You Don't Own Me'. Later, at different moments, first the brides and then the grooms throw themselves to the ground again and again with brute force, cursing and shouting as deafening music plays. At one point, one of the men hurls circular saw blades across the stage into a wall wheeled on for that purpose. These theatrical paroxysms, central to the experience of the play, build to the murderous rampage that stops the wedding and fills the stage with utter pandemonium.

Two topics dominate the play's spoken text: the nature of men and women and the matter of force or being taken against one's will. The three sisters can be seen to represent three different archetypes of womanhood: Thyona is a man-hating arch-feminist who thinks 'boy babies should be flushed down the toilet at birth'; Olympia is a girly girl who likes to be submissive and pampered and 'wear short skirts that blow up in the wind'; and Lydia is a level-headed idealist who trusts her gut and thinks men and women should 'learn to live together/in common justice/reconciling our differences in peaceful conversation/reaching out with goodwill towards one another'. Their spectrum of views is contrasted with the men and in particular with Constantine, who delivers a disquisition on why 'it's not easy to be a man'. He begins by observing that historically men have been socialized to develop the capacity for violence because in times of war 'when push comes to shove/ and people need defending/then no one wants a good guy any more/ then they want a man who can fuck someone up'. When the war is over, he points out, a man is expected 'to carry on with life/as though he didn't have such impulses' for violence and destruction. This leads Constantine to a radical, provocative and disturbing conclusion: if the impulse to hurt is 'an inextricable part of civilization', then 'when a man turns this violence on a woman/in her bedroom, or in the midst of war' he is sharing with her an essential aspect of what it is to be a human being. Without that experience, she would not 'know the truth of how it is to live on earth'. So it is that he concludes, in effect, that rape 'is a gift that a man can give a woman'. As objectionable as this idea is, it has a perverse logic within the play's start-and-stop symposium on what is fair in love and war. 'People are taken against their will every day,' Constantine says to Thyona when the men first arrive, adding:

> Tomorrow will take today by force
> whether you like it or not.
> Time itself is an act of rape.
> Life is rape.
> No one asks to be born.
> No one asks to die.
> We are all taken by force, all the time.
> You make the best of it.
> You do what you have to do.

Other characters complicate matters when they point out paradoxically that being taken by force can be a choice. Olympia is unapologetic when she admits that 'I myself enjoy the freedom that submission gives me.' Giuliano, a mama's boy who sings Rodgers and Hart's 'Bewitched, bothered, and bewildered' at one point, observes that 'some people like to be taken forcibly. / If that's what they like, then that's okay. / And if not, then not. / I myself happen to like it.'

Big Love does not trouble itself to resolve the many dialectical questions that it raises. In the end, Bella's assertion that 'love is the highest law' takes place on a stage littered with corpses. The text indicates that Lydia and Nikos are 'shellshocked and devastated' as they leave the stage in a happy-ending sequence filled with wedding clichés (throwing rice, tossing the bouquet, taking pictures, Mendelssohn's 'Wedding March'). The forced note of canonical harmony in this moment rings with wishful sincerity and mocking irony both at once, a yin-and-yang duality typical of Mee's work that prompted one reviewer of *Big Love* to accuse the playwright of wanting to 'have his wedding cake and eat it too and smear it on everyone's faces'.[10] The observation is apt, and critics and other spectators have used similar ideas both to dismiss and to celebrate Mee's theatre, which is often raucous to the point of being cacophonous and anarchic.

Nevertheless, as the play made its way around the country, it struck many critics as a breath of fresh air. Writing of the Long Wharf production directed by Waters, Alvin Klein wrote, 'In theatrical scale, intellectual size and stylistic scope, "Big Love" bravely traverses expansive terrain ... [Mee's] leap of boundless imagination has refashioned tragedy into a theatrical statement that is comedic, gymnastic, musical, sensual, shocking and redemptive.'[11] The critic for the *San Francisco Chronicle* wrote, 'Part romantic vaudeville, part dramatic roundtable on marriage, power, violence and free will, and part nuptial wrestling match, Charles L. Mee's play works by its own intuitive logic.'[12] The *Hartford Courant* simply described it as 'crazy quilt theater'.[13] This boisterous hodgepodge quality can be frustrating or irritating or simply uninteresting for those who prefer a play with a coherent message and a clear narrative line. But a Mee play does not work that way. Instead, it asks to be experienced – at least in the moment of performance – on an affective and sensual basis, more like a musical concert, an evening of dance, a variety show or a gallery of paintings than an Aristotelian drama with a logical sequence of causally related events. No Mee play makes this more clear than *bobrauschenbergamerica*.

bobrauschenbergamerica

A year after *Big Love*, Mee returned to the Humana Festival in Louisville in March 2001 with *bobrauschenbergamerica*, a piece he wrote for Bogart and the SITI Company, the experimental ensemble theatre she co-founded with Japanese director Tadashi

Suzuki.[14] Bogart's 1992 staging of *Orestes 2.0* was the inaugural production of the SITI Company, and since then she and Mee had been looking for another opportunity to collaborate. After seeing a 1997 Robert Rauschenberg retrospective at the Guggenheim Museum in New York, Mee proposed to Bogart that they create a piece based on the artist: not a biography so much as a collage play in the manner of Rauschenberg, one that would borrow his themes, images and techniques to create a new theatrical composition. Rauschenberg's art, especially his pioneering work in the 1950s and 1960s, appealed to Mee for its combination of a wide range of found materials in a manner often described as democratic and populist. On that model, Mee decided to incorporate writings from as many other contributors as possible, including participants in a playwriting workshop organized for that purpose and members of the SITI Company, all of whom were well practised in the collective creation of devised work. As in other Mee plays, the early drafts of *bobrauschenbergamerica* contained general instructions for adding open-ended performance events to the action – including a scene that in its entirety simply read '*A beating occurs*' – and the SITI actors, designers and Bogart as director found clever and compelling ways to fulfil those provocations.[15]

Unlike many Mee plays, *bobrauschenbergamerica* is not based on a classic drama, although there are hints of Thornton Wilder's *Our Town* in the piece's celebration of ordinary, small-town American life. Instead, Rauschenberg's art – its playful, often jarring juxtapositions; its fascination with layering and the surfaces of things; its ethos of inclusiveness – provided the invisible substructure for the piece. The artist's presence was also insinuated by a character called Bob's Mom, who comes and goes through a screen door to deliver a series of monologues as if she is narrating a slide show about her dear son Bob when he was a boy. Mee's text explicitly states that the slides shown do not actually illustrate the moments she is describing, most of which are not in fact drawn from Rauschenberg's biography. As portrayed by Kelly Maurer in the original SITI production, Bob's Mom provided a comforting, maternal presence in the play, as if to reassure viewers that no matter how wild and disjointed the action became, everything was going to be okay in the end.

In addition to Bob's Mom, the play features seven other principals: three romantic couples – Phil the Trucker and Phil's Girl; Carl and Allen; and Susan and Wilson – and 'a derelict' named Becker, who Susan falls in and out of love with over the course of the action. As scholar Timothy Youker observes, a character's name is 'merely a label that Mee has affixed to a body of fragmentary source texts' that prompt 'the audience to attempt to read them as an organic whole' because they are spoken by a single actor wearing a costume that suggests a character to some degree.[16] And so, in the original SITI-Humana production designed by James Schuette, the performers seemed to represent a spectrum of American archetypes. Phil the Trucker, in a Harley Davidson T-shirt and green mesh cap, is a working man. Wilson's blue suit suggests he is a businessman or a lawyer, though he never speaks of such pursuits. Carl is a dancer (and by extension, an artist), and Allen seems to be a man of science, perhaps an astronomer or a physicist. In a soiled trench coat and wearing no shoes, Becker represents the poor and homeless. These demographic markers are superficial identities, surface indications of the American melting pot and not the sign of realistic characters with a personal psychology or individual past. In the original production, some casting choices helped to highlight the character type at work. For example, Phil's Girl, outfitted in a two-piece, orange-and-pink bathing suit reminiscent of actress Annette Funicello in 1960s beach movies, was played by Akiko Aizawa, a company member originally from Japan who speaks with a bit of an accent.

bobrauschenbergamerica begins with a prologue in which the play's characters crisscross the stage pushing or pulling one-of-a-kind prop constructions that allude to what Rauschenberg called his 'combines', collage sculptures whimsically fashioned from a miscellany of found materials and discarded objects. A voiceover provides what will prove to be a key to the performance ahead (and, for that matter, to Mee's work in general):

Look,
everything overlaps doesn't it?

Is connected some kind of way.
Once you put it all together, it's just obvious.
I mean, tie a string to something, and
see where it takes you.
The biggest thing is
don't worry about it.

A few moments later, in a similar vein, Becker reminisces about exploring the open country that stretched beyond the neighbourhood where he grew up:

> You could just go and go
> you didn't know where you were headed
> but you were a free person
> you'd see where it was you'd been
> after you came out of the woods at the end.

This trope of aimless wandering, heading out on an adventure without a map or a destination, improvising a journey based on whim and impulse, is the guiding principle of *bobrauschenbergamerica*, both thematically and structurally.

The piece proceeds to present forty-three distinct vignettes – monologues and dialogues, musical numbers, dance sequences, performance events – that add up to a kaleidoscopic, impressionist portrait of the United States of America in the second half of the twentieth century. There is a square dance, a line dance and a waltz, a backyard picnic, a yard sale and a game of checkers. At one point, Carl, a figure inspired in part by the Judson dancer Steve Paxton, takes a series of flying leaps into a huge pile of laundry that has just dropped from the flies overhead. Later, a series of shots ring out; Carl falls dead, the victim of an assassin's bullet; and a solemn mood overtakes the stage until Phil the Trucker enters and tells a series of corny chicken jokes. Then, Carl pops up from the floor and delivers a speech welcoming people to the opening of a gallery exhibition in which he admits, 'We don't often get to do a show like this/where we can just put on whatever we like.' At another overtly metatheatrical moment, a man in a full-body chicken suit slowly crosses the stage as a quiet, quizzical voice comes over the loudspeaker and says, 'A man in a chicken suit crosses the stage. Why does he cross the stage?' In this carefree, defiant manner, the action careens from one theatrical non sequitur to the next 'with giddy incongruity',[17] testing the audience's willingness to go with the flow and see where the performance is taking them.

Well over an hour into the performance, a figure who has not been seen before enters the stage as if he is not a member of the cast and had just walked in off the street. He is a pizza delivery boy coincidentally named Bob (not to be confused with Rauschenberg or the son of Bob's Mom). When he arrives, pizza box in hand and without introduction, he begins a long, rambling, confessional monologue by saying, 'And yet, I think, nonetheless, forgiveness is possible.' He proceeds to describe how years ago he stabbed his sister, her husband and their son to death in a delusional rage, his gruesome description made all the more menacing by a powerful stutter. The others listen to him with rapt attention, and when he finishes his troubling story, he simply says, with an irony that is typical of the play, 'Who ordered a pizza?' When no one claims it, he insists on being paid for 'the fucking pizza'; to avoid further excitement, the others scramble to give him money and he leaves without further comment. The tension of the scene, the longest in the play, is broken with a comic twist when Bob's Mom comes through the screen door, smiles when she spots the pizza she has been waiting for, grabs it and goes back inside.

This scene, titled 'The Dark Side', is conspicuous not only for its length but for its contrast in tone and content to the generally happy-go-lucky flow of events, marked by silliness one moment and sentimentality the next. It is also a prime example of Mee's common practice of using an extended piece of text, borrowed or not, in more than one play in order to see how it resonates in different contexts. 'I think I write plays the way painters paint paintings,' Mee says, pointing out, for example, that Van Gogh painted dozens of paintings of sunflowers, indoors and out, at different times of day, and so on.[18] In a similar vein, Mee feels free to use the same images or speeches in more than one play or the same speech twice in one play spoken by different characters and, for that matter, to write more than one play on the same subject. He rejects the expectation that each time a playwright writes a play it will be 'a great big new play about some subject they've absolutely never written about before. And there'll be different people in a different setting, talking about different stuff, living different lives.'[19] Mee feels no compunction about repeating himself, another way in which his work challenges the idea of originality.

Based on the transcript of a television interview with a convicted murderer, the haunting ten-minute monologue of Bob the Pizza Boy was first used in *Orestes 2.0* in 1991, and Mee also recycled it in *Summertime* and *Paradise Park*. For him, Bob the Pizza Boy:

reflects that strain of unfathomable violence in America. You listen to him speak and you think, this is weird and funny, and then, this is horrifying, and then you begin to have sympathy. And you finally conclude that you don't understand where his violence is coming from. I think human beings remain unfathomable.[20]

The insertion of Bob the Pizza Boy into *bobrauschenbergamerica* resonates with other eruptions of violence in the piece, including 'The Assassination' (described above) and 'The Beating', in which Allen methodically places earplugs in his ears and then beats an aluminium dustbin with a baseball bat until it is nearly flat. The abrupt discontinuity of these outbursts is Mee's way of making sure that his portrait of Middle America – as bucolic and nostalgic as it is at moments – includes the unfathomable and ubiquitous violence that is so much a part of the national culture.

With Bob the Pizza Boy's exit, the play turns toward home, and the rhythm of the performance becomes gentle and easygoing. A subtle, affective progression in the play from morning to noon to night now shifts into twilight and the tranquillity of a summer evening. Susan and Wilson have a short, sweet love scene and then waltz to Strauss. Becker delivers a panegyric ode to the common man lifted from Walt Whitman's *Leaves of Grass*. With crickets in the background and a night sky overhead, Bob's Mom reminisces one last time about her beloved boy, her words echoing the initial voiceover and the idea of tying a string to something to see where it leads:

You knew he was going to go somewhere,
you just didn't know where.

Isn't it something
how he can see the beauty in almost anything!

In the end, *bobrauschenbergamerica* celebrates a particularly American beauty, one rooted in the prosperity of the post-war era of the 1950s and 1960s and a particular sense of adventure and infinite possibility that Mee associates with boyhood, with the vast American landscape and with visionary artists such as Rauschenberg, Merce Cunningham, Cage and other twentieth-century figures who changed the understanding of what art is and can be. The character of Carl voices Mee's sentiments on the subject when he says:

> art is made in the freedom of the imagination
> with no rules
> it's the only human activity like that
> where it can do no one any harm
> so it is possible to be completely free
> and see what it may be that people think and feel
> when they are completely free
> in a way, what it is to be human when a human being is free
> and so art lets us practice freedom
> and helps us know what it is to be free
> and so what it is to be human.

Though not initially conceived as a touring show, the SITI production of *bobrauschenbergamerica* first seen at Humana went on to become one of the most widely travelled in the group's repertoire. Over the next five years, it toured to Stamford, Connecticut; the University of Illinois; the Brooklyn Academy of Music; Chicago; Minneapolis; Cambridge, Massachusetts; and internationally to Germany, France and Ireland. Critical response varied widely, based in part on a reviewer's inclination to give over to the play's now ludic, now nostalgic spirit and its unabashed preoccupation with whimsy, delight, joy and just having fun. While the critic for the *New York Times* found it 'brashly, unapologetically entertaining',[21] others took issue with all of the ebullience:

> *bobrauschenbergamerica* gets carried away by its own effervescence. Despite all the biographical source material, the production's joie de vivre seems divorced from *la vie* precisely because joy's counterweights – pain, sorrow, horror – are seldom explored with any honesty or risk.[22]
>
> This is not collage on stage, but a variety show, Anne Bogart and Charles Mee's *Laugh In* – in short, the perky postmodernism that the world has been waiting for. And perky is the word. The production's Will to Cheerfulness is positively exhausting. The actors eat fried chicken cheerfully; they caper cheerfully to Earth, Wind and Fire's 'September'; they square

dance cheerfully; they cheerfully appropriate Pilobolus and throw themselves headlong across wet plastic.[23]

If the giddy exuberance – so characteristic of Mee's work at this time – was too much (or not enough) for some critics, it generated an infectious spirit in general audiences that prompted the SITI Company to revive the piece in 2010 for a run at Dance Theatre Workshop (now Live Arts) in New York, affirming its status as a signature work for both Mee and the SITI. By that time, performance rights were more readily available and fringe companies and university theatre departments around the US were producing the play on a regular basis.

Wintertime

Wintertime premiered in August 2002 at the La Jolla Playhouse in a co-production with Long Wharf Theatre that was directed by Waters. The mounting interest in Mee's work at this time led to a flurry of other productions at regional theatres around the United States, including ACT Theatre in Seattle, the Guthrie Theatre in Minneapolis, San Jose Repertory Theatre, the Wilma Theater in Philadelphia and a co-production between the McCarter Theatre in Princeton and Second Stage Theatre in New York City. While *Wintertime* has not had the sustained popularity of *Big Love*, it advanced Mee's move into the mainstream of American theatre through its continued exploration of the mysteries of love and romance. Despite setting out to write 'a dark, anguished, tragic play' in the vein of his work in the 1990s, he surprised himself by turning out what he described as a 'frothy romantic comedy about a dysfunctional family in a summer house and a young couple trying to get together'.[24] The experience affirmed his Rauschenbergian conviction to follow his impulses wherever they might lead without trying to control or guide them, even if they yield a zany boulevard comedy with characters quoting Sappho, mooning the audience and wearing Viking party hats.

Wintertime was Mee's follow-up to an earlier play titled *Summertime*, which premiered in 2000 at the Magic Theatre in San Francisco in a production directed by Kenn Watt. It marked the first time that Mee used the same setting and the same characters in more than one play, and in 2004 he brought many of those characters back for a third time in *A Perfect Wedding*, which Gordon Davidson and Yehuda Hyman directed as the inaugural production in the Center Theatre Group's new Kirk Douglas Theatre in Los Angeles. Each play in the trilogy – another instance of Mee creating works in series – centres on one of the three children of an estranged middle-aged couple who own an elegant summer house in the woods. As in other Mee plays, this setting is presented as inside and outside at the same time. There are no walls or doors. Grass grows on the desk in *Summertime*, snow piles up on the piano and the mantel in *Wintertime* and the furniture is surrounded by a forest of white birch. This is Mee's version of Shakespeare's woods outside Athens or the Forest of Arden, a transformational Green World populated by impetuous lovers of various ages dashing to and fro guided only by quicksilver emotions and raging hormones.

Wintertime takes place between Christmas and New Year when the summer house is closed up for the winter. Jonathan and Ariel, two young lovers, arrive in pursuit of a private romantic getaway and are surprised to discover that Jonathan's mother Maria and her French lover François are already there for the same purpose. Moments later, Frank, Jonathan's father and Maria's husband, shows up, and he is followed shortly by his lover Edmund. This instantly comic situation leads to awkward small talk, which in turn leads to statements that are misconstrued by one lover or another, all of whom reveal a skittish uncertainty about the fidelity of their beloved. Frank warns of the dangers of seizing on 'any little thing/some doubt one has of another's love/or faithfulness/ and blow it up', but that, of course, is precisely what happens. One by one, the couples in the play – including a fourth couple, a pair of older lesbian neighbours named Hilda and Bertha – succumb to the same irrational suspicions, misunderstandings and jealousies.

When these surging emotions become unbearable, they erupt in paroxysms of theatrical violence similar to incidents in *Big Love* and other Mee plays. Jonathan smashes a desk chair until it is reduced to splinters. François writes fond memories of Maria on pieces of paper and then sets them on fire, explaining, 'When the last one is burned up/you will be gone from my heart.' In a sequence mentioned by many critics, Edmund rolls out a heavy door on wheels, and while an aria from Donizetti's *L'Elisir d'Amore* plays, the characters come out one by one and slam the door again and again until the feelings of hurt and jealousy and even homicidal rage are slaked. At these moments, what began as a mix of romantic comedy and bedroom farce opens out into all-out expressionistic comedy. Temper tantrums become operatic tirades filled with bitter recrimination. Characters excoriate each other with savage vitriol, and then the first act ends with the news that in desperation Maria has thrown herself into a nearby frozen lake and drowned.

Most of the second act involves a memorial service for Maria, filled with expressions of sorrow and regret, which climaxes with a ritualistic rending of garments that leaves all of the characters standing around in colourful underwear. At that point, Maria appears, alive and well, and reveals that her supposed suicide was a trick designed to teach them a lesson about how lucky they all are 'to have found someone who cares for you so completely' and how foolish they are to risk losing it over petty insecurities and perceived slights. Misgivings about her deception give way first to a celebratory dance (in which they all pull down their underwear and shake their butts at each other and the audience) and then a Viking New Year's Eve feast (complete with party hats). The play ends on a happily-ever-after note for three of the four couples with music, confetti, fireworks and a big kiss.

Critical response to the numerous productions of *Wintertime* around the US was mixed. In his 2002 *Variety* review of the La Jolla Playhouse premiere, Lawrence Christon accurately described *Wintertime* as

> a small encyclopedia of classic comedy. Its amorous deliberations recall Molière, its soulfulness echoes Chekhov, some of its speech rhythms derive from Noel Coward, a single door brought on for everyone to slam is an homage to Feydeau and its straight-ahead energies are a throwback to Kaufman & Hart.[25]

But for many reviewers, this unapologetic heterogeneity was a fault, reducing the play to what Marilyn Stasio called a 'stockpot of incompatible styles' in her 2004 *Variety* review of the Second Stage production in New York.[26] Others discredited the play's lengthy ruminations on the nature of love as grandiose, self-indulgent, logorrheic or mere pop psychology. In his 2004 *New York Times* review, Ben Brantley wrote:

> Mr. Mee specializes in that funny thing called love ... He brings an ingenuous and theatrical passion to the subject, rather like an adolescent boy who has discovered 'Oedipus Rex' and 'The Seven Year Itch' at the same time. The question with Mr. Mee is always whether his bubbly enthusiasm will prevail over the staleness of what he has to say.[27]

Here again, oddly, the ebullient spirit and underlying happiness of Mee's work at this time is presented as a flaw or a limitation, as if somehow he should act his age or move on to other subjects, having had his say about love.

Nevertheless, by the time *Wintertime* played in New York, Mee was arguably the most produced contemporary American playwright in the first years of the twenty-first century. Between 2000 and 2005, the following Mee plays premiered at significant theatres around the US: *Big Love, First Love, Summertime, bobrauschenbergamerica, True Love, Wintertime, Limonade Tous les Jours, Snow in June* (a version of *Utopia Parkway*), *A Perfect Wedding, Belle Époque* and *Fêtes de la Nuit*. Most of these plays received subsequent productions by other theatres with national profiles as well as by numerous local, fringe companies looking to make their mark. Something about Mee's anarchic sensibility and buoyant spirit captured the imagination of the American theatre, establishing him as a figure of enduring interest and influence.

Conclusion

In 1953, during the summer after his freshman year of high school, Charles Mee suffered a severe case of polio that nearly killed him. It left him permanently disabled, unable to run, play football, dance or even walk without the assistance of cuffed crutches. In *A Nearly Normal Life*, his memoir of his experience of polio, he associates his manner of writing with his physical condition:

> I like a book that feels like a crystal goblet that has been thrown to the floor and shattered, so that its pieces, when they are picked up and arranged on a table, still describe a whole glass, but the glass itself has been shattered. To me, sentences should veer and smash up, careen out of control; get under way and

find themselves unable to stop, switch directions suddenly and irrevocably, break off, come to a sighing inconclusiveness. If a writer's writings constitute a 'body of work', then my body of work, to feel true to me, must feel fragmented.[28]

That fragmentation is achieved by Mee's incorporation of miscellaneous borrowed texts in his scripts as well as his inclusion of movement sequences, performance events, dance breaks and eruptions of spectacle in his scripts, some of which are inspired by the work of visionary European directors such as Pina Bausch, Alain Platel, Sasha Waltz, Jan Lauwers and Ivo van Hove. Here again, Mee sees a link with his personal history:

> I'm not a very mobile person. I walk with crutches ... If I'm going to have vicarious pleasure, the vicarious pleasure for me is to write a play in which people jump up and run and throw things and smash stuff up and dance. So this is sort of what comes out of my soul, this fantasy of physical virtuosity.[29]

For that fantasy to be realized, a Mee play requires a confident, imaginative director who appreciates his eclecticism and will preserve the jagged edges built into the scripts. Waters describes it like this:

> With Chuck's work, you don't need to underline what is already there. You have to get out of the way of it and let the theatricality exist ... I rather like the fact that [the plays] are often a very bumpy ride. You are constantly surprised by where the play has ended up. You don't know how you got there. It's like a fast-moving train that will suddenly jump the tracks and end up on parallel rails.[30]

This helter-skelter quality includes a freedom in staging the plays that many directors are not accustomed to. More than conventional plays, Mee's experimental work is unfinished until directors, designers and performers bring their creativity to bear and build something on top of it. Bogart puts it this way:

> He just says, 'Go. I'll be curious to see what you're going to do.' That's really unusual. There is no playwright who has more

trust in a director. And I mean every director. You don't sense a responsibility to his career or to make sure that what he has imagined happens onstage. There is a lack of attachment to his own work and at the same time a deep, deep commitment to his work. Those two things create a paradox, which is him.[31]

As familiarity with Mee's work spread, more and more directors and theatres came to embrace his work. The Signature Theatre Company in New York made Mee their featured playwright for the 2007–8 season and for the first time in their history produced three world premieres by one playwright in a single, signature season: *Iphigenia 2.0*, a return to Mee's deconstructions of Greek tragedy directed by Landau; *Queens Boulevard*, a musical inspired by a *kathakali* dance drama directed by Davis McCallum; and *Paradise Park*, a freewheeling look at American escapism set in an amusement park directed by Fish. Around this time, Mee teamed up with celebrity Shakespeare scholar Stephen Greenblatt to write *Cardenio*, a contemporary romantic comedy and literary fantasy inspired by the lost play by Shakespeare and John Fletcher. Directed by Waters, the play premiered in 2008 at the American Repertory Theatre, Mee's sixth production there.

Mee also wrote several more scripts for Bogart and the SITI Company, including two more pieces about famous artists that also premiered at the Humana Festival. The first and more successful of these was *Hotel Cassiopeia* (2006), inspired by the American artist Joseph Cornell and his famous box constructions, whimsical and surreal juxtapositions of everyday objects and cut-out images arranged in a small wooden box or other container. In a manner similar to the Rauschenberg piece, Mee created a theatrical collage based on the motifs, methods and materials of Cornell, one that was more lyrical, dream-like, meditative and private than the earlier play. It was also more suggestively biographical and included figures representing Cornell, his disabled brother, his overbearing mother and the ballerina Allegra Kent, who fascinated him to the point of obsession. Mee, Bogart and the SITI Company went on to collaborate on *Under Construction* (2009), an intentionally open-ended, rough-hewn mash-up of the worlds of Norman Rockwell, the popular mid-twentieth-century illustrator famous for his idyllic *Saturday Evening Post* covers, and Jason Rhoades, the early twenty-first-century installation artist whose challenging, chaotic, often vulgar sculptural environments included *Black Pussy Soirée Cabaret Macramé*. Mee also wrote *Soot and Spit* for the SITI Company, a piece about the deaf outsider artist James Castle from Boise, Idaho, but Bogart and company never developed the piece.[32] And around this time, Mee rekindled his collaboration with Clarke, first on a 2002 reworking of *Vienna: Lusthaus* and then on *Belle Époque*, a 2004 piece about Toulouse-Lautrec that she directed at Lincoln Center Theater. Mee's practice of writing plays inspired by well-known painters and sculptors – organized on his website in a section called 'Lives of the Artists' – confirms him as a genuine aesthete, an identity that can be traced back to his days as editor of *Horizon* magazine.[33] As it turned out, in the new century, his ability to 'see the beauty in almost anything' (as Bob's Mom puts it) superseded his earlier focus as a citizen historian on diplomatic brinksmanship and the roots of American imperialism.

In the second decade of the century, attention to Mee's work has tapered off from the fever pitch of the decade before, but he remains a figure of note and continues to write plays and post them on his website for anybody who might want to experiment with them. Three of them – *Heaven on Earth* (2011), *Eterniday* (2013) and *Daily Life Everlasting* (2015) – were successfully staged at La MaMa ETC by director and choreographer Dan Safer and his experimental dance theatre group Witness Relocation. In 2015, as part of its Legacy series, Signature Theatre revived *Big Love* in a lavish and robust production directed by Landau. And Actors Theatre of Louisville premiered *Glory of the World* at the 2015 Humana Festival, a commission to mark the centenary of the birth of Thomas Merton, the Trappist monk and Catholic theologian who had a famous revelation in downtown Louisville just blocks from where the theatre is now. Staged as a wild party by Waters and choreographer Barney O'Hanlon of the SITI Company, the all-male production – seventeen performers plus Waters himself in a cameo role that bookends the mayhem – celebrated the paradoxical identities of Merton with a series of raucous toasts, a seemingly endless litany of quotations and a succession of masculine physical encounters that culminate in an all-out brawl.

All of this recent work harkens back to Mee's early collaboration with Clarke on *Vienna: Lusthaus*, a piece in which text, movement and image stand on equal footing. Clearly, in the late stages of his career, Mee regards himself more as the author of libretti for rambunctious dance-theatre pieces than a dramatist in the conventional sense. He writes blueprints for performance events. He instigates theatrical riots. He stages public symposia mixed with song and dance. In this and other ways, his career, his theatre and his writing – appropriated from other sources or not – have expanded the possibilities of what a play and a playwright can be.

4

Lynn Nottage

Cindy Rosenthal

Introduction

'There is no such thing as one Lynn Nottage voice in all her plays,' says Dan Sullivan, the director of Nottage's first 'hit' show in New York, *Intimate Apparel* (2003), which was produced at the Roundabout Theatre, Off-Broadway.[1] In the preface Nottage penned for *Crumbs from the Table of Joy and Other Plays* (2004), an anthology of five of her plays from the 1990s, she states that the unique gaze of her mother (Ruby Nottage) was an inspiration for her wide-ranging, provocative and political playwriting.[2] Nottage, who is also a screenwriter, sees herself as part of the legacy of African-American writer-activists, 'women of the vanguard', such as Paule Marshall, Alice Childress, Toni Morrison and Sonia Sanchez. The artwork on the walls of Nottage's Boerum Hill, Brooklyn, home (where she grew up and returned in the late 1990s), which includes paintings by Romare Bearden and Norman Lewis, one-time friends of her parents, has also inspired her. Musical soundtracks Nottage fashions and listens to as she writes plays are equally integral to her creative process.[3] Each soundscape Nottage carefully crafts for herself as she writes a play serves as a background to the journeys and conflicts and triumphs of the characters in the vividly detailed and far-flung theatrical worlds she creates.

Although Nottage declares that each of her playwriting processes is a bit different from the others, what characterizes all of her research is an active engagement with a variety of materials and subjects. For *Intimate Apparel*, the first of the plays discussed in this chapter, she spent many fruitful hours doing research at the New York Public Library, specifically at the Schomburg Center for Research in Black Culture in Harlem and at the main branch in midtown Manhattan where she uncovered 'one central image, and then buil[t] outward from there'.[4] For *Fabulation, or the Re-Education of Undine* (2004), the second play explored in this chapter, an article about African Americans who ignore their roots, which focused on Condoleezza Rice, was the initial inspiration. Nottage is an avid adventurer who loves to travel outside her comfort zone to a research destination that is or was the site of extreme upheavals, transformations and political crises. A journey to such a destination was the inciting event of the research process for *Ruined* (2008), the third play of Nottage's examined here, when she travelled to East Africa with her frequent collaborator, director Kate Whoriskey, to interview women who had been brutalized by the wars in the Congo. They were survivors, Nottage says, who wanted to tell their stories.[5]

In the aforementioned anthology of Nottage's earlier plays, *Las Meninas* (2002), the last play in the volume, takes its name from Diego Velázquez's celebrated 1656 painting *Las Meninas* (The Ladies in Waiting). The painting, considered a masterwork of Western art and culture, is a provocative representation of the seventeenth-century Spanish court, featuring two royal attendants of small stature in prominent positions on the canvas. Nottage's play, which had its world premiere at the San Jose Repertory Theatre in March 2002 (and was also produced at Brown University in 1997), was inspired by a research project that began when Nottage came across a single line in a history book that referenced a small-statured African man who was a favoured attendant of Queen Marie-Therese of Spain, wife of King Louis XIV of France. Nottage subsequently discovered that the dwarf servant, Nabo Sensugali, and Marie-Therese had a child together. Although there is very little evidence of this individual in history books, Nottage selected their daughter as her 'guide' and as a framing device for the play. Louise Marie-Therese, 'the Black Nun of Moret' (1664–1732), tells 'the *true* story of the seduction of Marie-Therese ... the Queen of France' to an audience of her 'sweet sisters'[6] – of course, she is actually addressing spectators of Nottage's play. 'This relationship [between the white Queen and her African servant] challenges the traditional roles of race and gender in the French court – and yet warrants only one sentence in most history books?!' Nottage exclaimed in a 2001 interview.[7] She published the following Yoruba proverb as the epigraph before her play: 'The white man who made the pencil also made the eraser' (246). In a 2010 interview, Nottage commented extensively on this erasure of members of the African diaspora from Western history:

> While I was doing my research, I felt as though I were pulling away a layer of history that had covered and obscured the relationship of the Queen and Nabo ... And part of my mission as a writer is to sort of resurrect some of these figures. Not only were we there, but we played a vital role in the shaping of the culture that we live in today, whether you want to call it 'western culture,' or ... I like to think of it as 'world culture,' because America is no longer Western culture. It reflects people from around the world.[8]

When asked in 2004 why she writes plays instead of novels or essays, Nottage replied that she is 'drawn to the interplay of voices on a stage' and that she 'love[s] the collaborative aspect of the theatre'.[9] Nottage is committed to creating socially engaged art and is interested in telling the stories of those on the margins, individuals whose experiences and perspectives are rarely expressed in theatre, whose voices are rarely heard. Often these individuals are women of African descent. Nottage declared in a 2015 interview that she is interested in being heard too, and is less interested in being successful. She also stated that she 'was taught you had to be twice as good in order to succeed as an African American woman. Because if you're just good you won't be seen, so you really have to strive to be better.'[10]

Nottage was born in 1964 in Brooklyn to a schoolteacher and a child psychologist; she graduated from the High School of Music and Art in Manhattan. She received her undergraduate degree from Brown University and graduate degree in playwriting from Yale. She worked in the press office of Amnesty International for four years after finishing her MFA at Yale. Nottage's works have been produced by nearly every major Off-Broadway theatre, but as of this writing, her work has not appeared on Broadway. Dozens of regional theatres across the US have produced her work, as have prestigious theatres across the globe – *Ruined* was even performed at a theatre in the Congo. Nottage was awarded a Guggenheim Fellowship in 2005, the MacArthur 'Genius' Grant in 2007 and a Pulitzer Prize for *Ruined* in 2009. Other honours she has received include the Steinberg 'Mimi' Distinguished Playwright Award, the Dramatists Guild Hull-Warriner Award, the inaugural Horton Foote Prize, the Lilly Award, the Helen Hayes Award, the Lee Reynolds Award and the Jewish World Watch iWitness Award. Like Charles Mee, Nottage began teaching playwriting at Columbia University School of the Arts during the first decade of the twenty-first century, where she is an Associate Professor as of this writing. Nottage is also on the faculty of Yale University, where her first day of teaching was the day after 11 September 2001.

Intimate Apparel

Intimate Apparel grew out of a tumultuous period in Nottage's life. In 1997, Nottage's mother Ruby died of Lou Gehrig's disease and two months later Nottage gave birth to a daughter, Ruby. Keenly feeling the difficult loss and her new identity as a mother, she set out to write a new play and in so doing 'rescue[d] the members of my family from storage', as she described it in an essay published in the *Los Angeles Times*.[11] With a sense of urgency to tap her roots, she turned to the story of her great-grandmother, Ethel Boyce, who arrived in New York City from Barbados in 1902, a seamstress skilled in creating ladies' undergarments. Ethel was the inspiration for the central character, Esther, in *Intimate Apparel*, set in New York City in 1905. Esther, like Nottage's great-grandmother, was lonely and seemed destined to be a spinster – until George came into her life. George in the play, and George Armstrong, Nottage's great-grandfather, was a labourer, who – like many thousands of West Indian men in the first two decades of the twentieth century – was conscripted to help build the Panama Canal. Nottage's great-grandfather, George Armstrong, was married to Ethel for about a year and died young; although this story may be family lore, he died when he was struck on the head as he orated on a soapbox.

During the *Intimate Apparel* writing process, Nottage was deeply engaged in library research; she sought 'a central image' to ground her story and found it at the main branch of the New York Public Library – the image of 'a beautiful white satin wedding corset embossed with orange blossoms. It was delicate and graceful – exactly what I imagined Esther would create for her wedding night. The image was dated 1905. That year became my departure point, my anchor.'[12] In *Intimate Apparel*, Nottage constructs a lyrical, long-distance relationship between the labourer and the seamstress via letters they send to each other, full of dreams and yearning. However, when the lovers finally meet face to face in New York, having agreed to marry, their literary personas wear thin very quickly. Over time, a number of unsettling truths are revealed: Esther is illiterate and had her clients – a prostitute/friend living in the Tenderloin district and a wealthy society woman on Fifth Avenue – read and write her letters for her; George has a quick temper and is crushed by the limited job opportunities he encounters as a Black man in America. Esther finally ends her relationship with George when she discovers he is involved with her closest friend, the piano-playing prostitute, Mayme.

Intimate Apparel won the American Theatre Critics' and the New York Drama Critics' awards for Best Play in 2004 and was the most produced play in the US in the 2005–6 season. 'People like plays about history, but people love doing *Intimate Apparel* because its characters are so pre-Freudian – they speak about their feelings through clothing and business relations,'[13] declares Whoriskey, who directed *Intimate Apparel* in its premier co-production, first at Baltimore's Center Stage and then at Costa Mesa's South Coast Repertory Theatre in 2003. 'Nobody actually talks about their emotional life,' says Whoriskey. 'You're constantly guessing at how people are feeling as you witness their actions. Lynn has written specific stage directions, and it would be a good idea for them to be followed. The story is in the behavior.'[14]

Reviews of the production at the Roundabout in New York in 2004 were more favourable than those of the Baltimore and Costa Mesa premiere productions in 2003. Viola Davis received uniformly glowing notices as Esther Off-Broadway, and aspects of Nottage's play that were seen as heavy-handed or melodramatic in Baltimore and Costa Mesa generally achieved a better balance in critics' assessments of the New York production. This was largely due to the power of Davis's performance, which foregrounded the delicacy and complexity in the 'big-heart' of the play (to use *New York Times* critic Margo Jefferson's phrase to describe Nottage's work). For Jefferson, Nottage's choice to write in the style of nineteenth-/early twentieth-century literature à la Edith Wharton was fitting, and she found Nottage's deep, exacting research to be impressive.[15] Jefferson also commended the designers' work on this production, but contrary to positive reviews from other New York critics, she was not enthusiastic about Sullivan's direction and felt that the play 'lagged'.[16] Contradictory critical responses to the play specifically centred on the question of melodrama. In the New York production, Esther's journey at the centre of the play, negotiating complex relationships with the women and men in her life, evolved artfully and not melodramatically in most critics' views. Mike Guiliano, who wrote of the Baltimore premiere in *Variety*, stated that supporting characters' 'dialogue tends to be overemphatic in letting us know what each of them represents ... [The second act contains] melodramatic plot twists [that] aren't completely convincing.'[17] In reviewing the Roundabout production, *Associated Press* critic Justin Glanville expressed the opposite point of view:

> A profound quiet arrives at the end of Lynn Nottage's new play 'Intimate Apparel' and not just because the lead character has been left alone on stage. It's the calm that descends when a production has achieved a near perfect balance between content and execution ... In the hand of a lesser writer, Esther's journey – complicated as it is by heart break and betrayal – might devolve into melodrama. But one of the wonders of the play is how it refuses to sentimentalize any of her relationships.[18]

Critics of Nottage's work often zero in on what Randy Gener aptly describes as Nottage's 'crush on strange romantic pairings as narrative devices';[19] in *Intimate Apparel*, the intensely charged, unfulfilled relationship between Esther and Mr Marks, the shy Orthodox Jewish fabric merchant from whom Esther buys exquisite and sensual silks and satins, is a prime example. 'Certainly what is not spoken between Esther and the Jewish fabric-seller Mr. Marks is the heart of the play,' asserts Sullivan. 'The sadness of it is that theirs is the deepest relationship in the play. What Lynn understood ... is what you don't say – the strictures of language that *don't* allow you to express yourself ... can be dramatically viable.'[20] The cultural divide between Esther and Mr Marks is powerfully etched into each of the characters' encounters; Marks, like Esther, George, Mayme and even the white socialite Mrs Van Buren, is subject to prejudice that is 'due to their several embodiments', as disability studies scholar Ann M. Fox explains it. In Fox's reading of Nottage's multicultural turn-of-the-twentieth-century terrain, each of the characters struggles with limitations and obstacles that society and culture have thrust upon them.[21] The men in Nottage's play – a Caribbean low-wage worker and a Jewish merchant – struggle with different constraints to those of the Black seamstress and the other women in the play, but they struggle nonetheless.

Nottage describes *Intimate Apparel* as her 'most deeply personal play' and as 'unabashedly emotional, beautiful, delicate'. She says these were '[e]lements that I felt, at the time I was writing, were absent from the stage'. She regrets that her mother 'never got to see the play, or to even hear a reading. It was very much a play for her.'[22] In developing the relationship between Esther and Mr Marks, Nottage said she imagined what it might have been like if she and her husband, filmmaker Tony Gerber, who like Marks in the play is Jewish and of Romanian descent, had met a hundred years earlier. '[W]hat would have been the nature of our relationship? Would we have been able to consummate that relationship? I explored that, so it is also deeply personal in that respect.'[23] All of the play's scenes take place in bedrooms, which in Nottage's view makes it 'possible to drop some of the social artifice and penetrate barriers, explore emotions'.[24] In the first scene between Esther and Mayme, which takes place in Mayme's Tenderloin boudoir, the prostitute had just been treated roughly by one of her male 'visitors'. The women share long-held dreams and hopes for the future. In a moment rich with unspoken emotion, Esther attempts to cover up her illicit attraction to Mr Marks: 'He a Jew', she explains. Mayme replies: 'And? I been with a Jew, with a Turk even. And let me tell ya, a gentle touch is gold in any country.'[25] The fact that Esther, at age thirty-five, is still a virgin is also revealed – although Esther utters no words on the subject:

(*Mayme laughs long and hard. Esther doesn't respond.*)
Mayme No kidding. I can't even remember what it was like.
    Ain't that something. (23)

Nottage acknowledges that the women in the play 'share a common struggle. But there also exists a racial and social gulf that divides them.'[26] Another subplot in *Intimate Apparel* evolves out of Esther's visits to the elegant boudoir of her uptown client, the white socialite, Mrs Van Buren, who helps pen the letters to George that foster Esther's romance with him. This subplot heats up when Mrs Van Buren, who grows increasingly fond of and attached to Esther, professes her love to her. In a scene where Esther is fitting Van Buren into a corset, Van Buren reveals that her husband mistreats her because she cannot bear him children. With Esther she is playful, even seductive. Van Buren tells Esther, 'It is so easy to be with you. (*Whispers*) Your visits are just about the only thing I look forward to these days. You, and our letters to George of course. Shall we write something dazzling to him? Something delicious?' (33). In a later scene, after Esther's marriage to George has begun to fall apart, the two women sit together on Van Buren's bed and Esther collapses in tears, admitting that her relationship with her husband is patched together with lies. She tells Van Buren (thinking of Mr Marks), 'I fear my love belongs someplace else' (59). Van Buren hears this as an acknowledgement of the love between the two women. Esther 'outs' the social divide between them and cannot accept their relationship as love or even true friendship: 'How we be friends? When I ain't never been through your front door. You love me? What of me do you love?'(59).

In an interview in 2010, Nottage cited Viola Davis's performance in the role of Esther (Davis received the 2004 Drama Desk Award for her performance in the Roundabout Theatre production) as one of her favourite performances of all time and shared how much she learned from Davis's work on the role. 'Davis has an exceptional ability to be still and yet go through a whole range of emotions,' observed Nottage. 'She can do everything just by standing there. Watching her, I felt that I did not need to write a line.'[27] In an interview in 2004, Davis opened up about the similarities between herself and Esther – and also about the challenge of performing a role when you rarely leave the stage:

> The major challenge in playing Esther is making her emotional journey seamless, to build each moment, and not play the last moment first. It's also challenging to be on the stage without a break. It's relentless ... One hundred years into the future Esther

would be me. Her story is my story. I went through my 20s feeling lonely and plain and wanting a man. In my 30s I woke up. Of course, I had six years of therapy that was not available to Esther. I found myself and eventually God.

Davis also responded to some of the criticisms Nottage received for how she depicted the central Black male character, George, who ultimately steals from and abandons Esther:

> As for George – yes, he is a negative depiction of a Black man, but I don't have problems with a Black character presented negatively; that's okay, as long as he is also human. And I believe George is human, unlike the portrayals of Black men on TV or in film who are just stereotypes. This play is unusual and important because of what it does. How often do you see a Black woman as the central character? Or a Black woman and an Orthodox Jewish man in love? Where do we see a white woman falling in love with a Black woman? All of it is meshed together here. The play is set in 1905, but reflects the multicultural world of today.[28]

As a woman with skills that are marketable and products that are desirable, Esther moves with ease across the geographical, social and racial 'neighborhoods' of Manhattan at the turn of the twentieth century. Esther's travels and the variety of intimate and fruitful transactions she makes speak to her particular fluency and agency, but also to the fascinating (if previously under-illuminated) details of the multicultural world of New York in 1905.

The idea of turning the clock back in time to view an African American woman's life at the turn of the twentieth century and then fast-forwarding to an African American woman's experiences and evolving identities today was a springboard for Nottage to write *Fabulation, or the Re-Education of Undine*, which she regards as a companion piece to *Intimate Apparel*. Nottage sees Esther as a forebear of Undine in *Fabulation* – a single woman staking her claim to financial independence who simultaneously seeks true friendship, love and career fulfilment. 'A century ago, a woman like that – who today would be considered very successful – would have been considered very cursed. I wanted to look into what it must have been like to have been imprisoned by the mores, the social strictures, of that time.'[29]

Fabulation, or the Re-Education of Undine

Nottage states that the job she had in the press office of Amnesty International after she finished her MFA at the Yale School of Drama helped her understand the central character of Undine in *Fabulation, or the Re-Education of Undine*.[30] *Fabulation* is set in New York in 'the present' – over 100 years after *Intimate Apparel*, in the twenty-first century. Undine, like Esther, is an upwardly mobile African American woman who is very good at what she does. When we meet Undine, she is on the phone – sharp-edged, fast-talking, all about the glamour and celebrity of being a wildly successful owner of a Manhattan PR firm. But then her Latino husband Herve steals all of her money and leaves her pregnant. Undine, the ultimate diva, returns home to her working-class Brooklyn roots and to the family she cleanly dumped out of her history years earlier when she claimed they all died in a fire. The dialogue in *Fabulation* swings along at a clip, and serious subjects often flip over into hilarity. Written at approximately the same time Nottage wrote *Intimate Apparel*, and opening in New York at Playwrights Horizons only three months after *Intimate Apparel* opened at the Roundabout, *Fabulation* covers completely different stylistic ground, sometimes dipping into Theatre of the Absurd, as it slam-dunks critical commentary about race and class in urban America. This is a contemporary 'riches to rags' tale and the moral of the story may be that nothing good ever comes of trying to erase your roots – in this case, by figuratively burning down the house and family into which you were born.

As Undine's privileged world crashes into bits, she takes the recommendation of her accountant and consults a Yoruba priest. In one of Undine's many 'asides' to the audience where the playwright has a tongue firmly planted in cheek, Undine tells us, 'They were roommates at Harvard Business School. So, I thought, Why not?'[31] The priest explains that Undine's downfall was the direct result of having enraged the African spirit, Elegba. Undine's penance is her returning home (and paying Elegba her last $1,000). Undine returns to the Walt Whitman housing project in Brooklyn where her mother, father and brother are all security guards. Her brother, 'Flow', is also a hipster poet, who was 'never the same', Undine tells us, 'after his tour of Desert Storm' (97). After her family takes her back, she is assigned the task of looking after her aged, ill grandmother, with whom she must share a bed. Undine discovers that her grandmother's injections for 'diabetes' are a cover-up for the old woman's heroin use. Undine is arrested while trying to score drugs for her grandmother; when she is hauled off to treatment, she horrifies the others in her counselling group when she reveals that she is not, and never has been, a drug addict. Like Esther, Undine is a woman 'done wrong' by her man, and like Esther, Undine digs deep, pulls herself up and starts all over again. These are survivors with complicated success stories. Nottage's central characters are powerful, independent women. Undine and Esther are smart, talented, skilled and brave iconoclasts who chart unique and groundbreaking paths that inspire intense envy, admiration and hostility along the way. Faced with numerous societal obstacles, each of their career and financial achievements is the result of hard work, creativity and ingenuity. But when they take a fall – and each does, painfully – Esther and Undine rise from the ashes, stronger and wiser than before. In the play's final scenes, Undine finds love and support with 'Guy' – a working-class, down-to-earth, one-time addict, who, in Nottage's clever cast breakdown, is played by the same actor that portrayed Undine's suave and slimy husband, Herve. And Undine's spacey, upwardly mobile assistant, Stephie, follows her boss in a downward spiral that lands her in a position at the local pharmacy where Undine buys her pregnancy vitamins:

> **Loudspeaker** Stephie, you're needed in aisle two. Pronto!
> **Stephie** Coming! Like nothing changes. I gotta run.
> **Undine** Go ... *(To audience)* ... I slip the calcium tablets into my pocket, unpaid, and I keep walking. I walk all the way home fighting a tinge of envy, because Stephie, my former assistant, might actually be named Employee of the Month at the pharmacy. (127)

In the author's note to *Fabulation*, published in a two-play volume with *Intimate Apparel* (2006), Nottage is specific in her recommendations for how the eight-member ensemble of four women and four men (in addition to Undine) should be cast. Each actor should play at least three or more roles, according to

Nottage's schema. The triple, quadruple and quintuple casting she suggests is carefully constructed for maximum satiric impact – no doubt great fun for actors and spectators alike, but also a set-up that magnifies Nottage's social critique along age, gender and class lines. (For instance, the actor playing Undine's grandmother doubles as a Kafka-esque caseworker and triples as the upscale internist that diagnoses Undine's pregnancy.) Needless to say, *Fabulation*'s storytelling and *mise-en-scène* play out very differently from *Intimate Apparel*'s straightforward – one actor = one character – mode. In *Intimate Apparel*, the delicate exchanges between Esther and Mr Marks, where fathoms of emotional depths are plumbed in-between the lines, are a far cry from the following satirical exchange between Undine and the aforementioned caseworker:

> **Caseworker** You don't know how to fill out a form?
> **Undine** I didn't know there was even a form to be filled out.
> **Caseworker** What do the sign say?
> **Undine** Please ill out he orm.
> **Caseworker** So what do that tell you?
> **Undine** Nothing intelligible. (120)

A playful connection between the two Nottage productions in New York was made by Walt Spangler, *Fabulation*'s set designer, in his choice to include a mannequin on the set. (The set for *Intimate Apparel*, designed by Derek McLane at the Roundabout, featured several mannequins suspended from poles.) Nottage, however, was not concerned or particularly interested in forging a connection between *Intimate Apparel* and *Fabulation*. In Jason Zinoman's article in the *New York Times*, published prior to the first performance of *Fabulation*, Nottage stated that audiences shouldn't expect similarities between the two plays. Charlayne Woodard, playing Undine in the premiere, said she was surprised at the differences. About *Fabulation* she said, 'This play is a little dangerous, a little politically incorrect.'[32] As previously mentioned, Nottage said that a profile of Condoleezza Rice in *The New Yorker* helped her craft the character of Undine – for her 'single-minded pursuit of success ... [she was] willing to give up anything'. In Nottage's view, Rice's belief system and choices were not uncommon – the tendency was to think, as Undine did, that success could only be achieved if family ties were cut. 'This is an unspoken issue in the African American community,'[33] Nottage explained. Although Nottage denies any straightforward autobiographical connection with *Fabulation*, she finds it funny that she and her family returned (as Undine did) to live in the home where she grew up. The same is true of Jonathan Lethem, the author of *The Fortress of Solitude*, a coming-of-age novel set in gentrifying Boerum Hill, who, like Nottage, rode the subway from Brooklyn to high school in Manhattan. '[We] had this notion that once we left Brooklyn we would never come back and it's so ironic that we've both returned.'[34]

Fabulation received mixed reviews in its New York premiere. Michael Sommers pointed out that Nottage took the central character's 'moniker' Undine 'from the social-climbing beauty of Edith Wharton's "The Custom of the Country"'.[35] Undine admits in one of many direct, facade-stripping addresses to the audience that she first encountered Wharton's character, a fortune-hunter who has been described as 'one of the most appalling and fascinating heroines ever created',[36] 'in an American literature course at Dartmouth College' (133). Sommers continued:

> The play is too uncertain in tone to be really effective, however, as is the author's ambivalent attitude toward the mostly unrepentant Undine, who refuses to wise up until the final moments. Clocking in at a bit more than two hours, the overlong play contains some sharp, funny material but is burdened both by laborious exposition and a lack of focus.[37]

Ben Brantley in the *New York Times* agreed that Nottage's 'sprawling, picaresque play ... could benefit from tightening'. But even as he stated that *Fabulation* 'lacks the structural cleanness and symmetry of "Intimate Apparel"', he affirmed that the play

> possesses a freedom of imagination that 'Intimate Apparel' barely hinted at. While both works deal with disorienting social flux and imprisoning social stereotypes, it is their differences that bode so well for Ms. Nottage's creative future. It seems that having found her feet as a playwright, she is not about to stand in one place.[38]

The Brantley review was largely positive; he described *Fabulation* as 'one of the livelier comedies available at the moment'. He ended his review with an excerpt from Undine's (nee Sharona Watkins's) brother 'Flow's' unfinished epic poem (described as a 'fabulation'), which is based on the fable *Bre'er Rabbit*. Brantley cogently argued that the following lines 'captur[e] the essence of a play that defines contemporary life as a distorting hall of mirrors': 'It's a circle that been run. That ain't no one ever won. It that silly rabbit grin, 'bout runnin' from your skin.'[39]

Contrary to more critical responses to this work, Peter Marks, writing of the New York production in the *Washington Post*, declared that with *Fabulation* Nottage 'may have at last found her true voice and it is one laced with sardonic wit … [H]er eye for the one-upsmanship rituals of fast-lane New York is unsparing and her ear for the misery of the down and out is acute.' He described Charlayne Woodard's performance as Undine as 'endearing' and Whoriskey's direction as 'snappy'. In his view, 'Whoriskey's staging takes the full measure of all the bumps and twists in Nottage's story of a life in freefall.'[40]

For no apparent reason, *Fabulation* premiered in Great Britain years earlier than *Intimate Apparel*, which was not produced there until 2014. Reviews of a 2006 production at the Tricycle in London were mostly favourable. Fiona Mountford's review in London's *Evening Standard*, 'PR Fable Is Absolutely Fabulous', is a rave; she called actor Jenny Jules, playing Undine, 'magnificent' and gave high praise to director Indhu Rubasingham for her staging and work with actors. Mountford wrote that 'Nottage is in supreme, glorious control of her material … *Fabulation* by name, fabulous by nature.'[41]

Michael Billington wrote in the *Guardian* that 'in a world filled with solemnity, it is good to see racial politics for once given a comic spin. But behind Nottage's sprightly fable lurks a big, unanswered question: what is actually wrong with impoverished African-Americans aspiring to be part of the bourgeoisie?'[42] It appears that Billington missed Nottage's main point, which is not questioning whether Undine/Sharona deserved success in the 'game' of marketing or capitalism, but whether there might be a more ethical way of achieving that success. Did Undine have to change her name or kill off her family? Isn't Nottage instead suggesting with her choice of title that for some upwardly mobile Blacks a re-education is in order?

Ruined

Ruined had its world premiere under Whoriskey's direction at Chicago's Goodman Theatre on 8 November 2008 in a co-production with New York's Manhattan Theatre Club, where it opened Off-Broadway on 10 February 2009. By that time, Nottage had visited East Africa to meet with women who were refugees from the Congo conflict and listened to their testimonies twice: once with Whoriskey in 2004, and again, after receiving the Guggenheim Grant in 2005, with her husband, Tony Gerber, her father and her daughter. A powerhouse of a play about the brutal rape and torture of women during the Democratic Republic of Congo's long wars, *Ruined* exploded on stages across the US, becoming one of the most produced plays of the 2010–11 season. Since none of the characters in Nottage's play are American, the fact that *Ruined* won the Pulitzer Prize for Drama in 2009 was especially significant. According to published information about the prize, the Pulitzer is usually reserved for plays by American writers that are 'preferably original in its source and deal with American life'.[43]

Bertolt Brecht's *Mother Courage* had an impact on Nottage's thinking about strong women characters, the horrors of war, difficult mothering choices and powerful political performances years before she began working on *Ruined*. When asked in 2010 (in a previously cited article from the *Observer*) what were the 'best' performances she had ever seen, before bringing up Davis as Esther in *Intimate Apparel*, the performance that came immediately to Nottage's mind was Judi Dench as Mother Courage at the Barbican Theatre in London in 1984:

> What I remember about her performance is she played low to the ground with a fierce wiliness ... It was as if Mother Courage were someone who had ripped herself out of the earth and yet was still somehow bound to it. She was a woman who, no matter how intractable the thirty years war in Europe ... still ... had an incredible regenerative power.
>
> One of the things that drew me to the part – and the performance – is that Mother Courage is morally ambiguous. She makes compromised choices to survive. Ultimately she is a

mother worrying about the care and survival of her children, and to feed her children she has to make dubious choices.[44]

How Nottage's play compares with Brecht's, and how it has been inspired by Brecht's, has been a subject of debate among critics and spectators and a frequent question for Nottage in interviews. In *American Theatre* (2010), Nottage claimed, 'I think my play is written from a woman's point of view, so there's much more compassion, there's much more optimism, than in *Mother Courage*. Mama [Nadi] embodies the role of "mama" in a much more traditional way.'[45]

There are fundamental differences between Mother Courage and Mama Nadi (the lead character in *Ruined*). Mother Courage is itinerant: she sells wares from her cart, travelling from one battle-scarred landscape to another. Mama Nadi's canteen/nightclub/brothel is the one setting in *Ruined*. Both Courage and Nadi refuse to take sides in the wars fought around them – they are on their own side. Under Nadi's roof an endless stream of brutalized and raped women are corralled; they sell their bodies to miners and soldiers for Mama's profit, in exchange for food, clothes and a bed. Nadi does not have children of her own, although her attachment to and affection for 'her girls' in the brothel grow stronger as the play continues. Nonetheless, as Nottage points out, 'like Mother Courage, [Nadi] is also exploiting the situation and doing something that, in some respects, is horrific'.[46] Brecht's 1939 epic drama – an example of 'theatre of alienation' – is a socialist diatribe exposing the absence of ethics and morality in a world at war. When he wrote *Mother Courage*, Europe was on the brink of the Second World War, but Brecht set his play centuries earlier during the Thirty Years' War. Nottage's play has a different agenda: with *Ruined*, she sounds a clarion call against using women's bodies as the spoils of war during the turn-of-the-twenty-first-century conflict in the Congo. Nottage stresses that '*Ruined* is a huge departure [from *Mother Courage*]. I didn't want to use a Western theatrical construct. I felt that was totally the antithesis of what I wanted to do with the play.'[47]

Ruined begins when the ironically named Christian, a travelling salesman (much in the mode of a latter-day Mother Courage), stops by to haggle with Mama Nadi over supplies in his truck and to persuade her to take in two new 'girls' at her brothel.

The young women, Salima and Sophie, endured gang rapes, were subsequently shunned by their families and communities, and have nowhere to go. Salima's baby was killed before her eyes and she was made the sex slave of a group of soldiers for months; Sophie's mutilation by a gang of men with a bayonet resulted in her being 'ruined'.

Nottage explains that many of the women she spoke with in Africa were subject to horrific sexual assaults that wreaked terrible physical damage on their bodies, which was the cause of their ongoing shame and pain. At the time of Nottage's first interviews in Africa, many of the Congolese women were unaware of the surgical procedure that can correct most vaginal fistulas. Even so, Nottage found the women to be remarkably optimistic about their futures, in spite of the challenges they faced day to day caused by the leakage and odours that accompanied their condition. *Ruined* hits audiences with an onslaught of violent sexual imagery; the impact is intensely emotional, intimately so – not akin to Brecht's 'distancing' approach at all. Yet, sensitive to the fact that spectators might want to flee the theatre given the graphic nature of the play's content, Nottage employs a Brechtian 'distancing' technique in *Ruined* – regular song-breaks. In the scene after Christian describes Sophie's gang rape story in some detail, Sophie takes a mic in hand and sings her soul out to the audience in Nadi's bar. Her performance is lively and disarmingly 'natural'. We are in the thrall of a self-assured young performer, and the presence of a fragile rape victim is suddenly elided – or is it? There is the sense of the Brechtian 'NOT/BUT' at work in Sophie's direct address to the audience as a skilled, confident 'chanteuse'. Witnessing this interstitial 'entertainment', audiences may feel jarred – but in a different way from their wrenched-in-the-gut responses to the visceral wartime imagery. Brecht and Nottage understood the use-value of this 'gear shift' and counted on it (the flow of *Mother Courage*, too, is interrupted by songs). For Nottage, the song-break affords spectators an essential moment to breathe, before being tossed back into the edge-of-one's-seat plot of *Ruined*. For Brecht, the gear shift had a different purpose; the song-breaks in Brecht's plays were meant to propel spectators to think – to reassess the issues of the play from an intellectual rather than an emotional perspective. In an interview with playwright Nilo Cruz (2010), Nottage shared that the notion of music came very early in the process. I don't know that anyone who has been to the [African] continent, leaves without having been touched by all of the delicious, wonderful music. I thought, 'If I'm going to write about Africa, then music is absolutely part of that tapestry.'[48]

Hence, creating a musical tapestry for *Ruined* that evoked a sense of the African experience and finding the right composer-collaborator became crucial. (Dominic Kanza composed the music for the play; Nottage contributed the lyrics.) Nottage told Cruz:

> We wanted a composer who was not necessarily a musical theatre person, but someone who really had their foot in world music and was very familiar with the vocabulary of the Congo. I do think as a result it lends a lot of authenticity to the piece. I know that Congolese who come to see the play say, 'Oh, this music is very familiar. It makes me think of home.'[49]

The sheer beauty of Sophie's voice and the rich quality of the East African-infused music adds warmth and poetry to the world of *Ruined* – otherwise a very cruel and harsh environment. In different but equally compelling and distinctive ways, each of Nottage's plays is connected to and imbued by a specific musical texture, rhythm and style. In *Intimate Apparel*, Mayme's swinging, sensual and upbeat piano rags add sweetness and a bluesy suppleness – furthering the lyricism and the romantic spirit of *Intimate Apparel*. *Fabulation* has a much more contemporary, edgy and energetic musical feel – much like the spoken word/hip-hop performance style of Flow's poetry.

With many of the song-breaks in *Ruined*, there are dance sequences as well – usually sexual, bump-and-grind movements performed by Mama's 'girls', or the sexualized slow dances Salima and Josephine engage in with soldiers. But a dance that occurs at the end of Nottage's play has generated some of the most heated criticism of *Ruined*. In the play's last scene, Mama Nadi is revealed to be ruined, like Sophie. Despite this new and shocking information about her disabled status, Christian asks Nadi to marry him and she dances with him in the bar. We assume that when she accepts his offer to dance, which at first she rejects, she will accept his marriage proposal. Christian also appears to have been cured of his alcoholism, which erupted a few scenes earlier when Nadi coerced him into drinking with the Commander, in order to smooth things over between them. In the final moments of the play, as Nadi and Christian – two unlikely partners – dance, Sophie and Josephine look on. Jill Dolan (in her 'Feminist Spectator' blog) suggests that this ending was Nottage's 'one false note'. In Dolan's view, Nottage should have 'maintained her singular, Brechtian vision of the consequences of war for women'. Dolan looked for 'a more bitter end, instead of capitulating to realism's mandate that narratives resolve with heterosexual marriage that solves everything'.[50] Brantley, however, admired Nottage's

> well-shaped, sentimental ending, [which] is the culmination of a carefully designed work allowing people who might ordinarily look away from horror stories of distant wars ... [to] find themselves bound in empathy to the unthinkably abused women that Ms. Nottage and the excellent actresses here have shaped with such care and warmth.[51]

Ann Fox offered yet another reading of the play's ending, reflecting a disability studies perspective that presents 'a counter narrative at the play's end; through Sophie, disability resists closure, and maintains the activist sensibility of the play. Sophie's body remains on stage in the play's final moment, still disabled. What has been done to her remains and cannot be glossed over.'[52] Fox also cited Ben Brantley's review, for its focus on Sophie's disability. Brantley underlines the disabled presence in the room, the disabled person bearing witness. The sheer fact of Sophie's survivor status and her keen awareness of a cure for her condition – although it has thus far eluded her grasp – gives spectators hope, and also leaves the ending open, unresolved. The women in the room may be 'ruined' but they are not broken, which, as Brantley says, 'transforms this tale of ruin into a clear-eyed celebration of endurance'.[53]

(Sophie pulls Josephine into the doorway. They watch the pair dance, incredulously.)
Josephine *(Smiling, whispers.)* Go, Mama.[54]

It was this optimism at the end of the play that evoked high praise from the Pulitzer Prize committee as well, who no doubt appreciated, as did Brantley and Fox, the complexity of the wartime circumstances as well as the potential for building audience empathy in Nottage's more open ending. Nonetheless, Nottage's tension-filled plotting of Mama Nadi's day-to-day living in a war zone was not always received well. Some critics were confused and disturbed by the scene when Nadi coerced Christian to drink with Osembenga, the army commander, since she knew that for Christian, maintaining his sobriety was a source of pride and a survival strategy. Nottage explained:

> [I]n war people are forced to make compromised, difficult choices. That moment with Christian in the bar is the kind of complicated, moral dilemma that people face day to day in war zones like the Congo. You might see it as an act of cruelty, but is it purely an act of cruelty? Or is she saving him and herself from an even worse fate by forcing him to have a drink?... I wanted to ask that very complicated question. How far are we willing to go to survive?[55]

The world of *Ruined*, one of unpredictability, extremes and often danger, is reflected in the sensorial richness and volatility of the rain forest surrounding Mama's bar, which in many productions is a palpable presence in the design of the show. This ever-present environment of shifting shapes and dark hues works on multiple levels, as Steven Oxman observed in his review of the Chicago production in *Variety*. Oxman praised designer Derek McLane's

> evocative set with its full-on jungle of trees in the background ... both realistic and metaphorical, a keen representation of the dense moral thicket at play. It's to Whoriskey and Nottage's credit that this environment, and these circumstances, quickly take on a disturbing ordinariness. The women's lives under Mama Nadi are treated neither as tragic nor filled with hope. It's a reality, a means of survival[56]

At the precise moment the play premiered in Chicago, Barack Obama won the November 2008 election and was about to become the first African American president of the United States. Obama's platform of hope ('Yes We Can') seemed in perfect harmony with the consciousness-raising, activist themes of Nottage's play. In his rave review in the *Chicago Tribune*, Chris Jones pointed out that because of *Ruined*'s sharp focus on 'the horrors ... of the DRC civil war ... one finds oneself wishing the Obamas would find time in their transitional schedule to attend, perhaps with a powerful talk-show host of their acquaintance'.[57]

Ruined opened to acclaim in London at the Almeida Theatre in 2010. Kate Kellaway in the London *Observer* wrote that the play was directed 'brilliantly by Indhu Rubasingham' (she also directed *Intimate Apparel* in London) and that 'sinuous, courageous' Jenny Jules gave a 'beautiful performance as Mama Nadi that holds the play – and its characters – together'.[58] Jules had played Esther and Undine in the London productions of *Intimate Apparel* and *Fabulation* as well.

Of the many stand-out moments in the play, none was singled out more by critics than Salima's 'indelible', 'agonizing' and 'harrowing' monologue, as Charles Isherwood described it in the *New York Times*.[59] Critics across the globe have cited this scene as the 'heart-wrenching' centre of the play. Calmly Salima tells Sophie about

> working in our garden, planting sweet tomatoes ... And I felt a shadow cut across my back ... And the tall soldier slammed the butt of his gun into my cheek. Just like that ... My baby was crying. She was a good baby. She never cried, but she was crying, screaming. 'Shhh,' I said. 'Shhh.' And right then (*Salima closes her eyes*) a soldier stomped on her head with his boot. And she was quiet. (47)

In the play's penultimate scene, Salima enters, haemorrhaging after a self-inflicted abortion. This grotesquely heroic, horrific, climactic act signifies one woman's last stand and ultimately her independence from the men and the wars that brutalized her:

> **Salima** *(To soldiers and Osembenga.)* You will not fight your battles on my body anymore. (64)

This line resonates as a battle cry for women who have been subjected to the violent tyranny of men at war the world over, throughout history.

Conclusion

In an interview in 2015, Nottage spoke about 'the canon' of American theatre – and about reframing it. Nottage is interested in articulating what 'American theatre should strive to be', which in her view 'is a reflection of the beauty and diversity of this culture'. She had just completed the foreword to an anthology on Arthur Miller that marked Miller's centennial. Nottage stated that it was crucial that women – and especially important that a Black woman – be part of the conversation of what was American theatre and what is American theatre going forward.[60] Social engagement was important to Miller as a playwright, and socially engaged art is clearly important to Nottage as well, as is evident from the plays examined in this chapter. In her foreword to *The Penguin Arthur Miller*, she writes, 'I found his plays to be like soul music, fusing the bitter truth of history with the urgency and incendiary spirit of a generation eager to be heard ... He understood that theatre had the potential to be more than a frivolous divertissement; it could be a powerful social art, designed to instigate and unsettle and ultimately pry people out of their complacency.'[61]

Aptly, in a review of *Intimate Apparel* in its 2014 British premiere at the Ustinov Studio Theatre in Bath, Susannah Clapp declared that Nottage's work has achieved canonicity. She wrote that 'Lawrence Boswell's first rate production shows the play's power and subtlety ... Quietly and subversive, its recovery of lost lives makes this a defining piece of American drama. First Death of a Salesman: white and male. Now Rebirth of a Seamstress: black and female.'[62] Here Clapp specifically cites Miller's play as a marker of canonical American theatre that Nottage has reached and reframed, with a production that reflects the kind of diversity and beauty Nottage believes American theatre 'should strive to be'.

In Nottage's foreword to the Miller collection, she writes, 'art should be in active conversation with the culture'. She is drawn to Miller because 'his work reminds us that theatre should be a place of transformation, a place where we can collectively explore society's wounds, unearth difficult truths, and wrestle with untidy human emotions'.[63] With this mission propelling her, Nottage created *One More River to Cross: A Verbatim Fugue* (2007),[64] an adaptation of the extraordinary WPA Federal Writers' Project (1936–8) interview transcripts with former slaves. This documentary/musical/ensemble work for eight or more performers and musicians builds a tapestry of 'difficult truths' that charts the journey from slavery to freedom from the vantage point of the late 1930s, looking back to the antebellum South and beyond. Nottage's contributions to the great African American canon continue to be in vibrant conversation with the works of Lorraine Hansberry, August Wilson and Suzan-Lori Parks, who have also reframed and revisioned our interrogation and understanding of decades of African American history – from the middle passage and into the twenty-first century.

5

Theresa Rebeck

Dorothy Chansky

Introduction

When *Omnium Gatherum*, co-written by Theresa Rebeck and Alexandra Gersten-Vassilaros, was named in 2004 a finalist for the 2003 Pulitzer Prize in Drama, Rebeck took the first big step in the eye of a general theatregoing public from being a yeoman Off-Broadway playwright and television scriptwriter to being someone whose first (of three as of 2015) Broadway play, *Mauritius*, would open in 2007, catapulting her to what might be called the major league of playwriting. Rebeck's own response to learning that the Manhattan Theatre Club wanted to take *Mauritius* to the Great White Way was, 'It's like moving from a studio to a penthouse.'[1]

'Studio' is a New Yorker's term for a single-room apartment, but it could also refer to the level of production to which Rebeck was accustomed for the first fifteen years of her career in theatres from Boston to Hartford, New Haven to Louisville, and in New York. By the time of that first Broadway production, she had published a dozen full-length plays (all of which had been professionally produced and not counting the co-written *Omnium*) and more than twice that number of one-acts. She had also written for television, starting with the short-lived sitcom *American Dreamer*, followed by a stint writing for another sitcom, *Brooklyn Bridge* (before being fired), shortly thereafter serving in a two-and-a-half-year position with *NYPD Blue* as a staff writer from 1994 to 1997. She then wrote for *L.A. Law*, subsequently serving as writer and producer for *Law & Order: Criminal Intent* until 2003.[2] Her television work was nominated for several Emmy awards.

If the extensive experience with television would cause some to turn up their noses and accuse Rebeck of selling out, and although she would say she considers herself primarily a playwright,[3] work on television made her confident in her ability to be productive within a timeframe, to hone her craft, to privilege discipline and to 'deliver what's needed'.[4] In 1999, she wrote a letter to the editor of the *New York Times* in response to an article entitled 'Unlocking Broadway: Outsiders Seek the Key', whose writer asserted that writing for television or film was 'at best distracting and at worst damaging to [a playwright's] craft'; actors featured in the article, however, were praised for precisely such goings back and forth. In Rebeck's words, 'Writing for television and the movies is no more damaging to one's craft than sitting around a tiny apartment and stewing over why you're broke.'[5] Later she would emphasize that she 'never thought accessibility was a bad word, either'.[6]

Rebeck's plays largely feature rapid changes of direction, high-stakes conflict and characters who are never at a loss for a snappy rejoinder to an adversarial interlocutor. Readers and audiences may find her work facile, but her subject matter is always socially conscious, never shallow and is powerfully of the moment. With a PhD in English literature, she is deeply informed; with a specialty in Victorian melodrama (her dissertation was called 'Your Cries Are in Vain'), she is finely attuned to holding audiences rapt as she takes them on emotional roller-coaster rides engineered around surprise and morality. And in *The Butterfly Collection*, first produced in 2000, she would pen a well-read young writer who praises a Pulitzer Prize-winning novelist precisely for his 'facile' prose, explaining that she means it 'in the academic sense ... fluid, easy'.[7] This almost reads as a sly comeback to her critics, nodding eerily *avant la lettre* to her own nomination for a Pulitzer. Rebeck's plays are page-turners but the situations in which she places her characters force them to show their true moral and ethical colours, often under tremendous pressure, and often to unflattering ends. 'I'm not interested,' she told a journalist in 2011, 'in writing that doesn't leave blood on the floor.'[8] At one point she told a reporter that her plays are about 'betrayal and treason and poor behavior – a lot of poor behavior', later writing a play actually called *Poor Behavior*.[9] Since her characters are almost always upper-middle-class urbanites with education, verbal dexterity and a sense of entitlement, Rebeck specializes in skewering, flattering and troubling a particular population all at once. Other than Lillian Hellman and Rachel Crothers, it is hard to think of an American woman playwright as prolific, produced and adept at social critique packaged to sell.

Theresa Rebeck was born in 1958 in Kenwood, Ohio. Her father was an engineer, her mother a social worker. The playwright has five siblings. Rebeck was brought up Catholic and graduated from Cincinnati's Ursuline Academy in 1976. She earned her undergraduate degree in 1980 from the University of Notre Dame, where she met her future husband, Jess Lynn, a one-time stage manager. From Notre Dame she went to Brandeis University, where she earned an MA in literature in 1983, an MFA in playwriting in 1986 and the PhD in 1989. She would marry Lynn in 1990 and spend the next decade writing plays, scripts for television series, and screenplays – in the latter category perhaps most notably the 1996 *Harriet the Spy* in collaboration with Douglas Petrie. Rebeck and Lynn's son was born in 1995 and their daughter in 2002. The family lives in Brooklyn.

The first full-length Rebeck play to garner attention was *Spike Heels*, completed and workshopped by the New York Stage and Film Company in association with the Powerhouse Theater at Vassar College in 1990, turned down by a number of regional theatres in 1991 for being both written by an unknown and perceived as feminist, and finally produced in New York by Second Stage Theatre in 1992. ('Apparently,' wrote Rebeck, regarding the feminist label as some kind of box office poison, 'when a woman writes about an actual incident of sexual harassment, it's pillow talk; and when a man writes about a woman lying about sexual harassment [here referring to David Mamet's *Oleanna*], it's a searing commentary.')[10] Actress Julie White, who played the second female lead in *Spike Heels*, would become a Theresa Rebeck regular and Rebeck would write the solo piece *Bad Dates* for White in 2003.[11] *Spike Heels* features a lower-class and very sexy young woman (she sports the shoes of the title) who is passed back and forth between a middle-aged male professor and his lawyer friend, the latter of whom is guilty of workplace harassment. The woman, Georgie, recognizes that she is part of a Pygmalion scheme on the part of the professor (Pygmalion is specifically invoked), who is engaged to another woman, Lydia, but clearly prefers Georgie's verve and shoes to Lydia's monied propriety. The play is direct about how language creates power and how clothing choices influence self-esteem and public perception. In the end, perhaps unsatisfyingly, Georgie dumps the professor and is willing to negotiate a relationship with the manipulative and abusive lawyer, from whom she has learned the idea of bargaining for advantage.

The 1993 *Loose Knit* (premiered at New York's Second Stage Theatre) and the 1994 *Sunday on the Rocks* (premiered at Long Wharf Theatre, New Haven) both feature groups of women friends in the throes of what might very broadly be called relationship and self-esteem 'issues'. Both plays traffic in the problems and milieu made famous and popular in the 1970s and 1980s by Wendy Wasserstein in such plays as *Uncommon Women, Isn't It Romantic* and *The Heidi Chronicles*. *Loose Knit*'s quintet meet regularly to knit and kvetch. One of them sets the others up on dates with the same man, Miles, a controlling and monied egomaniac, who takes them all to the same restaurant and treats each first date like a job interview. One woman loses her job; one's husband is cheating on her with her sister; one is the sister sleeping with her brother-in-law; one is a therapist who does not have all the answers. A reviewer for a 1999 revival called *Loose Knit* a 'wicked take on gender alienation' whose 'unspoken agenda is really group therapy'.[12] The quartet in *Sunday on the Rocks* are younger and unmarried, sharing a house and working out questions about careers, marriage, children and religion. Again, abuse and the tension between wanting to be one's own woman and the terror of being without a man take centre stage. *Sunday on the Rocks* ends with a group trip of solidarity to the hospital in the wake of one of the women being beaten by a date. The conclusion does not so much solve (much less resolve) anything as it reaches a plateau and serves as a springboard for (audience) contemplation. *Loose Knit* similarly ends less with any plot resolution than with a kind of bonding (again) around group solidarity, the possibility of selling the sweaters created by the best of the knitters, rapprochement around Miles's sleaziness and grounds for post-show conversation. One reviewer called *Loose Knit* a 'rigged comedy' whose characters 'represent a rough cross-section of middle-class New Yorkers'.[13] That a lawyer, a therapist and access to a man who drives a Rolls-Royce comprise an idea of middle class says everything about the audience Rebeck addresses – an idea that emerges with full force in *Omnium Gatherum* and its marketing and reception.

Two other plays from the 1990s move outside domestic settings to take up questions of manipulation, sexism and abuse of power in the heady realms of Washington politics and Tinseltown television. *The Family of Mann*, which premiered in 1994 at New York's Second Stage, centres on a young writer, Belinda, who has a PhD in literature and is the new darling in a stable of Hollywood writers for a glossy, glib, domestic sitcom sharing its title with that of the play. According to one interview, Rebeck claimed that '90 per cent of what happens in the play could be labeled as documentary'.[14] *Mann*'s egomaniacal producer is not-so-subtly based on *Brooklyn Bridge* producer Gary David Goldberg, who, in Rebeck's telling, fired her for using the wrong tone of voice in responding to him one day.[15] In the course of the play, we see good ideas trashed, actors ridiculed for their bodies, sexual harassment trumpeted and Belinda's soul beginning to be crushed. When Belinda spends a frantic weekend rewriting a scene to specification only to find on Monday that the producer changed his mind and wanted something entirely different but failed to inform her, she begins to lose it. A less talented junior colleague is first an ally, then her boyfriend and finally her replacement and betrayer. The play exemplifies Rebeck's description of herself as 'a comic realist, a misanthrope, and an idealist'.[16]

The 1996 *View of the Dome* centres on the scales falling from the eyes of an idealistic protagonist, Emma, whose efforts to help elect a seemingly moral and visionary candidate to office in Washington lead to the revelation that ideals only last so long as they are expedient. As one character tells the newly shunned Emma, 'It's everybody's favorite pastime, deciding who is more important than whom … [Y]ou were the least dangerous. The most expendable.'[17] Emma, summarily dumped by the people she has tried to help, also becomes pregnant by a senator who is ready to have sex with her but is even more ready to drop her when she inquires about his loyalty to his campaign manager seeming to trump his loyalty to her. A Polaroid of the two in the bedroom becomes a weapon in an anti-corruption effort, and Emma's cause is taken up by extreme religious conservatives seeking to use her for their own ends. The *New York Times* reviewer called *View of the Dome* 'the dismally familiar story of a ... Candide-like naïf in the nation's capital', whose 'not very surprising lesson can be summed up simply: corruption is contagious and unavoidable'.[18] Another way to situate this play, however, is as a zingy, highly readable and performable snapshot of a set of familiar 1990s hot-button subjects. The same review compared Emma to Anita Hill and Gennifer Flowers, the former put through a highly public and unpleasant set of hearings when she accused Supreme Court nominee Clarence Thomas of sexual harassment and the latter a one-time consort of President Bill Clinton. In retrospect, a play featuring Polaroids (old technology?, failure to realize how easily even a paper image can 'go viral?') and the revelation that women (here especially the campaign manager) can play behind-the-scenes hardball with the best of the guys, along with precisely the connections to then headline-making scandals, is arguably an engaging package of shorthand situations that could serve as pedagogical enticement in undergraduate classes on American social history.

It would be wrong to regard Rebeck's dramatic output of the 1990s simply as a kind of training ground for the plays she would write in the first decade of the new century. The plays remain readable, playable and representative of their era. But the terrain she staked out in her first successful decade would be revisited, refreshed and re-seen in the 2000s. *Omnium Gatherum* was a finalist for the Pulitzer; *Mauritius* was the Broadway breakthrough; and *The Understudy* is the sort of philosophical and literary achievement that uses the immediacy of its setting (here not bound to the immediacy of its moment – no hot-button issues) to theatricalize questions about the value of artistic work and integrity beyond marketability and the difficulty of assessing artistic value under capitalism.

Omnium Gatherum

The co-authored *Omnium Gatherum* was written in response to the 11 September 2001 attacks on the World Trade Center in New York. Rebeck and Alexandra Gersten-Vassilaros claimed they began writing the play 'even as ground zero continued to smoke' (the reference is to the location of the destroyed WTC twin towers), arguing with each other about the circumstances of the event 'in an effort to try to pin it down or understand it'.[19] The pair had known each other for a decade; both specialized in 'plays populated by smart, unhappy, erudite characters', with Gersten-Vassilaros's having been produced Off-Broadway, at Steppenwolf (Chicago) and at the McCarter (Princeton, New Jersey).[20] Neither woman had ever written with a co-playwright before. *Omnium*'s plethora of hot-button issues were what Gersten-Vassilaros called an attempt at a 'marriage – of fact, fiction, social criticism, and heartfelt satire'.[21] Rebeck would note in a 2006 interview that the more the duo investigated and argued about 9/11 'the less [the play] became a lesson about that specific event and more about: What do you do, how do you act as a moral and constructive person, in a world that's evolving in truly terrifying ways?'[22] The first readings of the play took place in the spring of 2002 at New York's Actors Studio; there was a reading at the Public Theater that September; and the Naked Angels company offered workshop performances at the start of 2003, just ahead of the world premiere at Actors Theatre of Louisville in April. The play opened Off-Broadway at the Variety Arts Theatre in New York in September, just slightly over two years after the event that prompted it.

Set in an immediately post-9/11 world of anxious urbanites, *Omnium Gatherum* stages a dinner party with conversation among people who cover a spectrum of political and ideological interests.[23] The politics, the food and food politics are the components in this loosely plotted, energetically talky work. The guests are wealthy, famous personalities including thinly disguised stand-ins for figures from Martha Stewart (the hostess, Suzie, played in New York by Kristine Nielsen) to Tom Clancy to the late Edward Said. The party also includes a fireman and a terrorist, the latter the surprise guest of honour, unveiled at the meal's end. Suzie hosts what critic John Lahr calls 'a pinball machine of educated debate', through which 'we come to understand the rumble of panic behind both dialectic and desire'.[24] Occurring in real time, the 'little plot per se' in which 'eight points of view that are bound to clash' is set in motion over the dinner that is itself highly structured, while the topics of conversation are more of a 'smorgasbord'; subjects range from free-market capitalism to the Bible to warfare to corporate-controlled media – all politicized by the guests.[25] At the level of dialogue, the self-contained world onstage winked at the world of the audience by nodding to local chefs, whose actual menus and fame were part of the show's appeal. The New York summoned by *Omnium Gatherum* is a rhetorical one; the play is set in hell. Hostess Suzie's line, 'The whole meal has been designed by [insert name of famous local chef here]' evokes a 'hereness' that pokes fun at New York's 'hellishness', while simultaneously addressing the audiences as sophisticated urbanites in the know.[26]

The New York producers, hedging their bets as to whether political discourse and 'potentially somber subject matter' might scare audiences so soon after the attacks, didn't mention 9/11 in their press and promotional materials.[27] Instead, publicity name-dropped the cast of famous types and held forth on the bill of fare that would be prepared by celebrity chefs for the production; press packets for critics also included a detailed description of the play's menu and the line-up of cordon bleus.[28] The publicist for the Variety Arts Theatre production, Richard Kornberg, and the set designer, David Rockwell, who designed chef Alfred Portale's restaurant Gotham, dreamed up the collaboration with celebrity chefs. While this seems to have been a marketing strategy, the spectacle and novelty of an elaborately staged meal became much of what the play 'was about' in New York, and later outside Chicago. The *New York Times* and *Chicago Tribune* each also featured stories on the respective productions in which actors quipped about the irony of growing tired of the delicious dishes and recounted the trials of negotiating acting and chewing, while props crews explained the logistical gymnastics of retrieving, heating and plating the courses in time for their onstage appearances.[29]

Critics, of course, did mention 9/11 in their reviews of *Omnium Gatherum*. Not all were impressed, and on several occasions, New York audience members walked out 'due to the subject matter', perhaps a result of the bait-and-switch from publicity to performance.[30] Reviewers tended to judge *Omnium Gatherum*'s success as a play through a metrics that measured its contemporary relevance against its potential to become dated quickly, as well as whether the play offered satisfactory explanations for the 2001 calamity and subsequent conflicts in Iraq and Afghanistan. While Robert Brustein called the New York production 'a strong piece of political theatre' that 'struck me as surprisingly intelligent', Frank Rich labelled it 'Tom Wolfe for dummies'. Charles Isherwood described it as having a 'middlebrow TV-chatshow essence', and Mark Steyn was disappointed by the 'hackneyed premise [which] proceeds in predictable directions', but Ben Brantley praised it as a 'piping hot slice of satire', adding that the play 'never feels merely derivative and schematic'.[31]

It is worth presenting the dinner menu (as it appears in the published script) in toto to get the full effect of its delights as well as its pretension. The meal starts with an amuse-bouche the size of a dime, described as a 'marvelous mini sweet potato scotch bonnet raviolini ... with a spoonful of chanterelle ... mushroom sauce, garnished with fresh cilantro shoots' (11). The appetizer proper is 'a beautiful wild salmon ... rubbed with rock salt and exotic Spanish spices, pan-roasted and ... served on a tower of sliced ruby crescent fingerlings' (which the hostess explains are potatoes) with a side portion of 'a lovely warmish yellow pepper sauce with threads of saffron and young scallions' (13–14). There is no bread, as the fireman Jeff (not from the ranks of the privileged, but nevertheless a fashionable hero to have at the table) who asks for it is told it is 'over!' and that 'all that starch just interferes with the complexity of the meal. Besides, it's very bad for you' (18). The main course is described as being from southern Pakistan but 'reimagined with a lively Southwestern flair. Comprised of freshly blessed lamb. Treated with a glaze made from vedalia [sic] onions, garlic, cane sugar, ancho chile powder, dried apricots and the blackest of black pepper ... Roasted and served with coush coush, that's it's [sic] correct pronunciation ... tossed with tender root vegetables' and a side dish of 'charred corn salsa' (27). Salad, served after the main course, is a 'nice mélange of microgreens and baby arugula dotted with pomegranate seeds in a spicy orange vinaigrette [sic] tossed with whole toasted walnuts' (42). Khalid tastes spearmint in the dressing and Suzie compliments him for recognizing it (45). Dessert is a 'cavalcade of brown sugar twills, lemon poppy seed Madelines [sic], hazelnut financiers and, finally, a tri-star strawberry and mascarpone mill-foo-ee-ay' (71).

Still, the characters in *Omnium Gatherum* cannot be understood as food snobs with tastes and skills wholly beyond the ken of the anticipated audience. That is, characters may indeed be food snobs, but not to an extent that would utterly alienate spectators. The play holds in tension envy and criticism, but it ultimately reassures the audience that bestselling writers ask for ranch dressing, that doyennes of domesticity still forget red wine is a no-no with fish and that keeping Saltines in the cupboard is not above even the fanciest hostess's practices. *Omnium Gatherum* pokes fun at the pretensions of foodies, but it also seems to shrug as if to say, 'What can you do? This is the world as we know it.'[32]

From the start, politics vie with food for the guests' attention. Food serves dramaturgically to create rhythm, pauses and metaphorical meaning as it is strategically introduced and discussed in such a way as to help shape audience interest and to structure attention. Each course arrives with a pronouncement by Suzie that either clears the air after a stand-off in an argument or an embarrassing joke, or that contextualizes politics within the consumer entertainment that is expensive, trendy food, rather than leaving the meal as a backdrop to extended discourse. The hostess, in other words, is the authors' device to manage the more difficult ideas in small sound bites, something they accomplish by making Suzie a wealthy media figure (important to listen to) and a ditz (a safety valve for anything the audience doesn't quite follow). Before the arrival of the salad, for instance, she deflects an argument about Israel and Palestinian rights with 'Such a lively debate. Wonderful, really, bravo to everyone. Now for the salad' (42).

Omnium Gatherum assumes that its audience recognizes all its topics but that it is not really an expert in any of them. In fact, it barely requires competence. A Leftist argument challenging the idea that terrorist acts by reactionaries are an expression of international outrage is met with, 'Whoa. What?' and the reply that it's 'Cambridge', where one had to 'keep up'. Since the audience can't be taxed with the obligation of a Cambridge University degree, it is allowed to expect the speaker to repeat his argument. He does so, and this time, one character says, 'I understand what you are saying' but another replies, 'I don't' (16). Only when the argument is repeated for the third time, much further into the play, do the two least educated of the guests pause and say, 'I followed that.' 'I did too' (48).

Debate about food politics in *Omnium Gatherum* coalesces around themes that were, and still are, frequent, topical subjects in the specialist as well as the popular press: the horrors of processed and fast food; the distastefulness of food that isn't stylish or exotic or both; dietary guidelines; dieting; genetically engineered food; the difference between colitis and diverticulitis; the biology of fish and shellfish; choosing the proper wine to accompany a dish; food allergies; veganism vs. vegetarianism; global hunger; and the tacit expectation that familiar foods (even if they are packaged or have too many carbs) are good to have around for fussy eaters or guests with pregnancy-related nausea. These topics are not addressed systematically, or in detail, and sometimes are inaccurately represented; characters interrupt, go off on tangents and get distracted in the same manner that they derail attempts at a sustained discussion of any one complex geopolitical issue.

The play's limited view of 'bad' foods (carbohydrates, bread in particular, and anything processed) accepts the wealth of some and the hunger of many as parallel but unconnected realities for which political entities but not wealthy (-enough) consumers bear responsibility. *New Yorker* reviewer John Lahr praised this critical ignorance of *Omnium Gatherum*'s characters as keen satire: 'Here American plenty is a source of percolating disgust ... [Suzie] eats the food of foreign countries, but, when the notion of sharing with them is raised, she draws a blank. "Share more with whom?" she asks, startled.'[33] The undefined 'others' who include people in/from foreign countries, people of colour and people who might be called 'natives' or 'peasants' are exactly the people who make the exotic meal possible. Not only has their labour facilitated Suzie's empire but their menus and native comestibles are what she poaches to create her own. The lamb has been blessed by 'not the rabbi, it's whatsitcalled, the the the Muslim version of kosher – ' (67). The origins of the Southwestern salsa are Native American, and the promise of dessert calls to mind for the very drunk Cambridge pundit a panna cotta eaten in southern Italy that 'was sexual, it was sensual. It was mother's milk reconceived ... This dish quelled all desire, all anxiety, all the world fell to a generous hush all about me' (72). As Peggy Phelan notes, 'Seeing the other is a social form of self-reproduction. For in looking at/for the other, we seek to re-present ourselves to ourselves.'[34] In the drama, the exotic foods serve as unproblematic metaphors for how global corporate capitalism benefits rich nations to the detriment of poor states and peoples, although one could also argue that the 'me' the food becomes 'all about' is one that fails to see the other as more than a stereotype – a 'me' one seeks to re-present to oneself as perfect in one's privilege.

In *Theatre and War: Theatrical Responses since 1991*, Jeanne Colleran's study of 'how theatre enacts a politic/ethical critique during a time when dissent has been termed unpatriotic and when media technologies manage public opinion', the author situates *Omnium Gatherum* among a handful of plays written in the immediate aftermath of the 9/11 attacks, all of them 'in tacit conversation with some part of the public codification of 9/11' and most failing to critique either American exceptionalism or first-person concerns (generally with individual safety and the possible disruption of a consumerist way of life).[35] *Omnium* is the only one of the plays appearing hot on the heels of the event to offer 'unexpected comic relief through a different kind of listening: one where [audience members] might well be overhearing themselves or listening with new ears to opinionated drivel passed off as thoughtful analysis'.[36] Colleran's study is rare for being a scholarly consideration of Rebeck's work, and its balanced conclusion is that while the play does little to further understanding of the enemy or the other, it succeeds in doing the work of asking us to face ourselves, as 'all the guests are revealed as self-contradictory and self-interested but reconcilable members of the human race'.[37] *Omnium Gatherum* earns high marks for ultimately being life-affirming in its reverence for 'food, travel, talk, and, most of all, company'.[38]

Mauritius

High marks were not forthcoming for Rebeck's Broadway debut, *Mauritius*, which opened at the Biltmore Theatre in October 2007, following a premiere at Boston's Center for the Arts almost exactly a year earlier. The play's action centres on a battle between two half sisters for a stamp collection that may contain a pair of stamps worth more than $6 million. Two professional philatelists – both greedy and cruel – and a third sort of young, shady, charming con man also enter the fray. In Rebeck style, what is at stake is not only the money that could radically change the lives of at least two of the characters; it is the sorts of choices and behaviours emerging from temptation, wealth, opportunity (however understood), family relationships and buried resentments that prompt ideas of deserving or entitlement. The play received subsequent productions in locations including San Francisco, Los Angeles, New Orleans and Austin, Texas. Reading reviews from the various cities suggests that the scale of production expected on Broadway and the metrics applied by the major press in that city do not always tell the same, therefore the full, story about a dramatist's work or appeal.

The title of *Mauritius* comes from the island where, in 1847 and under British rule, one of the first postage stamps in the world was printed. In Rebeck's play, a crucial printing error has made two stamps in a family album worth millions of dollars. Instead of 'post paid', the stamps bear the words 'post office'. They are in pristine condition and part of a collection, assembled by the grandfather of one of the two half sisters, Mary (Katie Finneran on Broadway), who has returned to the family homestead following her mother's death from cancer. Mary's father, who died young, seems to have come from wealth, and Mary was sent to boarding school at the age of 16, effectively leaving home at that point. The younger sister, Jackie (Alison Pill), is canny, impoverished and seemingly both uneducated and streetwise (she reads comic books and has been beaten up often enough to shrug off being slugged during the play's climactic encounter as something that will yield a black eye but nothing worth a trip to a doctor). She is also the one who stayed with their mother during the latter's final illness, while Mary, when summoned, waffled about visiting until it was too late.

We know little of the women's personal lives, but they both carry emotional baggage. For Jackie, the stamps are a means to money – although at first she has no idea how much – and a way out. For Mary, until she comes to realize their dollar value, the stamps are a cultural legacy. Indeed, towards the end of the play she snootily tells Jackie 'You clearly haven't had the opportunity to develop an appreciation for for [sic] something as elegant and precious and *timeless* as that stamp collection. I know what things must have been like for you all those years.' Jackie's comeback is, 'You don't, actually.'[39] Jackie and Mary are variously courted and conned by philatelist Philip (Dylan Baker), whose expertise is sought by all the others, but who has hardly gained wealth through his knowledge; Sterling (F. Murray Abraham), an imperious, ruthless collector with a potty mouth and a great deal of money; and Dennis (Bobby Cannevale), a young grifter and wannabe collector, who plays Philip and Sterling off each other and whose answer to Jackie's query about his once having had money that he lost is 'I'm actually not terribly interested in the past ... I mean, you know what they say about the stamps. It's the errors that make them valuable. That's kind of my theory on people' (51). It is Dennis who, in the play's disastrous showdown, tries to broker calm by sharing blame all around via invoking a Rebeck leitmotif: 'People have been behaving poorly' (75). Critic Charles McNulty, reviewing the 2009 Los Angeles production, thumbnailed Rebeck's creation as a 'chess match to maximize profit over the stamps'.[40]

Virtually all reviewers compared *Mauritius* to David Mamet's *American Buffalo*, that playwright's Broadway 1975 breakout in which con men try to con a hapless owner out of a rare nickel. Comparing New York reviewers' handling of this matter to that of critics in other cities points to how New York theatre cannot uncomplicatedly be taken for (all) US theatre. For *The New Yorker*'s Robert Risko, *Mauritius* is 'David Mamet for girls ... [as] Rebeck channels Mamet's rhythms and his comic tropes of linguistic self-inflation'.[41] Los Angeles's McNulty, however, argued that 'it's not entirely fair to fault Rebeck for borrowing a setup when her style doesn't otherwise have a lot in common with a dramatist who gets his kicks from verbal cocaine'.[42] In New York, the *Times*'s Ben Brantley complained of Rebeck's dramatis personae: 'These are less complete characters than exercises in style: components in a ritual of negotiation on which they take turns commenting self-consciously.'[43] Risko went further in this vein, calling the play 'psychologically bogus' and wanting to know why one sister has had more advantages in life than the other and what the issue was between Mary and the mother, finally whining, 'Who *are* these people?' If one insists on kitchen sink realism, these are perhaps legitimate questions. But Rebeck is, as she has stated in interviews, interested in behaviour, something observable and on which we pass judgement daily whether or not we have 'backstory'. (Do we care about what might earlier have transpired between Romeo and Rosaline prior to his walking out on her? Is the specific source of Iago's over-the-top propensity to jealousy of primary importance in appreciating his horrifyingly effective machinations? Do the childhood or workplace experiences of the characters matter in assessing the characters' existential situation in *Waiting for Godot*?) Frank Rizzo's *Variety* review of the Boston production seems to grasp this difference, as he commends Rebeck's 'just hint[ing] at each character's simmering backstory of family trauma, betrayal, and lost chances', an idea also embraced in Sandy MacDonald's review of the Boston run: '[Rebeck] reveals just enough about her quintet of characters to keep you guessing as to their motives and capabilities, and leaves just enough questions unanswered to keep you mulling long after the curtain has fallen.'[44] MacDonald even calls Sterling, as played with a Cockney accent by James Gales, 'a figure out of Pinter', the latter a playwright famous for tense, life-changing encounters in everyday settings between characters whose backgrounds are generally offered sketchily at best.

Mauritius is neatly structured to feature two or three of the five characters in varying configurations in every scene until nearly the end of the play, when the quintet converges for a brief, confrontational and violent five pages (of 77). Alliances shift throughout the play in accordance with newly acquired information and perceived opportunities. For Brantley, *Mauritius* is 'deftly formulaic'. Risko accused Rebeck of being 'so slick that Gucci wears *her* shoes', adding that *Mauritius* is 'an act of prestidigitation, a confidence trick ... [an] ersatz ... sleight of hand [that] follows the old boulevard recipe of complication without depth'. Matthew Murray of the online 'Talkin' Broadway' warned, 'Whatever you do, don't take it too seriously.'[45] For Los Angeles's McNulty, however, the operative description of the script is 'taut dramatic intrigue ... [that] draws you in with its twists and turns'.[46] MacDonald in Boston called the play 'a definite keeper', in keeping with Rizzo's admiration of *Mauritius*'s 'dandy plot and character twists', and Beverly Creasey's labelling the work 'an elegant, downright hilarious play ... a sassy suspense comedy with delicious flights of philosophical fantasy'.[47]

Certainly one could say that the New York reviewers are sophisticated and others more easily pleased, but doing so negates the appeal Rebeck's work has more broadly than on the Great White Way. Moreover, producers' ideas of what belongs on Broadway differ from ideas about what could win interest and favour in other contexts.

The Understudy

It would not be an overstatement to call *The Understudy* a play unafraid to be identified with the quest for the meaning of life – at least contemporary life for actors and possibly, by association, other artists. Set in a Broadway theatre, the play features three Rebeck characters at a rehearsal of a previously undiscovered masterpiece by Kafka. Both the subject of the play being rehearsed and the setting of Rebeck's own play in a theatre – a world of doubling and artifice-with-belief – lend themselves to questions about reality, hierarchy, power and helplessness. The eponymous character is a talented but down-on-his-luck actor grateful for this job because he needs the paycheck. In his past are some undisclosed financial problems, a fiancée jilted two weeks before the wedding, a change of name and recent unemployment. This actor, Harry, has been hired to understudy Jake, a movie star described as '*so handsome and sure of himself you truly want to faint, or puke. He does in fact carry with him an air of reality that the rest of us sadly can only yearn for in the blackest parts of our souls.*'[48] Jake's newest film, an action flick packed full of special effects, for which he was paid $2.3 million, has grossed $67 million the previous weekend, marking him in Harry's mind as an overpaid, talentless sort of stud who holds all the right cards for all the wrong reasons. Jake's role in the Kafka play is one of two, the other belonging to an even bigger movie star, Bruce, who never appears in Rebeck's play, but who commands $22 million per film and whose ego is legendary. The third onstage character is the stage manager, Roxanne, a former actress whose talent was not enough to keep her from ending up largely unemployed, hence her current backstage position. Roxanne is also the woman on whom Harry walked out.

In a way all three characters are understudies unlikely to get to play roles worthy of the true professional selves in which they believe, except in the context of rehearsal. Jake reveals himself to be not only an able actor, but more knowledgeable about the play than Harry is. Roxanne not only understands the play's characters better than either of the actors, but she also knows more about Kafka's life and mistreatment of women than does either of the men. When she reads and fully acts Bruce's role to show Jake what she means about a character (to wit, that the play's power dynamics would be far more powerful and frightening with a woman in the role), Jake is awed and inspired. Harry admits that the joy of playing his part – even as an understudy and even only in a rehearsal – is worth his full effort. It is an effort he makes even as the company learns the play is to close because its star attraction has suddenly decided to depart. In a surprise move, the unseen Bruce has taken the film role Jake has hoped would be his, scuttling Jake's hopes for more serious parts, Harry's hope of ever going onstage in the Kafka play and perhaps even Roxanne's hope of staying employed, albeit in a second-choice capacity.

For the original New York production at Roundabout's Laura Pels Theatre in 2009, critics generally read *The Understudy* as an 'amusing riff on theater-world pecking order'[49] or a 'slight but breezy backstage comedy',[50] locating 'the primary object of Ms. Rebeck's comic scorn [in] the corruption of the American theater by the public's and the industry's obsession with celebrity'.[51] Rebeck herself acknowledges that obvious assessment, noting, however, 'it's also about more. A lot of what happens in show business is just horrible ... and with next to no reason for it. Your life is out of your control ... And after a while I came to see that the capitalist cruelty growing out of the drive for profit was behind it ... It's kind of a senseless, dehumanizing, totalitarian force.'[52] Actress Danielle Skraakstad, who played Roxanne at the McCarter Theatre in Princeton in 2014, observed that surely 'it's not just in theatre that people feel underappreciated or think they could do things better than people who get promoted whom [*sic*] they don't think are as good at that job as they are'.[53] Adam Immerwahr, who directed the McCarter production, taking the long view of the world of the play, simply observed, 'It can be daunting to face those unknown forces that direct our lives.'[54]

As with *Mauritius*, critical responses outside New York for later productions (Princeton, New Jersey; Baltimore, Maryland; Philadelphia; and Hartford, Connecticut, among others) were more favourable, again perhaps inviting thinking about how a New York playwright and an American playwright are not, or at least need not be read as, precisely one and the same thing. (Nearly all productions of *The Understudy* earned high praise for their actors. Indeed, this is a play one is unlikely to assay without three strong, versatile performers. In New York, Rebeck regular Julie White played Roxanne to an outstanding response.) Baltimore reviewer Amanda Gunther led her assessment of the 2014 Everyman Theatre production with the clear assertion that *The Understudy* is 'more than just a metaplay about real life actors and Kafka. Proving to be a mordant blast of focused dark wit, Rebeck's work is ... unpredictably enthralling, keeping the audience engaged with the three characters and their intertwined stories to the very Kafkaesque ending.'[55] Anita Gates, reviewing a 2011 revival at Hartford's Theatreworks for the Connecticut section of the *New York Times*, focused on how casting determines which of the three characters dominates the play and perhaps gains greatest audience sympathy. (For Gates, it had been Julie White in New York, while in Hartford it was Andrew Benator's Harry.) She called the production 'saucy', concluding that Rebeck is 'one of her generation's major talents'.[56]

In *The Understudy*, Rebeck's dramaturgy works in a manner akin to that of *Omnium Gatherum*. The focus is on character, situation and large questions rather than on plot twists, scheming or even really what's going to happen. Again, as in *Omnium*, Rebeck makes complex questions legible and intelligible to an audience expected to recognize topics but not to have real mastery. Nods to *The Trial* and *The Castle* as well as a couple of references to bugs and judicious invocations of Kafka's name serve to assure the audience that it is in sophisticates' territory without actually going so far as to demand knowledge beyond what one might vaguely recall from a college lecture, if that. While food service provides *Omnium*'s excuse for shifting gears and changing the subject, here it is the imperatives and problems of the rehearsal. Characters leave the stage to locate a missing prop or look for an absent technician, to place a phone call or simply to go to the bathroom. The continued appearance of the wrong lighting cue or the wrong setting moving into place at the hands of the unseen (and presumably high on marijuana) technician forces the rehearsal to mix up the order of the scenes in the play-within-the-play, deliberately messing with any notion of chronology or logical causality. The play opens with a monologue, ends with a dance performed by all three characters and in between features scenes of two or three characters, with the two-handers mixing up the partners and changing the stakes and topics as new information is revealed. A sample of dialogue illustrates what journalist John Timpane calls the play's 'three kinds of writing: Broadway drama, Hollywood script, and Kafka':[57]

Jake Nobody gets sick on Broadway. People leave shows. Bruce could leave the show ... and then I would go on for him and they would cast some other movie star as me.
Harry So you wouldn't be you anymore, you would be Bruce.
Jake That's right.
Harry But I would still be me. I would still be the understudy.
Jake Yeah.
Harry So I might go on.
Jake You're not going on!
Harry I just don't choose to see it that way.
Jake Dude, it doesn't matter how you choose to see it.
Harry It matters to me.
Jake It doesn't matter to anyone else.
Harry If it doesn't matter, then I can choose what I want.
Jake You can choose what you want, but what you want is not your choice.
Harry You sound like Kafka now.
Jake Awesome. 'Cause he was really smart.[58]

While Timpane the journalist, looking from the outside, sees three kinds of writing, Rebeck the playwright articulates three kinds of needs in this work, and arguably in all her plays: 'to entertain; to tell the truth about our lives; and to let that spiritual thing called *drama* happen'.[59]

Conclusion

In 2010, a group of 150 playwrights assembled in New York at a meeting organized by two of their own, Sarah Schulman and Julia Jordan, to discuss bias against female playwrights.[60] Their keynote speaker was Theresa Rebeck.

Rebeck started with a story in which she described her own experience with her 2000 play *The Butterfly Collection*. In her telling, the play is about a family of artists and it was enthusiastically embraced by artistic director Tim Sanford of Playwrights Horizons (who produced it), leading to interest from nine regional theatres. But the *New York Times* review, in Rebeck's telling, 'dismissed the play ... as a feminist diatribe'[61] (critic Bruce Weber's exact words were 'bilious' and 'agenda-based writing'),[62] scuttling any chance of the play remaining open or moving. Rebeck went on to describe follow-up conversations in which friends suggested she write under a male pseudonym or switch to writing novels; she also reported that her agent refused to represent *Omnium Gatherum* or *Bad Dates*, calling both 'unproduceable'.[63] Rebeck claims that she fell off the radar for two years. 'It turned out that being a woman playwright was just in and of itself suspect; if you are a woman playwright by definition you have a feminist agenda, which was so bad, it annihilated the work itself.'[64] Her real purpose in the keynote, however, was to put teeth into an argument against systemic gender bias throughout the entertainment industry and beyond, and to do so via statistics.

> Generally, over the last 25 years, the number of plays produced that were written by women seems to have vacillated between 12 and 17 percent ... So women playwrights live in a world where we are told it is a bad thing if women are 57 percent of the undergraduate population, because that's too big an imbalance, but it's an okay thing if women are only getting 17 percent or 6 percent or 9 percent of the best jobs in show business (and elsewhere, in America) and if we tried to rectify that it would be unfair because it would involve 'quotas.'[65]

Rebeck's parting shots were two. First, she pointed out that women buy the majority of theatre and film tickets. Therefore, appealing to this constituency by representing their interests is surely a wise business move. Second, she stated that pointing out imbalance and contradiction, far from being a feminist agenda, is simply telling the truth.[66]

Readers attuned to gender bias may have noticed that, throughout this chapter, the favourable, non-New York reviews of Rebeck's plays were often written by women. With one exception, the New York reviews – many mixed or negative – were written by men. Indeed, the Women's Media Center published a 2007 article by Melissa Silverstein suggesting clearly that the overwhelming preponderance of male theatre critics has an effect on how ideas about plays reach the public. Silverstein's 'exhibit A' was Theresa Rebeck. *Newsday*'s Linda Winer, at the time the only first-string critic for a New York daily paper, offered her own observation after twenty years on the job: 'I can't tell you how many plays I've been to that have been fascinating, and my colleagues will say, "It wasn't about anything: they were just talking."'⁶⁷

If one looks at statistics, however, Rebeck could easily thumb her nose at a set-up whose odds she has opposed and beaten. She enjoyed numerous productions of new plays (i.e., not revivals) Off-Broadway and outside of New York in the mid-2000s, and a brief look at their reception tells much about assessments of new plays for a playwright in mid-career. *The Scene*, like *Mauritius*, premiered outside New York in 2006 and opened in Gotham at Second Stage in 2007. Its subject is the obsessive, mindless capitulation of New Yorkers who work in theatre, television and other media-driven fields to the imperatives of publicity, money and youth culture. Gordon Cox, reviewing the premiere at Actors Theatre of Louisville, used the word 'soulless' for the characters' lives, observing that Rebeck's play was a favourite at Actors Theatre of Louisville's Humana Festival and predicting it would move to New York but concluding that its ideas 'won't be a revelation to anyone who's been paying attention', with the added observation, '"The Scene" will surely play well outside of Gotham, in places where the blather and desperation of the entertainment world might still seem exotic.'⁶⁸ Yet the *New York Times* review praised text and production, calling the play a 'sharp-witted, sharp-elbowed comedy about the savage economies of sex and show business in contemporary Manhattan', concluding with the label 'dark-hued morality tale [offering] fresh insights into the cultural landscape', along the way applauding the 'high-octane' production and all four cast members.⁶⁹ Here the reviewer for *Variety*, a show-business industry publication, tripped on his own sense of one-upmanship in a miscalculation concerning sophistication and 'paying attention'.

One might also argue that adventurous, non-plot-driven, not entirely realist plays lacking contemporary settings are simply not Broadway's mainstays. Rebeck ventured twice in the first decade of the new millennium (as well as once before and once after) into territory fitting that description – a clear indication that Broadway for its own sake is hardly her sole aspiration. She has expressed a special fondness for *The Bells*, her 2005 reworking of one of the most popular of late nineteenth-century British melodramas, also called *The Bells*, by Leopold Lewis. In the original play, an Alsatian town councillor and innkeeper, Mathias, suffers guilt for having murdered a Polish-Jewish grain merchant 15 years earlier after robbing the merchant in order to pay off his mortgage. The protagonist keeps hearing his victim's sleigh bells, ultimately succumbing to madness and a heart attack. Rebeck set her play in the Yukon in the waning days of the Alaska gold rush, her Mathias the proprietor of a saloon-cum-hotel whose reason for killing a Chinese prospector years earlier was impending starvation and the need to take care of his child. For Rebeck, her play 'really is about America ... *The Bells* ... was finally about the way, in American history, we've seen people commit terrible violence, in the name of domestic security, on peoples of color.'[70] One might interpret the 'domestic' writ small as well as large. Protecting one's nuclear family has become almost a kneejerk trope in popular narrative entertainment used to excuse violence and breaking all kinds of laws, official and otherwise.[71] Rebeck praised Emily Mann's direction of *The Bells* at Princeton's McCarter Theatre, calling the production 'very European' and describing it as ending up 'looking like a cross between Charles Dickens and Robert Wilson', with the entire stage 'deconstruct[ing]' when Mathias goes mad, and featuring an 'expressionistic' ending 'where he finds himself locked in the memory of what has happened forever'.[72] Critics carped about her use of melodrama, but Rebeck believes that 'the form works' if it is psychologically grounded. 'It becomes epic rather than silly.'[73]

Aspirations to the epic perhaps also undergirded the 2006 *The Water's Edge*, Rebeck's harnessing of the Agamemnon story set in a New England lakeside home and where the father returns not from war but from making a killing in finance. Here, he is the parent who left home after his toddler daughter drowned, seventeen years earlier, when he was on the telephone brokering a deal rather than watching the known-to-be-impulsive child. Rebeck's invocation of *Pygmalion* (or at least Pygmalion) in the 1991–2 *Spike Heels*, the mid-2006 work with Aeschylus and *The Bells*, and a 2012 update of William Congreve's *The Way of the World*, called *The Way of Things*, workshopped at the O'Neill National Playwrights Conference (featuring *Omnium Gatherum*'s Kristine Nielsen), bespeak a writer for whom Broadway success is only one piece of a writing life in which homage to her forbears, social critique and engagement in current affairs drive her playwriting. Certainly, in the first decade of the twenty-first century, Rebeck had earned the status to merit productions of her plays, whether read as silly, biting or far-reaching. In 2011, she had professional productions of three plays, all at high-profile, prestigious theatres. *Poor Behavior*, about two couples' squabbles and betrayals, opened at Los Angeles's Mark Taper Forum, prior to moving to New York. (Rebeck once told an interviewer that 'discourse among driven New Yorkers ... often consists of alternating arias of angry or aggrieved self-obsession',[74] both in evidence in this play.) *Seminar* opened on Broadway starring Alan Rickman and Lily Rabe. It explores how aspiring writers pin their hopes on mentors and betray each other, with the mentor himself an egomaniac and opportunist. *Dead Accounts* premiered at the Cincinnati Playhouse in the Park. That play looks at a Cincinnati family, one of whose members has mysteriously managed to make quite a lot of money and who returns to a roost of impending death and overbearing neediness. Also in 2011, Rebeck's play *O Beautiful* was produced at the University of Delaware, where the project was funded by a $50,000 grant from the (public) university's humanities centre. *O Beautiful* takes on teenage bullying, abortion and restrictions on high school teaching materials under the aegis of stick-to-the-textbook/teach-to-the-test. It features a time travelling Jesus who motors with a pregnant teen to a state where she can have an abortion without parental consent. Throughout the play, both Jesus and various American Founding Fathers deny claims to having made statements attributed to them that serve as present-day conservative battle cries.

Dead Accounts opened on Broadway at the end of 2012. Elsewhere in 2012, Rebeck was co-creator and a lead writer on the NBC television series *Smash*, which centred on the creation of a (fictional) Broadway musical about Marilyn Monroe. Reviews were mixed and the series was cancelled after two seasons but not before being nominated for a Golden Globe Award for Best Television Series – Musical or Comedy. In 2014, Rebeck's *Zealot* looked at Muslim unrest through the eyes of an Iranian woman protestor, an American undersecretary of state (also a woman) and two men – a British civil servant and a Saudi minister. It ran at South Coast Repertory in California.

Is the jury out on the importance of Theresa Rebeck's work – especially during the key years of 2000–9? Prolific playwrights are few in the American theatre, perhaps because of the popularity of the workshopping process, which can delay production, and perhaps because few can afford to keep writing in the absence of guaranteed productions. Those who do write frequently and regularly – Israel Horovitz and Neil Simon come to mind, as does the less mainstream Charles Ludlam – often suffer the fate of prophets in their own lands. Rebeck's crime may be her popularity, accessibility, lack of writer's block and willingness to move on and keep at it. Perhaps seen in some circles as little better than a kind of word-count mill for dramatic fodder, her finger-on-the-pulse-of-the-times immediacy, cliffhanging scene endings and high-definition characters call to mind another prolific writer once seen as almost a populist tabloid fiction writer and now revered as one of the greats of his era: Charles Dickens.

6

Sarah Ruhl

Wendy Arons

Introduction

It would hardly be an overstatement to observe that in many ways the first decade of the twenty-first century was Sarah Ruhl's decade in the American theatre. After graduating with an MFA in playwriting from Brown University in 2001, Ruhl first came to widespread attention in 2004 with the premiere of her play *The Clean House* at the Yale Repertory Theatre. The success of that play – which won the Susan Smith Blackburn Prize in 2004 and was also a Pulitzer Prize finalist in the same year – was quickly followed in succeeding years by critically acclaimed productions of several new plays, including *Eurydice*, *Late: a cowboy song*, *Melancholy Play*, *Dead Man's Cell Phone*, *Passion Play* and *In the Next Room or the vibrator play*, all of which premiered both regionally and in New York before the end of the decade. Ruhl's receipt of a half-million-dollar MacArthur Fellowship in 2006, at the age of thirty-two, confirmed her status as a writer who, in the words of her mentor playwright Paula Vogel, had already 'made an impact on the next generation all over the country'.[1] The boldly theatrical productions inspired by Ruhl's genre-defying approach to making theatre electrified audiences both in the US and internationally throughout the first decade of the century.

Ruhl's writing resists unification in terms of subject matter or thematic concern – the focus of her plays ranges from the reworking of one of the oldest stories from Greek mythology to an exploration of the social and interpersonal disruptions generated by the use of cell phones in the modern era. What links all her plays together is her highly theatrical use of space and image to create a complex emotional landscape for characters and audiences alike. Ruhl's work deals with big, unruly and often mystifying emotions like unbearable grief, head-over-heels love and aching desire – emotions that are not readily captured by dialogue alone. The difficulty of communicating – or more precisely, the failure of words to adequately express our passions and our hurts – is also at the root of her theatrical poetics, in which, at moments when language fails or is inadequate, the space transforms or an image metamorphoses to produce a psychological or emotional shortcut. Ruhl's writing could thus be seen to have a structural similarity to the American musical: where, in the latter, characters burst into song at moments of heightened emotion, Ruhl's plays explode into metaphor, abstraction and magical realism when the emotion of a moment exceeds the boundaries of realistic dialogue.[2] Ruhl's interest in what Vogel called 'the emotional vocabulary of theater' cut against a trend in late twentieth-century playwriting that appealed primarily to intellect and irony. As Vogel observed, in a conversation with Ruhl, 'We're used to plays that build into their structure a kind of rational mousetrap, but you're exploring emotional resonance without embarrassment. There is an impulse to be ashamed of emotions in theater, which is rather odd because one would think that's why we have theater.'[3] A hallmark of Ruhl's theatre is the emotional response her work receives, even from critics, who are otherwise often loathe to admit that a play has moved them or made them cry. *Eurydice*, in particular – as I discuss in the next section – created deep emotional resonance with audiences and critics, at times robbing them of a full capacity to describe its effects.

Ruhl's strategic deployment of image and spectacle to heighten the emotional impact of her storytelling connects her to a line of American playwrights and directors who have rejected realism and naturalism in favour of a theatre that is non-linear, intangible, associative, obscure and evocative – writers like her mentors Paula Vogel and Mac Wellman and her early inspiration, Maria Irene

Fornes, and directors like Anne Bogart, who staged the premieres of both Vogel's *The Baltimore Waltz* and Ruhl's *Dead Man's Cell Phone*, and Les Waters, who directed the New York productions of both *Eurydice* and *In the Next Room*. For Ruhl, non-realism is essential to making a theatre that has both an emotional and intellectual impact. In her essay 'Six Small Thoughts on Fornes', Ruhl outlines her beef with what she calls 'good playwriting in more traditional American circles': it is that the dramaturgical school of thought undergirding such writing insists on a clarity of intention, on the idea that emotions have to have aims and that characters must possess identifiable wants and desires.[4] Ruhl counters this naturalist conceit with an approach that takes as a given that some emotions have no specific aims and are, for that reason, more compelling. In her essay on Fornes, Ruhl argues that 'the most interesting emotions are those for which it is hard to identify the cause or motive. And if those emotions are more interesting, those are the emotions it would be nice to see onstage. Because interesting moments are more interesting than noninteresting moments.'[5] A quintessential aspect of Ruhl's writing is its lack of psychological motivation for characters' actions and reactions. Her characters often swing wildly from one emotional state to another, or seem to be experiencing two emotions simultaneously. A characteristic stage direction asks the actor to make huge leaps, as in this one, from *The Clean House*:

A pause.
For a moment,
Lane and Virginia experience
a primal moment during which they
are seven and nine years old,
inside the mind, respectively.
They are mad.
Then they return quite naturally
to language, as adults do.[6]

Emotions in Ruhl's plays are neither rational nor readily explained, and often they are conveyed more by magical metamorphoses of the scene than by language. 'If you transform space and atmosphere,' Ruhl told Vogel, 'you don't have to connect the dots psychologically in a linear way.'[7] Ruhl's activation of imagery and space lends her work a magical realism reminiscent of the novelistic worlds created by writers like Gabriel García Márquez or the theatrical worlds created by playwrights like Fornes, Tony Kushner, Cherríe Moraga, José Rivera and José Cruz González: they are worlds in which the extraordinary coexists on the same matter-of-fact plane as the ordinary, in which spaces and times collide in non-logical and non-linear ways, and in which people quotidianly possess supernatural powers. Her stage directions and imagery may seem, at first glance, to ask directors and designers to make impossible things happen on stage, but these are challenges that have inspired directors and designers to expand the range of storytelling tools theatre has at its disposal.

Because her plays depend on image, sound, space and atmosphere to convey so much of their emotional content, Ruhl's plays only really achieve their full impact in production. As such, an important context for the emergence of Ruhl's work was the culture of new play development that reigned in the US theatre in the late twentieth and early twenty-first century. In 2004, Ruhl's contemporary, the playwright Julia Cho, mused about being 'a playwright in the age of readings'. She reflected that 'people of my generation can be playwrights without actually being produced' and that the system of readings and development often meant 'you end up with a reading of the play that may not even convey what the play really is'.[8] Ruhl, too, saw many of her plays linger in the 'reading' stage of the process: she estimated at one point that *Eurydice* had had fourteen workshop readings before its first full production.[9] In response to this situation, in 2003 Ruhl and twelve other playwrights joined together to form 13P, an artistic collective that had the simple but revolutionary mission to self-produce a play by each playwright, thus making an entrepreneurial end-run around the US regional theatre new play development process and allowing the playwrights to gain some artistic control over the trajectory of their careers.[10] 13P's mission statement articulated the group's concern 'about what the trend of endless readings and new play development programs was doing to the texture and ambition of new American plays. Together we took matters into our hands.'[11] Many of those playwrights, like Ruhl, have gone on to earn major recognition and have been widely produced in the US regional theatres and in New York, and 13P has served as a model for emerging playwrights who seek, like them, to take matters into their own hands (the group has made its history available online to allow others to copy their process). While Ruhl's career took off independently of 13P, her involvement in this collective linked her to a cohort of playwrights who sought to reinvigorate US theatre through experimentation and risk, and who demonstrated the 'produceability' of 'challenging' plays that the regional theatres had been unwilling to take a chance on. In Ruhl's case, 13P provided an opportunity to rework one of her earliest plays, *Melancholy Play*, and produce it in New York, where previously she had not been able to find a venue.[12]

The burgeoning of feminist theatre in the late twentieth century forms another key context for Ruhl's work. While, with the exception of *In the Next Room*, most of Ruhl's work does not specifically address issues of gender oppression or women's equality, all of her plays speak to a feminist consciousness insofar as they primarily put focus on women's experiences and women's lives. Ruhl might be said to be practising a form of 'post-feminism' in her writing, in that her work has moved beyond the consciousness-raising play and beyond speaking to women about the causes and effects of gender inequality, and instead takes as a given that women's stories and women's experiences are universally important and of interest, and that they are linked to concerns and issues that affect a wide diversity of people. At the same time, the relative paucity of women's plays on the US regional and Broadway stages at the end of the twentieth century meant that the mere production of women's work remained a feminist political issue, regardless of the politics of the work itself.[13] Ruhl acknowledged in an interview with Anita Greene that her work is implicitly feminist, explaining, 'I personally have never experienced any particular discrimination. I can remember Paula Vogel saying, "If you're a woman writing for the theater, you are a feminist." And I think that's right.'[14] As I note in the following discussions of three of Ruhl's plays, for many scholars and reviewers there is certainly a feminist undercurrent to Ruhl's work, even where her aims are not explicitly political.

Eurydice

Eurydice is one of Ruhl's earliest plays, and its genesis can be traced to two impulses. On one hand, it came out of a desire to think through the ancient Greek myth of Orpheus and Eurydice from Eurydice's point of view and to rectify a literary-historical silence regarding Eurydice's experience. '[I]n the long history of artists putting their teeth marks into the story of Orpheus,' Ruhl explained to Caridad Svich in a 2001 interview, 'no one has expressed much interest in Eurydice; she merely evaporates. She facilitates Orpheus' faith, Orpheus' guilt, Orpheus' music, by being looked at or not looked at.'[15] This first impulse aligns with the interest throughout Ruhl's body of work in telling stories that centre on women's experience. On the other hand, the play also springs directly from Ruhl's own personal experience of grief and loss. In an interview with Wendy Weckwerth, Ruhl explained:

> I was caught with this idea of memory and language and the idea of Eurydice going into the underworld and meeting her father there. The play is really dedicated to my father, who died when I was twenty and he was fifty-five. *Eurydice* is a transparently personal play. I wanted to write something where I would be allowed to have a few more conversations with him. A myth exploring the underworld and the connection between the dead and the living was a way to negotiate that terrain.[16]

The play's navigation through that terrain of memory, grief and loss would prove timely for the twenty-first century. Although Ruhl began work on the play before 11 September 2001, it only first received a professional production in 2003, at which point the play could be received and experienced by audiences and critics alike as an opportunity for both personal and collective mourning over the immense losses of life precipitated by the terrorist attacks of 9/11.

The plot of the play varies in key ways from other tellings of the myth. *Eurydice* begins with Orpheus and Eurydice's betrothal and introduces them as inhabitants of two different spheres: Orpheus is a man who lives for and communicates through music; Eurydice is a woman of words. From the start, their relationship seems breathlessly romantic, but also a tiny bit off: Eurydice disappoints Orpheus by not being able to reproduce his melody, and he, in turn, lets her down by thinking about music instead of her. In the second scene, Ruhl introduces Eurydice's dead father, 'one of the few dead people who still remembers how to read and write', who sends her a letter on her wedding day from the underworld.[17] This letter becomes the device that leads to Eurydice's death and establishes the central conflict in the play between Eurydice's desire to reconnect with her father and her love for Orpheus. Eurydice's arrival in the underworld, via an elevator in which it rains, is heralded by a chorus of three Stones who explain her inability to communicate: she's been dipped in the River of Forgetfulness and has lost the capacity for language. Eurydice's father takes it upon himself to nurture her back into language and memory, so that by the time Orpheus has figured out how to travel to the underworld to retrieve Eurydice, her father has, in a sense, re-established himself as her first love. In Ruhl's telling, then, Orpheus's arrival provokes a profound ambivalence in Eurydice, since following him back to the world of the living means leaving her father behind. Unlike in canonical versions of the myth, where an uncertain Orpheus turns to reassure himself that Eurydice is following, here it is the uncertain Eurydice who calls out to Orpheus and prompts him to turn to look at her, sending her back to the underworld. Moreover, as Leslie Atkins Durham has noted, 'this is not the point of greatest devastation in Ruhl's tale. Rather than Orpheus's loss of Eurydice ... the true climax comes with Eurydice's second loss of her father.'[18] For when Eurydice returns to the underworld, she finds her father curled up asleep on the ground, having voluntarily given up all memory and language in the River of Forgetfulness. She writes a final letter to Orpheus, releasing him to find another woman to love, and consigns herself to oblivion as well. The play ends with Orpheus's arrival in the elevator, the obliteration of his capacity for language and his memory through its rain, and his subsequent inability to read the last letter Eurydice left for him: a heartbreaking metaphoric image of what is taken from us when a loved one dies.

Eurydice received its first workshop production at Brown University in January 2001, and went on to receive multiple workshop productions and staged readings across the US before its first professional production at Madison Repertory Theatre two years later, under the direction of Richard Corley. The following year, Les Waters directed a production at Berkeley Repertory Theatre, with Maria Dizzia in the role of Eurydice and Charles Shaw Robinson as her father; this production was remounted at the Yale Repertory Theatre in New Haven, Connecticut, in 2006 and then again at Second Stage Theatre in New York in 2007. The influential critic Charles Isherwood raved about the play in his *New York Times* review of the Yale Rep production, calling it a 'magical play' with 'some of the sublime potency of music, the head-scratching surprise of a modernist poem and the cockeyed allure of a surrealist painting'.[19] Isherwood conceded that the play's cryptic nature might not be every spectator's cup of tea, but 'if the play's powerful emotional core draws you into its strange currents, you may find yourself taken to heights of emotion ... I fought off tears for half the play, not always successfully.'[20] His enthusiasm for what he called Ruhl's 'idiosyncratic' theatrical imagination remained unabated when the play finally premiered in New York: he wrote that the play itself was 'weird and wonderful' and described the production as 'rhapsodically beautiful', confessing that 'I staggered out of the theater in the same state of sad-happy disorientation that I recall from my initial viewing.'[21] Other reviewers echoed Isherwood's assessment of the play's powerful emotional impact. *New York Times* critic Anita Gates described how, in the final moments of the play, 'the tears came with the suddenness of grief' and Louise Kennedy, of the *Boston Globe*, writes of breaking down into 'heaving, wracking sobs' in her car after leaving the theatre: 'I cry for a long time ... this play, more than most I have seen this year, continues to haunt me.'[22] While some subsequent productions seem to have fallen into the cloying preciousness Isherwood predicted for a 'less felicitous production', nonetheless in multiple remountings critics and audiences alike have embraced the play's shimmering imagery, its lyrical evocation of grief and loss, and its emotional allure.[23]

Such responses reveal that *Eurydice* offered to audiences a welcome opportunity to linger, without embarrassment or reserve, in grief – something Americans had not been encouraged to do in the first decade of the century. President George W. Bush's appeal to US citizens in the aftermath of 9/11 for 'continued participation and confidence in the American economy' – a statement jeeringly interpreted as an encouragement to 'keep shopping' – expressed a masculinist dismissal of grief and mourning as cowardly and effeminate and hailed Americans as stoic survivors who did not stop to lick their wounds.[24] In telling Americans to '[g]et on board. Do your business around the country ... Get down to Disney World in Florida. Take your families and enjoy life, the way we want it to be enjoyed,' Bush seemed to be advocating a collective forgetting and urging Americans to simply move on.[25] But what does it mean to forget and move on? *Eurydice* meditates on the complex interplay between memory and forgetting, and holding on and letting go, involved in the process of grieving and mourning. In the play, to remember is to be trapped with the dead; to forget is to enter a state of oblivion and loss of language. In either case, 'enjoying life, the way we want it to be enjoyed' is not an option; the best advice the Stones can give Eurydice is to 'learn the art of keeping busy' (407) – a command that sounds suspiciously like 'go shopping' and seems equally dismissive of the process of grieving. In staging what Isherwood calls 'the discombobulating experience of grief and loss', the play invites audiences to (re)experience what they were exhorted to move beyond in the name of patriotism and national interest.[26] Thus the play's resonance with audiences can be traced, in part, to a perhaps hitherto unacknowledged need to comprehend and cope with loss on both a collective and personal level. For many critics, this connection was immediately evident: as Gates observed, 'while *Eurydice* is certainly a play for our fearful times, it is about every death, every loss, every paralyzing pang of grief'.[27]

Because it is a work that pulls spectators into a dreamlike experience of subconscious emotion, *Eurydice* is not an easy play to write about analytically. *Boston Globe* critic Leslie Kennedy confessed, on seeing the play a second time, 'I feel as if I need a new language to talk about Sarah Ruhl's *Eurydice* ... [It] evokes so many emotions and thoughts at once that I find myself groping for words that don't sound like hollow clichés next to its complexity and depth.'[28] The critic's loss of words in response to the play is reminiscent of a common response to grief: we often say 'there are no words to express' what we feel when a loved one has died (or when we seek to provide consolation to someone in mourning). Loss of language is not only an aspect of the world of the play (when characters die, their capacity for language is eradicated, replaced by the 'language of Stones'); the play fundamentally dwells where language butts up against the inexpressible, its metaphoric images and cryptic utterances evoking emotions and associations that words fail to compass. Ruhl translates her desire to have one more conversation with her father into a theatrical experience that pulses with the yearning to communicate. The Stones tell us that their language is a very quiet one, 'like if the pores in your face opened up and talked'; later, they help the audience understand Eurydice's attempts to speak by advising them to 'listen to her the way you would listen to your own daughter if she died too young and tried to speak to you across long distances' (359–60). The play asks audience members to suspend expectations of direct understanding and tune in to a form of communication that exceeds words – it has an opacity that invites comparison with the work of Fornes, whose plays are likewise often simultaneously perplexing and moving. As Ruhl put it, in an interview with Caridad Svich, 'if we can suspend long enough to alter perception, what is it that we might let in that we might not otherwise let in'?[29]

Ruhl creates that state of suspension not only through her poetic dialogue, but also by conjuring some of the most remarkable and evocative images and soundscapes of the early twenty-first-century American stage. The raining elevator, the room laboriously made of string by Eurydice's father, the drip of water and 'ping' of forgetting, the Lord of the Underworld riding a tricycle, Eurydice – and later Orpheus – standing on a letter in an attempt to absorb its meaning – such highly theatrical and often absurdly comic images contribute to the play's thrilling strangeness and give it tonal variety and complexity. Ruhl describes her Underworld as resembling 'the world of *Alice in Wonderland* more than it resembles Hades' (332), and the topsy-turviness of that world – in which the Stones might be bratty kids at a birthday party, and the Lord of the Underworld might topple in on stilts – serves as an important playful counterpoint to the overarching mood of melancholy and nostalgia. As John Lahr observed in his *New Yorker* profile of Ruhl, 'lightness – the distillation of things into a quick, terse, almost innocent directness – is a value on which Ruhl puts much weight'.[30] The slippage created by the stage elements between the ordinary and the strange and between the comic and the tragic promotes a sense of suspended reality and offers access to the irrational and invisible through seemingly illogical juxtapositions.

Eurydice may be a 'transparently personal' play, but it's also one that for some critics speaks, albeit obliquely, to feminist concerns. Leslie Atkins Durham reads the play in the context of other women's plays of the decade that refigure and reconsider the gendering of grief as a 'feminine' activity, arguing that 'they replace a transformed vision of grief in public life, recuperating it as a valid force on [sic] contemporary, and potentially political, expression'.[31] To her, the play's primary political intervention lies in its capacity to 'help us reconsider an experience that cultures political and social have encouraged us to renounce and forget'.[32] Other critics look to the play's figuration of the relationship between Eurydice and the male characters to tease out a feminist analysis. Núria Casado-Gual finds in the play 'aspects that evoke the specific history of women's emancipation, as well as their struggle to exist and signify as distinctive individuals alongside their male partners', but she also notes that the play 'both defies and confirms straightforward feminist readings'.[33] Indeed, Eurydice's complex relationship to her father, to Orpheus and to the aptly named Nasty Interesting Man resists a reductive feminist reading, but its complexity likely rings true for many contemporary women, who may continue to feel conflicted about their desire to have their fathers give them away at their wedding or their toxic attraction to nasty interesting men. For the most part, however, *Eurydice* speaks less specifically to women's experience as women than to the experience of loss and grief in general; the next two plays under discussion are more pointedly aimed at excavating and exploring contemporary women's experience.

The Clean House

In a 2006 interview with *New York Times* writer Dinitia Smith, Ruhl recounted the origins of her play *The Clean House*. She was at a cocktail party, and

> a doctor walked in and said, 'I've had such a hard month. My cleaning lady from Brazil wouldn't clean, and I took her to the hospital and got her medicated, and she still wouldn't clean. So I had to clean my own house. I didn't go to medical school to clean house.' I thought, 'What does this mean about gender and about class?' I thought, 'What about the poor woman? Is she clinically depressed or does she just hate cleaning?'[34]

Out of those ruminations grew a funny and poignant play that not only captures the complicated dynamic of class between working women and the women they pay to do their domestic work, but also meditates on love, loss, grief and the 'big, invisible things that come unannounced' to which we simply have to 'give way'.[35]

In the play, Matilde, a young woman who has come from Brazil after the death of both her parents, has been hired to clean for Lane, an accomplished but emotionally buttoned-up doctor, and her husband Charles, a surgeon. But Matilde has little interest in cleaning houses; her passion is for comedy. Comedy is in her genes: her parents were master comedians who loved laughing and making each other laugh. Comedy is also Matilde's tragedy – in her first monologue she tells us that her mother died laughing at one of her father's jokes, at which point he shot himself, taking that lethally funny joke with him to his grave. Matilde's sadness runs deep, and the medication Lane has given her to lift her out of her depression and get her motivated to clean the house can't begin to address it (especially since Matilde doesn't actually take the medication). Into this stalemate steps Lane's sister, Virginia, who regards cleaning as a privilege and as a practice that gives purpose and meaning to her life. Virginia offers Matilde a deal: if Matilde will agree not to tell Lane, Virginia will come by each day to clean Lane's house and free Matilde to spend her time thinking up good jokes. This arrangement works nicely for a short while: Lane's house is finally clean, and all three women are engaged in occupations they find personally satisfying and rewarding. But when Lane discovers that her husband is having an affair with one of his patients, the sensuous and vivacious Ana, this domestic arrangement, along with everything else in Lane's ordered life, falls apart. Charles moves in with Ana; Matilde goes to work at Ana's, where her joke inventing becomes prolific; and Virginia takes over the care and cleaning of Lane's house, to Lane's great irritation. Then Matilde returns with bad news: Ana's illness has returned and Charles has left on a quest to find a tree that will cure her. She needs medical care, so Lane agrees, reluctantly at first, to help her, opening her heart and home to her husband's lover. In the process, she also finally reaches out to her sister and Matilde for help, and, in the end, Matilde, having thought up the world's funniest joke, whispers it to Ana – who then dies laughing.

The Clean House premiered at the Yale Repertory Theatre in 2004 and played at several regional theatres before opening in New York in 2006 (the two-year delay was mainly due to Ruhl's desire to have the play staged at Lincoln Center, where the height of the stage could accommodate the balcony required for the set). Although Ruhl wrote *The Clean House* after *Eurydice*, this was the play that first drew significant critical and public attention to her work. Critical reception of the play was almost uniformly enthusiastic: in 2004, *Variety*'s Frank Rizzo called Ruhl a 'unique comic voice', praised the play as a 'wondrously mad and moving work' and predicted that it was 'sure to have a life far beyond the three major regional productions planned this season'.[36] Two years later, Isherwood of the *New York Times* called it 'one of the finest and funniest new plays you're likely to see in New York this season'.[37] Critics were particularly taken by what Isherwood labelled Ruhl's 'alchemical imagination': they called her aesthetic 'whimsical realism',[38] 'a blend of humor and lyricism, built of blocks of light and magic'[39] and 'American magical realism'.[40] *The Clean House* received the Susan Smith Blackburn Prize in 2004, was a finalist for the Pulitzer Prize in 2005 and has been produced subsequently at dozens of regional theatres in the US as well as in Canada, the UK and New Zealand.

Thematically, the play takes up, and toys with, the questions about domestic work prompted by the complaint Ruhl overheard at that cocktail party. In the first decades of the twenty-first century, sedimented assumptions and expectations continue to devalue domestic work and render housewives and domestic labourers socially and economically invisible. Leslie Durham sees in this play a feminist exploration of the dynamics of caring and argues that it proposes 'a revaluation of caring work and principles', thereby allowing audiences to recognize and appreciate 'new dimensions of contemporary lived experience'.[41] As such, the play speaks powerfully to that prominent demographic of US theatre ticket buyers – middle-class and upper-middle-class women – for whom the problems of domestic labour and caregiving as well as the class issues involved in hiring another woman (especially a migrant woman) are particularly acute. Audience members may laugh at Lane's declaration that she didn't go to medical school to clean her own house, but that laugh will likely also be tinged with self-recognition: many women who have achieved the high level of professional status and income formerly reserved to men might likewise feel that they should also receive the perk of not having to perform domestic labour. But the labour of care is complicated, as Ruhl noted in an interview: 'Does class get us beyond the obligation to clean for ourselves, to care for our own dirt in a daily way? Does medical school supersede our gender? As women are we supposed to clean up after other people?'[42]

As paradoxical as it may seem, for many in Ruhl's audience the attitude toward domestic work expressed by all of the women in the play will feel equally valid. That is, they may feel, with Lane, that they 'did not go to medical school to clean my own house'; with Virginia, that caring for one's own domestic space is a privilege; and with Matilde and Ana, that whether a house is clean or dirty is of little concern or value to a good life. And many in the audience will readily relate to Lane's discomfort with the class dynamic inherent in the hiring of domestic labour: 'I don't want an interesting person to clean my house. I just want my house – cleaned' (13). In interrogating the comic premise of the doctor exasperated with her hired help, Ruhl thus opens up a serious and multifaceted inquiry into women's employment of other women as domestic surrogates. As Ruhl explained in an interview with Wendy Weckwerth, the questions thus raised are not just economical, but existential as well: 'What does it mean to be alienated from your own dirt? What does it mean for the upper classes to be alienated from the exigencies of everyday living, so that they're not noticing what accumulates over time?'[43]

But although *The Clean House* takes off from a comic premise, like *Eurydice* it has grief and loss at its centre. Matilde is mourning the loss of both her parents; Virginia has realized, in middle age, that she has made almost nothing of what could have been a promising life; Lane, who thought she had it all, loses her husband to another woman; Ana faces imminent death; and Charles loses Ana, the love of his life, to cancer at its end. And like *Eurydice*, *The Clean House* touches poignantly on what is lost when a person dies: when Ana asks Matilde what was the joke her father told her mother before her mother died laughing, Matilde replies, 'I'll never know. Let's not talk about sad things' (72). But where *Eurydice* is haunting and mournful in tone, *The Clean House* celebrates the power of humour. It is not only a sublimely funny play, but also a play about the social, psychological and cultural work that comedy performs. In his critical study of Ruhl's plays, James Al-Shamma observes that jokes in this play have the power to generate two kinds of shifts. In addition to the semantic shift in frame of reference that produces their humour (as in the one-liner, 'I don't suffer from insanity; I enjoy every minute of it'), jokes in *The Clean House* are also capable of initiating an ontological shift, insofar as they have, within the world of this play, the shamanistic power to transport a person from life into death.[44] This comports with what Ruhl has speculated about comedy: 'There's something compassionate about humor; it has a saving power. It seemed to me that if you took the most sublime version of a joke – the Platonic ideal of a joke – that it could transport you somehow.'[45] Laughter is equated with both joy and grief not only within the world of the play but for the audience as well; Lane's richly complex reaction to a joke she can't understand mirrors what an audience might feel in response to the play itself: '*Lane cries. She laughs. She cries. She laughs. And this goes on for some time*' (48–9). Although death is no laughing matter in this play, laughter becomes a way of coping with loss. If, as Matilde claims, 'a good joke cleans your insides out' (26) and if, with Jung, we take houses to be symbols of minds, then the play's title, *The Clean House*, might be taken to refer to the cathartic work humour performs in purging the psyche, purifying the mind and helping to put our mental houses in order.

Humour is also one of the magic-realist elements Ruhl deploys in the play to forge metaphorical connections, effect psychological transformations and express what exceeds the boundaries of words alone. Ruhl's conferral of fatal powers to jokes delivered in a language that most of her audience will not be able to understand creates a channel between two things that defy full comprehension and explanation: death and humour. Matilde's raunchy opening joke, told in Portuguese, is made funny by the actress's embodiment of the joke's action, but the gap between what we see and hear and the joke's verbal content mirrors the gap between what we can know of death and what the experience of death really is. Like death, the perfect joke – according to Matilde – cannot be fully grasped:

> The perfect joke makes you forget about your life. The perfect joke makes you remember about your life. The perfect joke is stupid when you write it down. The perfect joke was not made up by one person. It passed through the air and you caught it. A perfect joke is somewhere between an angel and a fart. (24)

The essential inexplicability of humour – there is, after all, nothing so dry and dull as a scholarly study of comedy! – stands in, here, for life's most profound mystery. Yet the play also makes clear that even when jokes cannot be explained or translated, and even when they remain forever unknown – as with the joke that kills Matilde's mother – their effects are sublime and transformative, lifting people momentarily out of the ordinary and the routine and into a state of hyper-aliveness. When Matilde conjures the memory of her parents, they are always laughing, and in her final monologue she recounts being born laughing, as a result of laughter:

> My mother laughed.
> She laughed so hard that I popped out.
> She said I was the only baby who laughed when I came into the world. (109)

The Clean House is a play in which jokes can kill, but it's also a play in which laughter is quite literally life-affirming. The play's jokes thus form a kind of magical-realist bridge between life and death. Here again, as in *Eurydice*, the yearning to reconnect with the dead finds theatrical expression in a daughter's desire to communicate in the language of her lost parents. The double casting Ruhl specifies for the play has the same actors embody Matilde's parents and Ana and Charles. One effect of this, as Al-Shamma observes, is that in being able to help Ana die laughing, 'Matilde symbolically rectifies her mother's murder as an act of mercy rather than an accident.'[46] But the whispered fatal joke is more than that – it is also a love note to the mother who birthed Matilde in(to) laughter.

In addition to magic jokes and character doubling, Ruhl also makes effective use of space to transcend the real and to fashion poetic associations. The set begins as '*a white living room*' in a '*metaphysical Connecticut*', but it's a space that, according to Ruhl's stage directions, '*should transform and surprise*' (8). In the second act, that white living room has '*become a hospital. Or the idea of a hospital*' and a balcony high above the space has materialized (51). The spatial coexistence of living room, hospital and balcony allows the three worlds of the play to collide in evocative and lyrical ways, as, for example, when the apples that Matilde and Ana discard from Ana's balcony add to the mess and chaos in Lane's living room (and, by extension, in her life), or when it begins to snow on the balcony as Charles seeks a yew tree in Alaska. Such use of overlapping space (a technique reminiscent of the collision between the worlds of the living and the dead in *Eurydice*) connects the characters across space and time and theatricalizes their inner lives, creating shortcuts that connect emotional dots in a non-linear, but nonetheless profoundly expressive, fashion.

In the Next Room or the vibrator play

In the Next Room or the vibrator play may be Ruhl's most straightforward – and most straightforwardly feminist – play. Inspired by Rachel P. Maines's 1999 book *The Technology of Orgasm: 'Hysteria,' the Vibrator, and Women's Sexual Satisfaction*, the play is about the 'unique moment at the dawn of the age of electricity when doctors, who had actually been manually stimulating their patients to cure them of hysteria, could suddenly use the vibrator'.[47] The play uses this history to examine the emotional and interpersonal gulf between women and men in the late nineteenth century and to expose the extent of men's control over women's lives and bodies. As a result, in this largely comic exploration of American Victorian gender roles and attitudes toward sexual pleasure, Ruhl also crafts a serious and poignant reflection on the untapped emotional and intellectual potential of women through history and gestures toward the many ways in which modern women's sexuality continues to be shaped and determined by men's needs and expectations.

The play is set at the Givings's residence in a spa town in upstate New York circa 1880. The Givings's home, which has been newly electrified, is bifurcated into a domestic space and a clinical space. The living room is a space of unacknowledged marital difficulties between the Givings: Catherine Givings, having recently given birth, is unable to provide enough milk for her infant daughter and suffers from feelings of inadequacy and superfluousness, feelings that are exacerbated by her husband's clueless obliviousness to her emotional, psychological and (it turns out) physical needs. In the adjacent clinical space (the 'next room' of the play's title), Dr Givings solves other people's marital problems. With the help of his midwife assistant Annie and the recently invented vibrator, he cures women of hysteria by inducing 'paroxysms' that release 'congestion' in the womb, where hysteria was thought to originate.

The arrival of a new patient, Sabrina Daldry, sets the play's action in motion: after her first successful treatment, the Daldrys offer to arrange for their African American housekeeper, Elizabeth, to serve as a wet nurse for the Givings's baby, and over the course of subsequent treatment sessions Catherine befriends Sabrina and develops a curiosity about the sounds she hears emanating from the next room. When Sabrina returns to the house in Dr Givings's absence, the two women pick the lock on the surgery door so that Sabrina can demonstrate to Catherine how the vibrator is used. Their non-medical use of the device gives both women a dawning insight not only into their own capacity and need for sexual pleasure, but also into the extent to which their marriages have lacked both physical and emotional intimacy. Catherine implores her husband to use the device on her; at first he refuses, but then consents, thinking that her lack of milk could be interpreted as a symptom of hysteria. When, in the throes of orgasm, she asks him to kiss her, he is appalled by her linking of what he sees as a therapeutic medical treatment to sexual intimacy and abruptly cuts the treatment short. Rejected and despondent, Catherine begins to fall in love with another of her husband's patients, the artist Leo Irving; but he, in turn, has fallen in love with Elizabeth (who, of all the women, is actually happy and sexually fulfilled in her marriage). Meanwhile, Sabrina finds herself falling in love with Annie after a treatment session in which Annie has had to bring her to 'paroxysm' through manual stimulation (the vibrator having unexpectedly failed to produce the desired result). At play's end, Catherine breaks through her husband's emotional armour and – in the only scene in the play that deploys Ruhl's characteristic magical-realist transformation of space – the seemingly solid walls of the house disappear to transport the couple into their garden, where Catherine sees her husband naked for the first time and they make love – making a snow angel – together.

In the Next Room was commissioned by the Berkeley Repertory Theatre and received its first production there in February 2009 under the direction of Les Waters; later that year, Waters remounted the production with a different cast on Broadway at the Lyceum Theatre. Critics on both coasts recognized this as Ruhl's 'most traditional' play, although not all agreed that this was a compliment. *New Yorker* critic Lahr labelled the play 'her most commercial and her best to date' while *Washington Post* reviewer Peter Marks felt that it was 'both her most accessible offering – and her least impressive'.[48] Early reviewers were captivated both by the subject of the play and by Ruhl's handling of it. Isherwood called the play 'insightful, fresh, and funny ... as rich in thought as it is in feeling' and was impressed by its cultural and political relevancy:

> women's experience seems to have evaporated almost entirely from movie screens as a subject worthy of illumination through entertainment ... *In the Next Room* is a true novelty: a sex comedy designed not for sniggering teenage boys – or grown men who wish they were still sniggering teenage boys – but for adults with open hearts and minds.[49]

Likewise, Lahr waxed rhapsodically over Ruhl's deft comedic touch: 'Part of the comedy of Ruhl's play ... is her nonjudgmental attack on a sensational subject ... [She] never laughs at her bewildered, repressed characters, who are either lumbered by frustrations that they can't explain or reeling with a desire for which they have no words.'[50] Other critics – writing of later productions in the US regional theatre and abroad – were less smitten. Some agreed that the play was smart and funny, but felt that it 'lack[ed] dramatic momentum' and was built on 'a static premise', and a number of reviewers were even less kind, giving some variation of Australian critic Cameron Woodhead's complaint that 'it's hard to see the first act as anything but one long, laborious dirty joke' and calling its 'sappy, unconvincing' ending 'a wintry resolution of saccharine conventionality'.[51] The play has nevertheless been popular with audiences and recognized by the profession: including previews, it had 91 performances on Broadway; it was nominated in 2010 for the Pulitzer Prize, three Tony Awards and a Drama Desk Award; and, like *The Clean House*, it has had dozens of subsequent productions at professional and university theatres in the US, the UK, Canada, Australia and New Zealand.

In the Next Room readily brings to mind other plays in which women are shown (or encouraged) to awaken to the social, political and sexual structures that overdetermine their existence. Catherine's confinement to a role of dependent femininity, along with her chatty nervousness and birdlike fluttering around the room, invites comparison with the character of Nora in Ibsen's *A Doll's House*, while Sabrina's and Catherine's ignorance of their own potential for sexual pleasure – and their gradual understanding and embrace of their sexuality – evokes some of the more heartbreaking testimonials from Eve Ensler's *The Vagina Monologues*. The documentary nature of Ensler's play serves, as well, as an important inoculation against potential accusations that Ruhl's depiction of Victorian ignorance about female sexuality is far-fetched, as Ensler's interview-based research revealed the persistence of a lack of education and knowledge on the part of both men and women on the topic of female sexual pleasure well into our current day. The same-sex attraction between Sabrina and Annie recalls the lesbian affair depicted in Fornes's *Fefu and her Friends*, another play that looks to history to explore the root causes of female oppression.[52] Certainly the Brechtian technique of historicization deployed by Ruhl in this play is reminiscent of the use of history by both Fornes and Caryl Churchill to trace a genealogy of women's oppression and to magnify gender dynamics in the present day by looking at them through the telescope of history.

In fact, much of *In the Next Room*'s appeal and political punch comes from Ruhl's adroit handling of the distance between Victorian and twenty-first-century attitudes and prejudices. On the one hand, she gives us two central characters who are recognizable, sympathetic types – progressive early adopters of new ideas and technologies. The play opens with Catherine playing with the recently installed electric lights: 'Look baby, it's light! No candle, no rusty tool to snuff it out, but light ... straight from man's imagination into our living room. On, off, on, off, on – ' (7).[53] As the young wife of a man of science, she's a modern woman of her day, one who has already demonstrated a willingness and ability to transgress the conventions of accepted gender roles. She boasts to Mr Daldry that 'no one can keep up with me not even Dr. Givings – that is how he fell in love with me, he said he was determined to keep up with me – he only saw the back of my head before we married because I was always one step ahead' (25), and, later in the play, she describes how she courted her husband's affection by writing his name in the snow. Likewise, Dr Givings is a progressive man of science: he is current with the latest scientific experiments, he has embraced the newest medical technology, he is up to date on his era's most modern theories of hysteria, and he has rationally transcended many wrongheaded notions. For example, when Mr Daldry suggests that the Givings take on Elizabeth as a wet nurse, Catherine initially objects that a friend had said she 'wouldn't use a darkie, the morality goes right through the milk', but, as the son of an abolitionist, Dr Givings is unperturbed by her race, and sidesteps Catherine's misgivings with an appeal to a different sort of prejudice: 'You'd rather have a Negro Protestant than an Irish Catholic, wouldn't you?' (28).

But like Ibsen's Hedda and Nora, as a married woman Catherine is trapped by the gender conventions of her time, and, with historical hindsight, we can recognize her malaise (along with Sabrina's supposed hysteria) as symptomatic of women's lack of purposeful employment and full human status and dignity. Similarly, as ahead of his time as he may be in the social and scientific realms, it's clear to us that Dr Givings is thoroughly steeped in a Victorian sensibility when it comes to gender relations, and this contradiction generates much of the comedy of the play. As Katherine Kelly observes, knowing what we now know about how 'wrong' Dr Givings is regarding the efficaciousness of his device allows us to see the blindness of patriarchal assumptions and makes his scientific authority seem ridiculous. She notes:

> The portrait of Dr. Givings wryly captures the prejudice of nineteenth-century male physicians on the subject of women's sexuality. In this sense, it resurrects early psychotherapy and sexology as disciplines that produced harmful 'knowledge' of sex and gender. But the vibrator helps the patients in spite of Dr. Givings's pronouncements about its purpose. Part of the play's humor arises from the gap between the characters' scientific explanation of the device's therapeutic effects and the audience's post-Freudian dismissal of that interpretation.[54]

For a twenty-first-century audience, it beggars belief that Dr Givings wouldn't recognize his hysterical patients' paroxysms as a sexual response; but then, as he himself observes in a moment of high irony for the audience, 'What men do not observe because their intellect prevents them from seeing would fill many books' (68).

One of the more serious questions the play raises, then, has to do with our own blind spots and prejudices. The gap between the characters' knowledge and ours not only produces comedy but also provokes reflection on the sedimentation of Victorian attitudes in modern society. The play's representation of an era in which patriarchal power literally meant that husbands took the place of fathers to their wives with full legal and practical control over their finances, their movement, their daily occupations, their circle of acquaintances and, of course, their sexuality (and the age gap between both wives and their husbands reinforces this paternalistic aspect of marriage) shines an oblique light on modern forms of sex and gender oppression. As smugly superior as we may feel to the Victorians depicted in the play, it is not difficult to see the parallels between their world and our own. Sabrina Daldry's description of sex with her husband makes clear that she serves merely as a means for satisfying his desire: 'when he comes to my room at night, I am asleep – he tells me to keep my eyes shut, and I do – so I feel only the darkness – and then the pain – I lie very still – I do not see his face' (116). As appalling as this description of marital relations is to the modern ear, it also conjures to mind the modern-day use of alcohol and drugs by men to incapacitate women in order to rape them. While the context is clearly different, the attitude toward women and their 'use-value' to men remains the same: just three years after the play's premiere, the rape of an unconscious high school girl by a group of high-school football players in Steubenville, Ohio, along with a spate of other high-profile crimes against women would direct national attention to the persistent and pervasive attitudes and beliefs that seem to give men license to victimize women. We may not share the Victorian prurience about talking about sex, and we may have better sexual literacy, but Dr Givings's and Mr Daldry's view of women as bodies on which to gratify their own sexual needs and desires – as vessels for their semen and incubators for their children – is, unfortunately, still all too prevalent in the twenty-first century.

For modern audiences, moreover, Ruhl's play offers an antidote and alternative to media representations of sex and sexuality that, in systematically occluding or misrepresenting female desire, perpetuates the attitudes toward women her play exposes and rejects. As *New York Times* journalist Patricia Cohen observed, the mostly male-run media industry promulgates unrealistic and confusing messages about women's sexuality that mainly accord with masculine fantasies about women. Cohen writes that contemporary television and film 'frequently portray women as rapacious sexual predators, always in the mood for sex and without qualms about bedding down as many men as possible'.[55] Such portrayals have toxic social effects, pressuring women to believe they should conform to such models and, even worse, priming men to assume unrealistically that real women share a similar interest in casual and/or frequent sex, thereby contributing to the communicative and perceptual gap between men and women that perpetuates rape culture. In grappling with the issue of female sexual desire in the Victorian era, Ruhl's play puts female agency front and centre and importantly relinks sex and intimacy; as Cohen notes, Ruhl was 'interested in the search for an authentic connection between the physical and the emotional, between two people and within an individual as well'.[56] The positive, transformative moment at play's end thus represents an optimistic hope for real change, one brought about not merely by stage magic but through cultural and artistic representation that aims at changing both the tone and content of the conversation.

Conclusion

In her conversation with Vogel, Ruhl described what she considered 'the pinnacle of a great night at the theater': 'I come into the theater wanting to feel and think at the same time, to have the thought affect the emotion, and the emotion affect the thought.'[57] Ruhl's magic-realist, fabulist approach to theatre allows her to tell stories that appeal both to the rational intellect, insofar as they grapple with social and political issues, and to the irrational emotions, in the way their imagery and juxtapositions excavate invisible yearnings, longings and griefs. Her writing makes full use of the storytelling tools of the theatre – sound, lighting, scenery, music, atmosphere and mood, in addition to language – to transport both characters and audiences and, in so doing, create the kind of suspension that might 'alter perception' and let new things in. With the success of *The Clean House*, in particular, Ruhl proved that non-naturalistic plays could find an audience in the mainstream, commercial theatre. As playwright Rob Handel observed, that play, along with *Eurydice*, demonstrated to American playwrights (and producers) that 'you can do anything ... *The Clean House* made it all "safe" for regional theatre audiences.'[58] Playwrights whose work can be seen to have been inspired by the non-realist audacity of Ruhl's *oeuvre* include – among many others – emerging writers like Lucas Hnath (*The Christians*), Jennifer Haley (*Neighborhood*

3: Requisition of Doom), Clare Barron (*You Got Older*), Jen Silverman (*Crane Story*), Clarence Coo (*Beautiful Province [Belle Province]*), Mia Chung (*You for Me for You*) and Gregory S. Moss (*La Brea*). Thus, although she still has a long career ahead of her, Ruhl's unique theatrical imagination has already helped breathe new life into the American theatre, and her work will undoubtedly continue to have an impact on theatre writers and directors of the next several decades.

Afterword

Julia Listengarten

At this writing in early 2016, American theatre is celebrating arguably its most diverse season in many years. Broadway productions today embrace an extraordinary variety of styles and techniques – including hip-hop in *Hamilton*, a smash musical hit written and composed by Lin-Manuel Miranda; hand puppetry in Robert Askins's dark satire *Hand to God*; and sign language in the revival of *Spring Awakening* produced by Deaf West Theater, with deaf actors among the cast. Ben Brantley wrote in the *New York Times* that '2015 was a year of astonishments, of productions that bent and sometimes shattered the rules that govern traditional stage genres'.[1]

In addition to the dazzling production of *Hamilton*, which integrates rap and storytelling, Broadway 'game changers', in Brantley's opinion, included the gripping musical *Fun Home*, based on Alison Bechdel's autobiographical graphic novel, and three London imports – Ivo van Hove's 'stripped-naked'[2] revival of Arthur Miller's *A View from the Bridge*, Mike Bartlett's *King Charles III*, about the future of monarchy, and *The Curious Incident of the Dog in the Night-Time* (adapted by Simon Stephens from Mark Haddon's novel), tracing the physical adventures and emotional encounters of an autistic child. Off-Broadway theatres also demonstrated their commitment to diversity and experimentation, with many exciting productions of new plays such as Annie Baker's *John* (2015), 'a richly felt study of a relationship under strain' with 'intriguing hints of the supernatural',[3] staged at the Signature Theatre Company; Taylor Mac's gender-bending drama *Hir* (2015), produced at Playwrights Horizons; and Danai

Gurira's *Eclipsed* (2009), a heartfelt and powerful portrait of African women caught in the chaos of the 2003 Liberian civil war, which appeared at the Public Theater in 2015 and transferred to Broadway in 2016.[4]

Theatre has continued to build on the artistic developments of the 2000s, which included eco-theatre, ensemble-based work and puppet-making, among others. One notable undertaking, the Earth Matters on Stage (EMOS) Festival, is an international eco-drama festival and symposium representing a blend of artistic trends within eco-theatre. A combination of staged readings, workshop performances and scholarly panels, the festival is sponsored by the EMOS consortium, which playwright and director Theresa May founded in 2004 to encourage artistic responses to the environmental crisis. EMOS calls for the growth of 'an inclusive ecodrama ... that illuminates the complex connection between people and place ... [and] makes us all more aware of our ecological identities as people and communities'.[5] A growing number of eco-plays such as Chantal Bilodeau's *The Article Cycle* (planned as an eight-play series) and Karen Malpede's *Extreme Weather* (2013) have focused on the catastrophic impact of climate change. Several industry initiatives, among them the Broadway Green Alliance, have encouraged environmentally friendly practices in theatre-making, such as ecological design to promote sustainability.

As for ensemble theatres, which have flourished in recent years, Theatre Communications Group Executive Director Teresa Eyring wondered whether such theatres, 'with their mix of continuity and adaptability, and their focus on the artistic mission', might indeed 'point the way forward' for the entire field. Regardless of their organizational structures or artistic methodologies – immersive, site-specific or devising versus more traditional approaches to the text and creative process – ensemble theatres, she says, forge strong continuity and collective consciousness that help them adapt to economic circumstances and propel them forward artistically. The Network of Ensemble Theaters, for instance – an organization that was formed in 1996 – has grown exponentially to more than 250 theatre collectives.

The increasing integration of puppetry in theatre has been evident in both mainstream and non-traditional theatre, as well as undergraduate and graduate theatre curricula. In 2015, La MaMa, dedicated to presenting innovative puppet theatre work, hosted a puppet series, a biennial festival which featured the new work of American and international puppet theatre artists as well as multicultural theatre groups, among them Tom Lee (United States) and Koryu Nishikawa V (Japan) in *Shank's Mare* and the Loco7 Dance Puppet Theatre Company (United States and Colombia) in *Undefined Fraction*. Basil Twist, who continued to contribute puppet designs for Broadway musicals (*The Addams Family* and *The Pee-Wee Herman Show*, both in 2010), offered a dance-cum-puppetry rendition of Stravinsky's *The Rite of Spring* (2014) – his 'astonishing inventiveness with silk and other seemingly ordinary materials [such as] folded paper [and] curling smoke' resulted in an 'otherworldly melding of abstract puppetry and music'.[6] Julie Taymor's work after *Spider-Man: Turn Off the Dark* included a black-box production of *A Midsummer Night's Dream* (2014), which was staged in a new Brooklyn theatre (the Polonsky Shakespeare Center) and dazzled audiences with a spectacular marriage of puppets and projections.

As contemporary American theatre embraced a variety of styles and engaged in current cultural and political discourses, all four dramatists featured in this book have also continued to develop their writing careers. Charles Mee immersed himself in a series of collaborative projects in the second decade of this century. He conceived *American Document* (2010), a re-envisioning of the theatrical ballet that Martha Graham created in 1938, with dancers from the Martha Graham Company, Anne Bogart and SITI Company actors. Graham's original piece, a unique fusion of theatre and dance, combined elements of vaudeville, folk rhythms and spoken text that included excerpts from the Declaration of Independence and Walt Whitman's *Leaves of Grass*. Created at the height of fascism in Europe, it asked the fundamental question, 'What is an American?' which deeply resonates with Bogart and Mee, who often reflect on this question in their work. Bogart recalls that when presented with the challenge to reinvent Graham's work, she immediately turned to Mee, her long-time creative partner, to write a libretto for the production.[7] With no complete record of Graham's piece, Mee assembled a text from various sources, including filmed excerpts and written descriptions of the production, Graham's handwritten choreographic notes and Whitman's poetry. 'Less of a worshipful homage to Martha Graham's seminal work ... as it is a fecund riff on Graham herself',[8] the collaboration celebrates the union of theatre and dance and continues to ponder what makes 'an American', a difficult question about identity and politics that has resurfaced with renewed vigour in contemporary American drama and theatre. *American Document* had a few work-in-progress showings at the Public Theater's Under the Radar Festival in January 2010 and then, a few months later, premiered at New York City's Joyce Theater.

Mee's other collaborative projects in the 2010s included *Pool Play* (2014), an immersive theatre work conceived and directed by his daughter, Erin N. Mee, and three dance theatre pieces – *Heaven on Earth* (2011), *Eterniday* (2013) and *Daily Life Everlasting* (2015), staged by the dance theatre group Witness Relocation at La MaMa. As one of three writers, Mee contributed to the collage-driven text of *Pool Party*, an entertaining and contemplative piece made up of 'a collection of scenes and musical numbers, each of which is a meditation on water'[9] – actors and audience were literally and figuratively immersed in the swimming pool. Mee also developed a creative partnership with choreographer Dan Safer, whose New York-based Witness Relocation company emerged in 2000 as an ensemble group to fuse 'dance and theater with the energy of a rock show, exploding contemporary culture into intensely physical, outrageous, poetic, and sometimes brutal performances'.[10]

Mee's recent collage plays, directed and choreographed by Safer, contemplate the ending of the world (*Heaven on Earth*), the passing of life (*Eterniday*) and the collision of lives and destinies as people 'pass through the landscape at a yard sale – under the observant eye of a boy named Odysseus 2.0' (*Daily Life Everlasting*).[11] The marriage of these scripts, which intersect diverse historical, textual and cultural references, and the company's pop-culture style resulted in multilayered, often jubilant and raucous, dance-theatre productions that 'involved a variety of movement styles, ranging from vigorous modern dance to stylized everyday gestures'.[12] Mee continued to offer directors and choreographers great liberty in remaking his texts. As Safer interpreted Mee's writing in *Daily Life Everlasting*, he dispensed with Odysseus 2.0, who seems to be a key character in Mee's script. Commenting on the uniquely open experience of working with Mee's texts, Safer wrote that 'Chuck imagines a fully realized dance-theater production and then gives it to me ... The script's full of very evocative stage directions. My job is to look at what he wrote and ask, "What is the seed of that idea?" [and] "If I take that seed, where would I take it based on what he's given me?".[13]

Glory of the World (2015), Mee's most recent work to date, was commissioned by the Humana Festival to commemorate the centennial of Trappist monk, philosopher, writer and poet Thomas Merton. Conceived as a reflection on Merton's legacy and a celebration of his life and ideas in the spirit of Mee's earlier works exploring 'the lives of the artists', it premiered at the Actors Theatre of Louisville under the direction of Les Waters, one of Mee's collaborators. Critic Todd Ziegler pointed to the production's integration of the 'ridiculous and sublime' – contemplative toasts marking the beginning of Merton's birthday tribute turn into a wild birthday party that 'goes into overdrive with dance breaks, shirtless pose-downs, lip sync battles and more, crescendoing into a fit of violence over some of the more controversial elements of Merton's life that dissolves into pure anarchy'.[14] Mee's script captures the complexity of Merton's work and personality through metaphysical commentary and pop-culture references; in Waters's staging, the text is layered with 'the sheer abandonment of ecstasy' and 'violent frustration'. Asked in an interview for *American Theatre* magazine about the use of trampolines and a rhinoceros on stage, Mee responded, 'You have to talk to Les about that.'[15]

Lynn Nottage's work after the overwhelming success of *Ruined* (Pulitzer Prize in 2009) has encompassed an impressive range of topics and styles, from the satiric exploration of racial stereotypes in the film industry (*By the Way, Meet Vera Stark*, 2011) to a documentary-based inquiry into the shattering effects of America's industrial decline (*Sweat*, 2015). The playwright's transition from the harrowing realities of the Congo's civil war in *Ruined* to the parody of race-driven politics in Hollywood in *By the Way, Meet Vera Stark* might seem unexpected. Nottage, however, continues to represent female voices that have been largely absent from historical narratives. In creating the character of Vera Stark, Nottage was inspired by the work of African American actress Theresa Harris, who excelled in establishing a distinct film career in the 1930s but then virtually disappeared from the public arena and Hollywood biographical accounts. The play traces the story of Vera Stark from her early days as a maid and trusted companion of a Hollywood celebrity to her last appearance on a 1973 television show. Critic

Manohla Dargis of the *New York Times* described the play as 'an imaginary history that, like others of Ms. Nottage's plays, weaves the personal with the political'.

A fusion of 1930s-era movie screwball comedy and sharp commentary on persistent racial inequality in the entertainment industry, *Meet Vera Stark* premiered in 2011 at Off-Broadway's Second Stage Theatre, directed by Jo Bonney and starring Sanaa Lathan as Vera. The play received mixed reviews. Ben Brantley, for instance, compared its 'mix of cartoon broad strokes and grittier emotional detail that never quite blends smoothly' to the comic sensibility of *Fabulation*, but noted powerful moments that 'provoke[d] hearty laughter and troubling thoughts at the same time'.[16] After the New York production, *Meet Vera Stark* was produced by a number of regional theatres, including Chicago's Goodman in 2013. Nottage has called the play a 'transmedia piece' and pointed to the significance of the multimedia aspects of her work.[17] In addition to incorporating film footage that features Vera Stark's performance, Nottage – with the help of production company Market Road Films, which she started with her husband, Tony Gerber, in 2005 – created two websites, http://www.bythewaymeetverastark.com and http://www.meetverastark.com, which included documentaries on Stark's legacy. 'I wanted the conceit to be complete,' she said. 'I thought it would be fun for the audience.'[18]

A later work, *Sweat* is another collaborative multimedia project including a website, which takes the viewer through Reading, a Pennsylvania city impoverished by the decline of the steel industry, and presents a compelling story, through images and narrative, about its disillusioned inhabitants. The project also features an 'interactive transmedia installation' – a 'social sculpture' – created from the testimonials and images of residents,[19] to inspire community dialogues about unemployment, poverty and drug addiction in America's most economically disadvantaged places. As she did with her previous plays, Nottage applied her skills as a researcher and historian to the process of conceptualizing and creating *Sweat*. After Reading was identified in the 2010 US Census as the poorest city in the nation, she travelled there 'with an eye toward collecting the stories of people battling to survive in a city crippled by economic stagnation ... and plagued by rising crime and unemployment'.[20] The play then gradually developed from the interviews, stories and images that Nottage and her collaborator Kate Whoriskey meticulously collected over a period of time. Whoriskey subsequently directed its premiere in August 2015 at the Oregon Shakespeare Festival. The play was also co-commissioned by Arena Stage in Washington, DC, where it opened in January 2016.

Sweat centres on a group of friends struggling with the consequences of the city's failing economy and offers a compassionate yet critical look at the intersections of race, class, politics and culture in today's America. Nottage's 'scorching new play' is 'dark, even devastating' but also 'funny', Charles Isherwood of the *New York Times* remarked. Commenting on the playwright's ability to fuse the heartbreaking with the humorous, the poetic with the gritty, he observed, 'Ms. Nottage knows well that the natural reactions to the assaults of life faced by these particular people are a savage sense of humor, and, more damagingly, a swan dive into the comforts of alcohol and drugs.'[21]

Balancing her need for solitude as a writer and her craving for collaboration as a theatre-maker,[22] Nottage continued to engage in various collaborative projects. She contributed a one-act play, *The Odds*, to the multi-writer production of *Decade*, which Rupert Goold conceived and directed to commemorate the 10th anniversary of 11 September. Nottage has also worked in film, co-producing documentaries such as *First to Fall* (2013), on the journey of two Libyan friends to the 2011 uprising against Muammar Gaddafi's regime, and *The Notorious Mr. Bout* (2014), about an international arms dealer. More recently, her work includes a musical stage adaptation of the classic film *Black Orpheus,* planned for Broadway under the direction of George C. Wolfe.[23]

Theresa Rebeck has continued to write for both television and theatre. She created and co-produced the NBC musical series *Smash* (2012–13), and her post-2009 plays included *Seminar* (2011), *Poor Behavior* (2011), *O Beautiful* (2011), *Dead Accounts* (2012) and *Zealot* (2014) – witty, provocative, socially conscious comedies whose subjects range from personal and professional failures and betrayals to political and moral accountability. In *Seminar*, the hopes and aspirations of young writers are ruthlessly dashed during a writing workshop taught by an arrogant and self-absorbed writing guru; in *Dead Accounts*, an unexpected homecoming prompts a family to ponder questions of moral integrity and familial loyalty; in *Poor Behavior*, a getaway weekend in the country turns into a series of painful revelations about couples' infidelities. In *O Beautiful*, Rebeck addresses modern debates about abortion rights and gun control, as well as bullying, rape and suicide among teenagers. Set in Mecca, Saudi Arabia, *Zealot* likewise explores female empowerment – in this case, through the complicated lens of Middle East politics involving Western diplomacy and the Saudi government's repressive policies.

Despite mixed critical reception, Rebeck, who in 2010 received the PEN/Laura Pels International Foundation for Theater Award for an American playwright in mid-career, remains one of a few women playwrights in American theatre whose works are regularly produced on Broadway, Off-Broadway and in major regional theatres. In fact, two of her new plays from the current decade – *Seminar* and *Dead Accounts* – premiered on Broadway in 2011 and 2012, respectively, while *Poor Behavior* made its Off-Broadway debut in 2014, three years after its original production at the Mark Taper Forum in Los Angeles. Productions of Rebeck's plays frequently feature the work of renowned theatre-makers. Directed by Sam Gold, the Broadway production of *Seminar* starred the celebrated British stage actor Alan Rickman in the role of a legendary writing mentor. Director Jack O'Brian led the Broadway cast of *Dead Accounts* that included two-time Tony Award-winner Norbert Leo Butz and television/film actress Katie Holmes. *Poor Behavior* was developed at Off-Broadway's Primary Stages under the direction of Evan Cabnet, whose recent directing credits included the critically acclaimed production of *Therese Raquin* in 2015 at the Roundabout Theatre Company.

Seminar exemplifies Rebeck's talent for writing intellectually stimulating, contemporary comedies of manners full of playful repartee and biting satire. Ben Brantley, who somewhat condescendingly referred to Rebeck as 'a canny craftswoman with a sensibility poised somewhere between that of Yasmina Reza (queen of the quick, smart comedy) and Neil Simon (the longest-reigning king of the New York-style one-liner)',[24] nevertheless acknowledged the play's 'efficiently mapped reversals and revelations' as well as its 'astute use of topical and intellectual references'.[25] As career ambitions and sexual tensions coalesce in *Seminar*, the four writers, each of whom pays $5,000 to master the art of writing, are forced to confront personal and professional limitations. The play also explores gender parity, a recurring concern for Rebeck.

When providing his unorthodox, often-dismissive, instruction to the beginning writers, Leonard, a once-famous novelist turned disillusioned editor, engages in a sexual relationship with two women in the group. Power games involving gender biases, sex, personal respect and professional recognition are at the heart of the play. Claudia La Rocco of the *New York Times* noted that *Seminar* 'tackles gender politics head-on' by offering a 'sharp critique of gender inequality' through one of its female characters.[26] Kate, whose posh apartment on the Upper West Side becomes an ideal location for the characters' sharp-tongued, spirited banter about money and social privilege, sets up the play's argument about gender inequality and class-based assumptions: 'His [Leonard's] biggest objection to me is that I am a rich white girl. Maybe if I am not a rich white girl we can find out if I can write' (49).

Relentlessly pushing the boundaries of mainstream theatre, Rebeck works to interweave American history and religious figures into discourse about rape, abortion and bullying at a high school in *O Beautiful*. 'A satirical look at the politics of the Tea Party, Glenn Beck, and the failed Senate candidate Christine O'Donnell',[27] the play thrusts major historical figures – Founding Fathers as well as Jesus and Saint Paul, among others – into the ideologically driven polemic about teenage pregnancy, parental control and abortion rights. *O Beautiful* was the result of Rebeck's collaboration with the University of Delaware's Theatre and English departments, which commissioned the playwright to produce the work. The production was staged at the Resident Ensemble Players, the university's professional theatre company, featuring a cast of Equity actors and undergraduate students. Commenting on this opportunity to write a play that included more than 30 characters, unlike most Broadway and Off-Broadway shows with small casts, Rebeck recalled that she 'want[ed] to tell a sweeping story that [would benefit] the commission. And one thing that has stayed with me over time is that so many women's stories were not being told in the culture.'[28] Since its original production, *O Beautiful* has been staged at regional and university theatres, including Connecticut Repertory Theatre in 2012 and Penn State Centre Stage in 2014.

Sarah Ruhl's *Stage Kiss*, a meta-theatrical comedy exploring the tensions between art and life, was commissioned by Chicago's Goodman Theatre and premiered there in April 2011 under the direction of Jessica Thebus. The boundaries between life and theatre blur when ex-lovers are cast to perform romantic leads in a 1930s melodrama. Pointing to a lighter, rollicking quality in this work, critics noted a major shift in Ruhl's writing from her often-poetically evocative and abstract plays. Charles Isherwood wrote that *Stage Kiss* 'may be Ms. Ruhl's fluffiest, most accessible play',[29] whereas John Lahr of *The New Yorker* compared Ruhl's comedic sensibility to that of Noël Coward and observed that the play – 'at once a knowing sendup of the hazy half-truths of stage naturalism and a goofy meditation on the nature of desire and sexual fantasy' – was both 'original and instantly recognizable to the audience'.[30] Lahr applauded Ruhl's talent for grasping the sense of 'structure, immediacy, and frivolity' in the genre of comedy and shared her view about the significance of humour and lightheartedness in theatre. 'Lightness,' Ruhl suggests, 'is actually a philosophical and aesthetic viewpoint, deeply serious, and has a kind of wisdom – stepping back to be able to laugh at the horrible things even as you're experiencing them.'[31]

Although the genre and subject matter of Ruhl's plays since 2010 have varied considerably, she remains committed to revealing the expressive, poetic quality of language. *Dear Elizabeth* (2012) is a play in letters, a dramatization of the correspondence between American poets Elizabeth Bishop and Robert Lowell. Ruhl distilled 800 pages of letters – the words of the play came exclusively from the letters – into an epistolary poem about friendship driven by profound intimacy and passion for literature. She crafted *Dear Elizabeth* 'in the spirit of a contemporary hunger to hear poetry out loud' because 'we are starved for the sound of poetry'.[32] The play, Ruhl pointed out, could be performed in many different ways: 'from a simple reading focusing entirely on the language to a full spectacle ... complete with planets appearing and water rushing onto the stage'.[33] In Charles Isherwood's observation, the Yale Repertory Theatre's production of *Dear Elizabeth*, directed by Les Waters, existed 'somewhere between a staged reading, along the lines of A. R. Gurney's durable "Love Letters" ... and a fully staged play',[34] masterfully negotiating the intimacy of the piece with the richness of its imagery. Its premiere at the Yale Repertory Theatre in 2012 was followed by productions at major regional theatres, including Berkeley Rep in 2013 and Seattle Rep in 2015. The play premiered in New York City at the Women's Project Theater in October 2015.

Ruhl's *The Oldest Boy* is a family drama imbued with anguish, love and faith, 'extremely imaginative and hypnotically beautiful'.[35] Produced at Lincoln Center's Mitzi E. Newhouse Theater in December 2014 after it premiered at the Marin Theatre in San Francisco two months earlier, this work offers a glimpse into a family's spiritual journey of 'letting go'. When a Tibetan monk reveals that a child born to an American woman and a Tibetan man is a reincarnation of his departed spiritual master and should be sent to a monastery in India to study Buddhism, the parents grapple with impending loss and acceptance. Infused with Buddhist teachings, the play contains elements of puppetry – a puppet plays the role of this special child – and ritualistic performance. In Rebecca Taichman's imaginative staging of *The Oldest Boy* at Lincoln Center Theater, 'ritualistic dance sequences and luminous images evoking the natural beauty of India' underscored the play's poetic quality; a bunraku-style wooden-rod puppet, designed by puppeteer Matt Acheson and handled by two performers, heightened the magical and mystical in the story.

Ruhl's other recent works included her adaptation of Chekhov's *Three Sisters* (2011) and *100 Essays I Don't Have Time to Write* (2014), a collection of witty and eloquent contemplations on the art of writing and collaborating in life and theatre. In one essay, she muses about the transformative quality of Ovid's *Metamorphoses* and his talent to 'imitate the dreams and the unconscious', revealing her fascination with the transformative in theatre. As Ruhl describes the Ovidian form, she perhaps unwittingly articulates her own approach to playwriting: 'Gods become swans, people become trees, people fall in love and die, the supernatural world is permeable. This story structure is reminiscent of fairy tales. Objects have magical properties, people transform.'[36]

A new generation of exciting young playwrights has also emerged, their works sought after by leading New York and regional theatres and garnering significant recognition. The plays of Amy Herzog and Annie Baker, including the former's *Belleville* (2011) and the latter's *The Flick* (2013), create moments of intense emotional intimacy, expressed through hyper-realism that often borders on the poetic. 'A quietly devastating play',[37] *Belleville* masterfully probes the darker side of intimacy and the self-destructive relationship of a young American couple in Paris. *The Flick*, a descendant of Chekhovian drama, with its small talk and fragmented language that reveal the poetic essence of the unspoken, captures the beauty of the mundane, as three misfits – underpaid workers in a movie theatre – go on with their tedious daily labour.

Other plays penned in the 2010s challenge persistent racial discrimination (Bruce Norris's *Clybourne Park*, 2010; Branden Jacobs-Jenkins's *An Octoroon*, 2014; Stephen Adly Guirgis's *Between Riverside and Crazy*, 2014) and debate gender politics and identity conflicts over faith, ethnicity and sexual orientation (Gina Gionfriddo's *Rupture, Blister, Burn*, 2012; Ayad Akhtar's *Disgraced*, 2012; Samuel D. Hunter's *A Bright New Boise*, 2011; Young Jean Lee's *Straight White Men*, 2014). Contemporary plays have also addressed war's devastation of people and communities. Among these probing and compassionate new works that raise piercing questions about war's traumatic effects are Quiara Alegría Hudes's trilogy (*Elliot, A Soldier's Fugue*, 2007; *Water by the Spoonful*, 2011; and *The Happiest Song Plays Last*, 2015), Rajiv Joseph's *Bengal Tiger at the Baghdad Zoo* (2009) and Suzan-Lori Parks's *Father Comes Home from the Wars* (2014). Responding to the proliferation of digital culture, playwrights have explored the vexed relationship between technology and human interaction. Matthew Lopez in *Reverberation* (2015) asks his audience to contemplate the disturbing effects of technological advances on relationships. By contrast, Lee (*Untitled Feminist Show*, 2012; *We're Gonna Die*, 2014), whose 'irreverent, essayistic, collagist approach to storytelling' has established her as 'a troubling necessary presence',[38] embraces technology by including the audience through blogging. As American theatre continues to reimagine itself amid the new wave of racial protests over 'Black Lives Matter', the 2016 presidential election campaign, the rise of ISIS and the surge in domestic and global terrorism, there are many more histories to be written and performed and many new roads to be taken.

Documents

Charles Mee: Interview with Cindy Rosenthal, 17 April 2015, New York City

CR Can you speak about the period we are most concerned about in this volume – 2000–9? Can you talk about an event or something that happened in your life or in the world that had a particular impact on your work at that time?

CM I never thought about this before. But there are three huge things that happened at about that time. I met the woman that I'm now married to and we lived happily ever after. I received a grant from the Guthrie Theatre that enabled me to go see theatre anywhere in the world – and I called Joseph Melillo, the Executive Producer at BAM, and I said I'd like to go to a theatre festival – where should I go and he said I should go to Avignon. I asked him what would be his second choice and he said there is no second choice. So I went to the Avignon Festival in 2000 and saw all of this fantastic work. Mostly from Europe, and it had a huge impact on me. That moment was very much the world of Pina Bausch and her descendants. Alain Platel from Brussels who runs a company called Les Ballets C de la B was asked if he was influenced by Pina Bausch and he said, 'Pina Bausch was the mother of us all.' That kind of theatre – an astonishing mixture of movement, music and text – is what I love to do. So that was my first experience of Avignon. And I've gone back eight times since then.

I didn't go to Avignon in the sixties. I graduated from college in 1960 and wrote plays for La MaMa, Caffe Cino, and St. Marks in the Bowery. Then I got very involved in anti-Vietnam War politics, became an activist and wrote books about American international relations, which led to writing books about American foreign policy. I got caught up in an argument for twenty years that I couldn't get out of. I didn't go back to the theatre until 1985. But I saw a lot of the theatre work of the 1960s.

The third thing is – when I first got to New York, right out of college, a guy became my friend who worked in the admissions department at Princeton. He began to find that work kind of boring so he thought maybe it would be really fun to be an investment banker. So he went back to business school and got a job at Morgan Stanley when it had 153 employees. And by the time he retired as President and Chairman of the Board, Morgan Stanley had 63,000 employees worldwide and was, by some accounts, the largest investment bank in the world – and he had done it because it was fun. He was not greedy or rapacious. He did his work, went home and had dinner with his family. Then he went to the theatre. His name was Richard Fisher and he died in 2004. But he was a dear friend of mine all those years. There was a moment in about the year 1999 when Anne Bogart asked me to do a piece with her and I got the commission to do *Big Love* from the Actors Theatre of Louisville for the Humana Festival. I was talking to Dick and I said, 'Gee, I had so much to do but there was no way I could get it all done – I had to have a job in order to live.' And then I said, 'Oh – I have an idea. Why don't we start a playwriting company together? You put in all the money and I'll write all the plays.' And he said, 'I'd love to do that!' So he started totally supporting me, which he did from 1999 until he died in 2004. And then he left me an endowment and his widow (Jeanne Donovan Fisher) continued to support me until she couldn't anymore – a couple of years ago. But for that decade I wrote three plays a year. All the stuff that had been stored up for the previous couple of decades just came pouring out. I realized that I was just typing it out, not writing. It was what had been going around in my mind over and over again for twenty years and now I finally had the time to type it up.

And the love of my life was an actress who did a workshop of one of my plays at Sundance in 2001 – it was called *Wintertime*, directed by Les Waters. I hate workshops. I don't go to them. But I thought I should go to Sundance. So I arrived a week late and Les Waters said, 'Here's Chuck' – so just to catch me up to where they are, he said, 'Why don't we read through the whole play?' So they started a read through. As a playwright, you know every choice an actor can make on every line. The right choice, the sincerely felt honest choice, and then sometimes – several choices that you'd never thought of before. The woman sitting across the table from me made the right choice or better than the right choice every time. And I thought – wow, she's one in a million. And I thought – that's true. And if I don't act on that, I'm really stupid. So at the act break I said to her, 'Would you have a cup of coffee with me and a conversation leading to marriage?' And she said, 'Well, I'd have a cup of coffee.' And I thought – well, she didn't say no. And then I thought I've got her cornered on the top of a mountain in Utah. I should be arrested for this. So I backed off and I thought I'll wait until we're back in New York and then she can say, it's so nice to meet you but I'm too busy to get together, blah blah blah. So I phoned her when she was back in New York and I said, 'Are you free for dinner later this week?' and she said, 'Oh yes, I'd love to.' And then I knew we were getting married. I don't know if she knew.

CR How did your relationship, your connection with Anne Bogart come to be?

CM Let me back up a bit. When I came back into the theatre, after I had been out of it for twenty years, I didn't know anyone in the theatre, but I had been writing history books and taking them around the corner to a Xerox shop. And there was a guy working there – and I knew he was involved in the theatre. So when I wrote this play, I took it to him, and I asked him what I should do with it. He said, 'Let me take this to my friend Joe Papp at the Public Theater.' That was Wally Shawn. Joe Papp called me up

and said, 'I love your play and I want to do it. We need a
director and I have one – Martha Clarke.'

Martha and I got together for lunch and she said, 'I love
your play but I've been thinking about something I want to
do about Vienna at the turn of the century.' I said, 'I'll write
the text for you.' She said, 'No, no – it's not going to have
any text, it's a dance/theatre piece.' I said, 'No, don't worry,
I'll write the text and it'll be ok.' She said, 'ok', and she took
me to meet her producer Lyn Austin and Lyn Austin said,
'You understand – Martha is a right hemisphere genius, but
she has no left hemisphere. Organization and coherence is not
something she can do. So what would be the structure of this
piece?' I'd never thought of this before. But I said, 'Oh, that's
easy. It's Spring, Summer, Autumn, Winter.' Lyn said, 'Ok –
we open a year from next Wednesday.' So she financed the
whole production and hired the actors and dancers to work
in the rehearsal room for a year while we made the piece. Lyn
Austin introduced me to Anne Bogart. Then I understood
something – never work with anyone except for friends or
people that your friends introduce you to. That's all I've ever
done. I'll never send a play out to a stranger. When Anne
formed the SITI Company, the first play she did was a version
of *Orestes* that I had written. I had written that because I
had gotten to know Joanne Akalaitis who introduced me to
Robert Woodruff. Gordon Davidson who was running the
Mark Taper Forum then called Woodruff and said, 'We were
going to do a workshop here but it fell through – I have space
and money for a workshop – is there something you'd like to
do?' So Woodruff called me and said, 'We can do a workshop.
What do you want to do?' I told him, 'I don't have anything
and I can't go to Los Angeles now, but why don't you go and
I'll send you things you can work on.' This was back in the
days of the first war in Iraq. So he took *Orestes* out with him
to Los Angeles and started working with actors and I faxed
him pages to stick into it – those were the days of faxing.

CR Why *Orestes*?

CM It was a play that already existed about a time when a
war ended and the soldiers came home. That was what was

happening in America at that moment. So Woodruff brought it back to New York – and I thought, oh, here's this pile of junk. I can just throw away the original play and save the junk I sent to him – using that structure, theme and storyline – that will be my play today. It was my first Greek play. In working on *Orestes*, I understood how great the Greek plays are – I wanted to do another one and another one and another one. The genius of the Greeks is they understood – the principal characters advance the plot then the chorus riffs. The principals advance the plot, the chorus riffs. The principals advance the plot, the chorus riffs. By the time you get to Ibsen, it's just the principals advance the plot, the principals advance the plot, the principals advance the plot. By the time you get to Pina Bausch, it's just the chorus riffs, the chorus riffs, the chorus riffs. I thought right – I get to do both. The chorus sings and dances – so I get to put together the Greeks, Pina Bausch, and musical comedy and make a new kind of theatre that I really really love like crazy.

CR Can you speak about the nature of your collaborations with theatre and performance artists like Martha Clarke and Anne Bogart?

CM I have made pieces with Martha Clarke and Anne Bogart when I am in the rehearsal room and it is devised theatre. We begin with an empty room and nothing on paper at all. We make it up as we go along. I've done pieces that way but it's not usually like that. Usually I write a play, I hand it to a director, and I say I'll see you on opening night. That way the director and the actors are free to do whatever they want without my being in the room to inhibit them. Because at some point years ago, after going to Europe and seeing work, I realized that the playwrights who get the best productions are the dead playwrights – and it's probably because they don't go to rehearsal. I think I'm the only living playwright in the world who feels the way Euripides and Shakespeare feel right now when their plays are done. From the afterlife, they look back and they see the work being done. I come to opening night.

This is true of the piece at La MaMa right now (April 2015). It's a piece called *Daily Life Everlasting*. There is a twelve-year-old boy who wanders through this yard sale in his backyard in middle America and his grandmother is on the front porch. And people of his parents' generation open the garage door and they are all drinking and singing opera and the boy's name is Odysseus 2.0. It's a modern Odysseus, making a journey through his world, today. Dan Safer eliminated Odysseus and cast performers who are all in their twenties. So now it's a wild, sexy party with everyone interested in having sex and figuring out who they are. It's just not my play at all – Dan took my text and made it into a piece that made sense to him. The last two pieces he did of mine were more faithful to my original notions.

CR How do you relinquish control so fully and easily? How does that feel?

CM How does Euripides feel, looking on from the other world at his work being done in 2015? He must think – wow this is cool. Oh no – that's not what I had in mind at all, but that's cool. He gets to see that his plays still get done – and some of them are faithful productions but most of them are just people taking off and doing something else. And that's wonderful. I hope I'm that lucky. If I'm really lucky and my plays are being done after I'm dead I'll get to see how they get done.

Another thing that happened in the year 2000 – *Big Love* is the last big Greek play that I did. I still have to do *Iphigenia*. I've been thinking about it since 1991 and I still haven't typed it up. There was *Orestes*, and then in 1993 I did *Trojan Women* and I realized that *Iphigenia* would be the first play of this trilogy. But I had a couple of young daughters at the time and I couldn't bring myself to write the play then. But after they went off to college and were having their own wonderful independent lives I was able to get back to that play. In a way, *Big Love* is the capstone of the Greeks. *Wintertime* is a normal play in a way. It takes place in the living room of a middle-class home with middle-class people. The mother has her lover there; the father has his gay lover there. It's a bit more like today than Ibsen's day. It's more like a normal drawing room play. Then, *bobrauschenbergamerica* is a total collage, like Rauschenberg made. Choosing these three plays for your book is great because you have the Greek play, the normal drawing room play, and the collage. After 2003–4 I took off from Rauschenberg and went further out into collage and dance-theatre. More like the work of European artists like Alain Platel in Brussels, Pippo Delbono in Italy, Romeo Castellucci in Italy – these are people who have inspired my more recent work.

When I first got out of college, I got a job at a magazine called *Horizon*, which was a hardcover magazine of the arts. I worked my way up to being editor-in-chief. There I was – if I saw an exhibition by Joseph Cornell, I could call the greatest expert in the world on Cornell's work and have him write an article, get the picture researchers to do their work and I got to see it all come together. I spent years working on art history, archeology, architecture for a living – and it was unbelievable. A lot of my artists-pieces come from that time in my life. But they had been in there, in me, for years. Also, with Rauschenberg, the way he made his art is the way I make my plays. With Cornell – the way he makes his art is the way I made that play (*Hotel Cassiopeia*, 2006). The way I write a play is I make notes on thirty to forty paintings or sculptures, pieces of installation art, and they start talking, they start doing stuff, they start dancing and that's how the play gets made. I know a lot of playwrights start with a central character and the life of that character. I start with right hemisphere imagery. That stuff I see on the stage begins to sing and move and dance and speak and that's how a lot of these plays are made. Following Rauschenberg.

CR What about your site-specific work? Where did that originate? How did it come about?

CM It came directly from Annie Hamburger who ran En Garde Arts. When Lyn Austin introduced me to Anne Bogart, Anne asked me to do a piece with her for Annie

Hamburger. I couldn't do it at that time, but Anne and I came back to Annie later because we wanted to work with her and Annie took us around town and said, 'how about here, how about here, how about here?' And we finally settled on an abandoned nursing home on Central Park West and 106th Street and the piece came out of that. I wrote stuff that seemed appropriate for that space. One day an elderly woman who was in an old folks home down the block wandered in to watch rehearsals and Anne said, 'How would you like to be in the play?' And then a couple of other people wandered in and she put them in the play. That was fun – that was great.

CR Although, as we've discussed, you've been influenced by a number of European artists, do you feel your work (I'm thinking especially of *Wintertime* and *bobrauschenbergamerica* right now) speaks to and for the US?

CM I feel I'm speaking to and for the place I live today, starting with my family. My eldest daughter is married to a guy from India so their daughter is half American and half Indian. My wife's mother is Japanese; we have adopted a little girl from China – so, personally, in my own living room, I live in a global society. I think we today, in America, live in a global society. I write out of that – even without having to think about it very much. That's where I live.

CR Do you feel there is a community of spectators you want to reach – that you haven't as yet?

CM No – in the 1960s during my time of anti-Vietnam War activism, when I was trying to impeach Richard Nixon, I was ultra-aware of what kind of audiences we could speak with and get on our side. When I began to work in the theatre again, I think my operating principle is I do what I love – what *I* love. Since I am the world's leading expert on what I love, I cannot be wrong. And since I am not from Mars, there will be two or three other people who will like it too. And that's the whole deal. Pippo Delbono, who was at the Avignon Festival a few years ago, was interviewed by a Paris newspaper. He was asked, 'Do you think your work is political?' And he said, 'Oh, I hope not. I hope it is more profound than that. I believe it is about the culture from which the politics spring.' That feels right to me.

CR Did it surprise you when the Signature Theatre decided to devote their season to you in 2007–8?

CM Totally, totally! It was stunning. I loved it – it was wonderful. Jim Houghton [Signature Founding Artistic Director] is an amazing guy. He called me and said, 'Hi, Chuck. Would it be ok with you if we did a season of your plays next year?' I almost passed out. I had to be picked up from the floor. I said, 'I would love that!' He said, 'What would you like to do?' I said, 'Usually what you do is bring back a couple of plays from previous years and then you do one new play. But as it happens, I have three new plays that are on their way to productions somewhere. Could we bring them all together and do them all at the Signature?' And he said, 'Sure! Who would you like to direct them?' And I told him. And he said, 'Who would you like to design them?' And I said maybe we should wait and have a conversation with the directors about that. He really gives the playwright the world.

CR Can you talk a little bit about your collaboration with your daughter, Erin?

CM I loved it – and I'm loving it again. We're doing more. Erin went off and got a PhD and started teaching and had a daughter and has had years when she's been consumed by other things. But now, in the last couple of years, she's getting back to directing. The first piece she did was called *Pool Play* – it was at a pool on East 22nd Street and East River Drive. And I wrote two little pieces of text for that. It was mostly written by a young woman named Jessie Bear. Jessie has written another play and we're in rehearsal right now for *Readymade Cabaret* at the Judson Church.

The audience gets to throw the dice deciding which scene goes next. A lot of scenes just aren't done. Jessie and I are going to write another play together. We've had a couple of lunches and conversations. Erin is also working on the *Pod Play*, when you get on the Staten Island Ferry and you have the play in your ear as you go across. You see the Statue of Liberty and the other passengers on the ferry. Otherwise it's all in your head.

CR Can you talk about your collaboration with Stephen Greenblatt?

CM We met at the Bellagio Center in Italy a few years ago and got to be friends. He was given a Mellon Grant – they give grants to ultra-established professors. They called Stephen and said – perhaps there was something else he wanted to do with his life. They gave him a million dollars and he could do whatever he liked. He immediately called me. He said, 'I'm doing what I want to do with my life – but maybe it would be fun to watch you write a play.' And I said, 'No, Stephen, it wouldn't. You'd sit there next to my desk and watch my fingers moving on the keyboard. But it would be fun to write a play together. Isn't there some lost play of Shakespeare's you'd like to work on?' And he said, 'oh – *Cardenio*'. And I said, 'Let's write that together.' He said, 'ok'. The story was taken from Cervantes's *Don Quixote*. So we went back and looked at *Don Quixote*. Stephen said, 'I'll share the money with you.' But I told him, 'No, Stephen, I'm taken care of.' So he rented a farmhouse in Umbria, because a lot of Shakespeare's romantic comedies are set in Italy, and we went there with his wife and little boy. We would get up in the morning and talk and make notes. Then in the afternoon we got in the car and would drive all around. (One summer I went to Ellen Stewart's place in Umbria and did a playwriting workshop there.)

It was fabulous. We had a cook who would come each day, bring things to the table, and say things about dinner. Much of the play is dialogue that I took down verbatim. The authentic pieces of Shakespeare are in there as plays within the play. Stephen taught a course at Harvard that

year (2003) about how Shakespeare wrote his plays for
this project. I got to spend a year with Stephen having
a personal graduate tutorial on how Shakespeare wrote
his plays as we wrote *Cardenio* together. The main thing
he did with the money was to give it to people around
the world for them to do their adaptations of our play,
provided it was suitable for their country – it didn't have
to be faithful. Les Waters directed it at ART in Cambridge
(2008). He did a beautiful job. Honestly, I don't think
it is a very good play. Some people loved it. But I think
I'm a bad collaborator. Because I work with people I like,
anything Stephen said, we did, and anything I said, he said,
'ok'. In fact, in our collaboration we indulged each other
too much.

CR How was adapting Shakespeare different for you from
adapting the Greek plays?

CM I think I felt I was trying to be more faithful to
Shakespeare than I ever try to be with the Greeks. I never
think of being faithful to a Greek play. I just take – I steal
what I want, what I like, I use it wherever I want.

CR Why did you feel the need to be more faithful to
Shakespeare?

CM Because I was working with Stephen, and he was a
Shakespeare scholar.

CR Where did your interest in creating dance-theatre work
and in plays with movement come from?

CM It came from seeing Pina Bausch beginning in about 1985.
But, I think it also came from when I was a boy. I played
football, basketball, baseball; I ran track. Then I got polio
at the age of fourteen. So I couldn't do any of that again.
I think if I put it in a play, I get to do it vicariously. And
this way I get to do all kinds of stuff vicariously that I never
could have done – even if I hadn't gotten polio. It's total
pleasure to me. It's not just dancers that get to do what they

want to do. I get to tell them what I want them to do. And then they do something else.

CR We spoke of your work on *Orestes*, which in some ways came out of your response to the first Iraq War. Were there other events or phenomena, or encounters with significant figures during the first decade of the twenty-first century that spoke to you or inspired you to make art?

CM With *Orestes*, there are also bits of text from the Vietnam War era and bits of text – verbatim quotations from Nazi soldiers from World War II. So, in fact, the way I deal with war is not to do a docudrama on Iraq, but to take from whatever I want to do with whatever I want. A tremendous amount of stuff in *Iphigenia* was taken from soldiers' blogs who were in Iraq at that time. Until the Defense Department shut down that website, I stole a lot of that stuff. It would have been around 2006.

I think I'm hugely inspired by the lives of visual artists – I think I wish I had been a painter. I'm terrible. Awful. But I've written a short play about Picasso – it's not a great play, but it's based on an anecdote that informs my entire life. When he painted *Les Demoiselles d'Avignon* and had it in his studio, his friends would come over and he would show it to them and they would say, 'I think you should probably throw that away.' It was in his studio from 1907 or 1908 and it did not get into an exhibition until 1925. This work is generally recognized as the beginning of modern art. I'll do like Picasso. I'll write stuff that people will say, 'You really should throw that away.' But if I love it – I'm keeping it.

Lynn Nottage: Interview with Cindy Rosenthal, 19 June 2015

CR You and I met briefly in 2008 when you came to Hofstra University to do a reading and you shared with us materials from your script for *Ruined*, then in development. I still have my notes from your talk on that occasion and I'd like to begin our conversation with one of the statements you made then that struck me particularly. I'd be interested in hearing your thoughts now on whether this still resonates, as you look back on your work from the first decade of the twenty-first century. You said, 'The audience is my final collaborator.'

LN That statement was particularly resonant with *Ruined*. I was very interested in having an open conversation with audiences about issues affecting women in the Congo. When Kate Whoriskey and I decided to do a modern adaptation of *Mother Courage* and make a trip to Uganda to interview refugee women who were fleeing the conflict in the DRC, we discovered that women were telling these very brutal, very raw stories of being sexually exploited. For us it was a revelation. We had a translator with us who was from Amnesty International, and some of the stories that were heard were also a revelation to him as well. He was unaware of the extent to which rape was being used as a weapon of war. When I returned home and sat down to write the play, I knew that many people experiencing the work would be hearing the stories about the Congolese for the first time. It was fascinating that when we did a production of the play in Kinshasa, Congo, for a number of the women who were in the production, the stories were also a revelation. Kinshasa is in the western part of the country and the war I was writing about was in the eastern part. It seems that there was a blackout of information between the two sides of the country. The women in Kinshasa were really quite shocked to learn that women in their own country were being abused to that extent.

CR Do you remember the circumstances, how and why you and Kate determined that sticking closely to the framework for *Mother Courage* didn't fit as you had thought it would?

LN When we heard the stories that women were telling – stories that spoke specifically to sexual exploitation – this was an issue that I felt *Mother Courage* circled around.

The stories were so specific to the circumstances of the Congo and I knew after the second or third story that I wanted and needed to share the experiences of the women I had interviewed.

CR I remember reading that your earlier play, *Mud, River, Stone*, was based on a newspaper article that covered the specifics of a particular day-to-day situation – was there a moment, one event, or stimulus that made you and Kate decide to go to the Congo?

LN I've always had a fascination with that country. It's a beautiful country with a rich literary tradition. I was drawn there first because of the kind of mystique of the culture. I was subsequently drawn to the region because of articles that I read about the protracted war in the Congo, and I became curious about what was happening to the women and the children. There was an absence of information. So in a way it was the opposite – it was because of the absence of an article that I needed to go and explore. Because of the lack of documentation. The lack of coverage. There were statistics – numbers of people killed – but there were no stories about the specifics of who their people were. I think the coverage of Africa has become more sophisticated, and people in the United States are more interested and invested in what is happening on that continent now.

CR It seems that much of your work in the 1990s and beyond has been dealing with place, has been situated in relationship to specific places. You've also been concerned with the body – specifically women's bodies. I wonder if you see these concentrations, focal points, as being connected to language – to the way you employ language in your plays.

LN That's an interesting question. It brings to mind something I wanted to clarify. When we were in Uganda, speaking with women who were coming out of the Congo, I remember my reaction to one of the first women we encountered. I had such a strong visceral reaction to what she said. I literally felt my heart come up into my throat and choke me. I thought – this is so horrible, how will it be possible to convey this kind of horror onstage and have people sit in their seats and actively engage with the character? I spent a lot of time thinking about how to tell the story and what language to use. How best to convey the horror and also the incredible resilience of the women we experienced. In 2005 when I got the Guggenheim grant, I went back and listened to more stories. A year later, I traveled with Erik Ehn and a group of theatre artists to Rwanda for two–three weeks to look at how art could be used as a tool for healing. I wanted to explore the techniques that other artists were using to get people to open up, listen and to create dialogue about trauma. When I finally sat down to write *Ruined*, I was thinking about the ways that songs could be used to move along the more difficult exposition. I also knew we needed to offer people a moment to exhale between the more challenging passages in the play. We didn't want them turning off emotionally to the stories of the women.

CR I also remember how beautiful Sophie's songs were. They taught us something else about that character – how she was still able to be a sensual being and be connected to beauty in the world.

LN It was extraordinary to see people find the capacity to resurrect themselves and escape circumstances. And for Sophie, music was a refuge. It was the one place she could reclaim herself and experience the beauty of her own voice – in ways she couldn't do in her everyday life. That's why those songs are there and why she's an essential singer. We need to see that the spirit is not broken.

CR That makes me think of the character of Mayme in *Intimate Apparel*. She is also a musician and she also brings beauty and a different kind of entertainment and experience to the audience.

LN I think what's interesting about the character of Mayme and the female characters in *Ruined* is that they are all women who become the victims of circumstance. Mayme is a free-spirited woman at the turn of the twentieth century; she wanted to be a singer, a musician. For a woman like her, there aren't many opportunities, and she found herself having to compromise in order to do what she loved. Similarly in *Ruined*, the women are forced to do things that they wouldn't under ordinary circumstances.

CR Your plays – needless to say – are political plays and they make us see or re-view the issues with fresh eyes.

LN When I was a younger playwright, I felt I had a mission – I shy away from using that word now but I still feel one of my purposes as a writer is to look into the places where there is no light, to look at characters who have been marginalized and whose narratives have by and large not been woven into the mainstream narrative, or into the accepted American narrative. I'm really struck by absence and the absence of our stories and how important it is to tell these stories. Just the other day – in the church, in Charleston, where those nine people were shot to death – the majority of them were women. Those women's stories were not told. That young man didn't know who they were. But when you don't know someone's story, it's very easy not to understand their full complexity. Because the stories of people of color have not been put on the stage or on the screen, people forget the roles we have played in the building of the culture. And they come to the conclusion that we are really not part of that. It's easier to ignore people when you don't understand them.

CR As you were talking, I made a connection with Undine in *Fabulation* and the fact that she had to undergo a re-education – she had 'burned' the traces and erased her own family – and this was something she needed to recognize and eventually learn to come to different conclusions about. And yet, *Fabulation* is such a funny play – I laughed out loud reading it. I don't think people consider you a comic writer. But there's a lot of humor in your plays.

LN That's interesting – because I think I've written an equal number of comedies and dramas. Until recently I think theatres in New York were reluctant to put Black comedies on stage because folks didn't know how to laugh at them. We just did a benefit reading of *Fabulation* with an absolutely remarkable cast and it *was very* funny. I am surprised the play doesn't get done more now because it's definitely in conversation with our culture.

CR From all of your work, a take-away is your portraits of women – women with very distinct voices. I wondered if you can illuminate how your focus on the women's experiences in *Intimate Apparel*, and on that time period in that play, came to be?

LN *Intimate Apparel* was a very specific experience for me – and in many ways it marked a breakthrough for me as a writer. I wrote the play shortly after my mother died. When I sat down to write it, I said to myself – I'm going to write a play that is unabashedly old fashioned and emotional. I wanted to write something for my mother. First and foremost, as I was writing the play I was thinking of her. I thought of her friends in the audience – they are wonderful theatre-goers – and I wanted to write the play for them. And I wanted to write from an emotional place, from my heart; I wanted you – audiences – to feel the emotional honesty in the play and to feel the love I felt for my mother as I was writing it.

CR There is a refreshing, surprising quality of nakedness in the letters between the two lovers in the play. And the music plays very profoundly in the lyricism of the piece.

LN The music moves between a fast, syncopated rhythm to something slower, more introspective and much more fluid, and lyrical. The play was a breakthrough for me because I really thought about – what it is I wanted to write. I wrote *Intimate Apparel* and *Fabulation* at exactly the same time. *Fabulation* was a kind of escape for me from the emotion of *Intimate Apparel*. I tried to imagine what would happen to someone like Esther if she had been a fully empowered woman, if she had a different vocabulary, if she had been through the feminist movement. Who would she be? And so, I came up with a twisted version of Esther that became Undine.

CR I'd like to see Viola Davis take on Undine.

LN Anika Noni Rose just did a wonderful job with Undine in the reading. I see *Fabulation* as being about my generation in particular, educated African Americans who are struggling with identity. We are one step removed from my parents' generation, people who fought in the Civil Rights Movement and the feminist movement. We're trying to move away and to sculpt something new based on the foundation they provided. We're living in a different world. We're called the nexus generation, the bridge between blues and hip-hop. Blues is mournful, soulful music that really speaks of the pain of the African American spirit whereas hip-hop is the ultimate deconstruction, reflecting the many layers – pain, joy, confusion – trying to figure out who we are now. That's the vocabulary we're drawn to – *Fabulation* is faster and more frantic than *Intimate Apparel*. It responds to many different traditions. *Intimate Apparel* is more blues. More soulful. *Fabulation* is more hip-hop.

CR What were the seismic events for you in the 2000–9 decade?

LN 9/11, of course. I can't tell you, or point to how exactly that event had an impact on my playwriting, but I know that it did. I think I write from a place of insecurity or rage that I didn't have prior to that. It's embedded in the work. Another seminal event was the election of Barack Obama. We were in the midst of rehearsal for *Ruined*. We were in Chicago. I remember we were tech-ing the show and someone had the election results on their computer and was streaming them. And the results came in and Kate said, we can't rehearse – we have to go to the park. There's no way we can focus anymore. And so the entire cast – unified and joyful – marched down to the park for Obama's acceptance speech. There was that sense of power – I think – in the play as well. We were unified as an ensemble because of this extraordinary moment we shared together. A moment of triumph and possibility.

CR The end of the play also speaks to that hope.

LN That was the moment we were in, in America – there was a tremendous sense of optimism. A sense that we could transcend the horrors of the past; we could leave behind the financial meltdown. We could leave behind 9/11 and resurrect ourselves with this new person in the White House, a Black man. I do believe that some of that optimism is woven into *Ruined*. That was the premiere production of the play.

CR Besides Kate, is there someone else in the category of director, designer, actor, collaborator, or comrade, who you'd like to mention – as an important contributor to your work?

LN I want to mention Dan Sullivan, who nurtured the New York production of *Intimate Apparel*. I appreciate that he was such a surgical dramaturge; he really helped me isolate the play. I also think that watching Viola Davis play Esther, with such grace and natural perfection, was a gift to me as an artist. Understanding that the play is not just about what's said but also what is not said. Infusing the silent, still moments with life. I understood through her how to incorporate the pause onstage in much more complicated ways than I had been doing prior to that.

CR You're now a professor of playwriting at Columbia. Were you teaching there at the beginning of the decade we're focusing on?

LN Actually, I began teaching at Yale the day after 9/11. I remember thinking – oh my God, I have to get up there. I had to bike up to Grand Central Station. And then get on a train to New Haven and begin teaching for the very first time in my life. It was great, in fact, to have a destination

and a purpose at that moment. It made me know I had to
move forward. And my students had to move forward. I
think the way I began to teach has a lot to do with why I
continue to teach – I know a lot of people who were drawn
to work in television and film. But for me, at a moment of
great need teaching was there and it provided comfort and
solace. And I think in some ways it was the engine that
kept me going. It forced me to articulate my philosophy; it
forced me to engage with ideas. It forced me to think about
writing.

CR Many of your plays are centered in New York. Of
course the play you're working on now – about Reading,
Pennsylvania – is the opposite of New York.

LN It *is* the opposite! But I do plays that focus on the
de-Industrial Revolution, which began in the late 1980s and
came to a head in the first decade of the 2000s. We found
a middle class struggling because of lack of work. And the
closing of industrial sectors in the United States. My new
play *Sweat* begins in 2000 and ends in 2008. It looks at a
group of friends in 2000 and how the choices they make
impact the lives of their children.

CR When you wrote *Ruined*, were any of the monologues or
material in the dialogue of the play taken directly from your
interviews with the women?

LN No. All of it was fictionalized. The play was inspired
by the interviews but you would not recognize any of the
people we interviewed in the play. I remember looking back
on the names from the interviews after I had finished the
play, and there was a woman whose name was Josephine –
certain names had imprinted in my head.

CR In working on *Sweat* – did you meet with many people
too?

LN Yes! This process was incredibly invigorating and
inspiring and took me out of myself in ways that I

appreciated. When I decided to write *Sweat*, I didn't know the story I wanted to tell but I thought let me go outside myself and see what stories people had to share. I didn't want to make it up. I really wanted to know what was happening. It's been two years now, going to Reading, Pennsylvania, and speaking with a wide swath of people – including the mayor, the first African American mayor elected in that city. I spoke with activists, people who were running Greenmarkets, I spoke with the unemployed, drug addicts, correction officers, and police chiefs. We cast a very wide net and were completely open. I finally landed on a story about steelworkers because it really represented the de-Industrial Revolution of America and would speak to a wider audience. That said, I became very connected to the city and the city became connected to me. And we are going to build a performance installation in the city, which puts the city in conversation with itself.

CR Does this play interrogate race at all?

LN It most absolutely does. On the surface, you would not think it is a play about race but it is about class struggles, and I think you can't separate the conversation about race from the conversation about class. It's not about race with a capital 'R' but thematically it's there.

CR Would you say your current work and this project connects with your interest in Brecht at all?

LN Yes, I would say that. I'm interested in Brecht because he was an unabashedly political playwright and someone who actively sought to engage audiences and get them to think. I'm always drawn to that.

CR Any other playwright, living or not, that you'd like to give a shout-out to, who is an important influence on your work?

LN I'm always worried that in making a selection I'll be excluding someone. There are so many plays and playwrights that have been important to me. I feel like I'm inspired by the field.

CR Would you describe this current project as a kind of community-based theatre project on some level?

LN When I think of community-based theatre, I think of the work of the Cornerstone Theater Company. But I would describe this work, *Sweat*, as community-inspired theatre. Right now we're trying to figure out language to help describe the way we built this project. I would say it's theatre of inclusion.

CR Is the cast for *Sweat* a multicultural, diverse group?

LN Yes, the cast is diverse and multicultural: white, Black, and Latino, which is the demographic of Reading, Pennsylvania. Reading is predominately Latino, making up about 65 per cent of the population. We will be bringing the play to Washington, DC, in January 2016 and to New York City in Fall 2016, so you'll get to see it.

CR I wondered if you'd like to say anything about *Theatre for One*, which just finished here in New York City last week.

LN I was asked to participate in *Theatre for One* by Christine Jones. I first experienced *Theatre for One* a few years ago when I happened to be on Governor's Island. It was very intense and very intimate. Very scary. And it excited me. It's something you don't usually experience in theatre – it forces you to be incredibly alert as the audience. And it really is about an exchange of energy. And I was curious about what that does to the storytelling.

CR This brings us back to where we began – 'The audience is my final collaborator.' One last question: was there one award, of the many prestigious awards you've received, that meant the most to you?

LN I think it was the MacArthur – because I had no idea I was being tracked. And it came at a moment of absolute need. I still remember when I got that phone call. I was on the phone with a writer I was mentoring, Katori Hall. And I was saying to her, 'I'm looking at next year and I have nothing. I have no means to make a living. I don't know what I'm going to do. I'm going have to make some big decisions.' Then I heard a click and I asked her to hold on and I got this phone call from the MacArthur Foundation saying I'd won a very generous 'genius' Grant. And I thought, WOW. It was the right moment in my life, when I needed a dose of validation. It allowed me to be an artist. It allowed me to focus on playwriting, which is, of course, what I wanted and needed to do.

Who is it for?

Theresa Rebeck[1]

I did a play once, which had the audiences roaring with approval – laughing, gasping, shouting at the stage. The actors and the director and the producer and I were all pretty pleased with the way things were going. Tickets were flying out of the box office. By all observable evidence, we were A Hit.

Then the critics came and some of them didn't like it. No one could quite tell why. One of them called me a phony, which I took personally. I never met this person! Another critic thought I was trying to be David Mamet. Not to say Mamet hasn't influenced me; the guy has influenced everybody. But in what universe would Theresa Rebeck wish she were David Mamet?

Anyway, a few days after we opened, one of my producers called me at home and said, 'You know, I hope you take consolation in the fact that the audiences are still loving it.'

I said, 'That's the consolation? I thought that's who we were doing it for.'

And then she said, 'That's great, Theresa; you have such a great attitude.'

What follows are some marginally interesting facts about how plays and musicals are built:

You write a play. You get your friends who are good actors to come read it to you. You ask your agent to read it. You take it to theatres that are interested in producing new plays. They do some more readings. Someone maybe gives you a workshop, and you have some actors read it to you a lot for a week or so, while you rewrite it. This is called 'development'.

This whole process can take quite a bit of time.

Then someone says they will produce your play. There is no better day, honestly, than the one where an artistic director says, 'I will produce this play.'

Then you hire a director, and you cast the play, and you do more rewrites, and you go into rehearsal. And then previews start.

The idea of previews is that you continue to work on the play with the audience in the house, so you can find out what parts of the play are working, and what parts are not. If your play, for instance, is a comedy and no one is laughing, then you have to figure out how to get the audience to laugh. Or, if you're presenting a tragedy and they all start to laugh, that's a different problem.

Everybody works hard during previews. We rehearse, we rewrite, we reinvent moments, we ponder the nature of narrative. We also ponder the nature of audiences. Is this crowd too old? Too small? Too drunk? Usually they are just right when they are laughing in the places we want them to laugh, and quiet when we want them to be, and gasping and shouting and clapping and popping to their feet at the end. If, as it turns out, the audience is just right several nights in a row, we come to believe that this is in fact because of the work we are doing to get the play just right.

Then the critics come in and do whatever they want. Which of course we all know they are going to do, and we also all know that they are fierce in their determination that it is their duty to do that. We have all read, over the years, that the critics in fact distrust audience response. They are firm in their belief that the audiences that surround them during previews are plants, friends of the production, people who are exaggerating their perfect responses in some misguided attempt to mislead the critic into believing the play is better than it actually is.

Also, I am told, some critics believe that audiences are stupid, and need to be instructed on how to respond. So an audience that is laughing and crying in all the right places needs to have a critic explain to it, and to other potential audiences, why they are/would be wrong to do so.

In any event, here you have one of the many contradictions theatre artists contend with. We are told it is our goal to connect with our audiences, and we go so far as to include the audience as part of the process, working diligently to make sure the show is connecting with them during previews. Then it turns out that while it is nice if the audience likes your play, in fact that is the consolation prize.

Plays that work for the audience are often called *commercial* and *accessible*. These are words that have sinister connotations. During the nineteenth century when melodrama ruled, plays were commercial and accessible but the critics disdained, with reason, the paucity of character, dialogue and intellectual rigor, which went into those plays. Melodramas were good at many other things – epic scope, spectacle, swordfights, extending emotion through music, to name a few. Charles Dickens embraced the excesses of melodrama, transmuting them into dazzlingly performative prose. Silent movies, surrealism and German expressionism all were born from the melodramatic aesthetic. Robert Wilson, Peter Sellars, and in fact anyone who has restaged an opera in the last 100 years owes a debt to nineteenth century melodrama. But one hundred and fifty years after its heyday, 'melodrama' remains an insult. In the nineteenth-century, 'populist' had come to be understood as 'bad'. If a lot of people liked it? It was by definition not good.

This disagreement about what good theatre is, and what it should be doing, and who should be doing it, actually started in Shakespeare's time, and he was at the center of it. The university wits famously just didn't like him. No one knows how Shakespeare himself felt about being called an upstart crow but it is unlikely he took it as a compliment. There is little question that his upstart crow-ness was connected to the fact that he was the son of a glover. Perhaps he would have been forgiven those middle-class roots if he hadn't been quite so successful – the son of a glover is not meant to attract the attention of the aristocracy. Certainly it made the history of Shakespeare himself suspect; people have been trying to prove for hundreds of years now that the man himself could never have written those timeless plays. Only an Earl, or a Duke, or Queen Elizabeth herself, was noble enough to pull that off.

Melodrama is suspect; Shakespeare is suspect. Plays that lots of people like are suspect.

That suspicion is currently having its way with us. Dramaturgs and literary managers and all sorts of university wits are still informing us that theatre is not for the masses and that if the masses like it, it's by definition not very good. If a lot of people like it, it must be Disney. If people are laughing, it must be Neil Simon. Forget them; forget Dickens, and Shakespeare and Chekov, Oscar Wilde and Charlie Chaplin; forget George Cukor and Orson Welles and Preston Sturges and Alfred Hitchcock. In the current discussion, they would all be suspect.

And so those of us who have chosen completely to make a life in the theatre find ourselves drifting apart from each other, into weirder and weirder camps. In the development community, there is a sneering uncertainty which has risen up between artists who get their plays produced because there is some sense that audiences might actually like them, and those who get their plays developed but never moved into production because the plays are too elusive and producers are afraid that audiences just won't get it.

That uncertainty continues to spread. If you get your plays produced and audiences like them, you are commercial. You don't want to be commercial, even though god knows it helps pay the bills. I don't know any playwrights who want to be commercial. We want to be artists.

Artists, on the other hand, really would like to make a little money. It's true that they get more grants, but living off of grants is not actually a tenable life choice. More importantly, you don't write plays without ultimately wanting to see them produced. Plays do not realize their full identity in a desk drawer. Someone has to step forward and produce them.

Which no artistic director actually wants to do, if it appears that no one will come see them.

And so there is no end of resentment that all those commercial sell-outs are getting their plays produced.

At the same time, playwrights who actually get their plays done are anxious. Unless you're an art star, and there aren't very many of those, your legitimacy is always on the line. When I was a young person, going to see revivals of Tennessee Williams and Eugene O'Neill and Arthur Miller at Cincinnati Playhouse in the Park, those writers were like gods to me. There was nothing higher to aspire to being than a playwright. They were telling stories for the ages. And it was fun to go see their very accessible and terrifying and human plays.

I was an ambitious little soul; I wanted to be Arthur Miller, or Tennessee Williams or Chekov or Molière. Now it's hard to know who to want to be. Maybe Tom Stoppard. Or Tracy Letts! The critics like him and the audiences too. Oh, to be Tom Stoppard or Tracy Letts.

Well, the theatre has hit weirder times. After the Greeks invented it – when everyone was welcome, the slave, the common man, the senator, the priest – the whole thing simply evaporated, for all intents and purposes, for hundreds of years. Where did it go? One theory is that those Romans were too in love with the spectacle of gladiators hacking each other to death. Audiences stopped going to see beautiful, mysterious stories enacted for them, when their other option was blood and guts.

Cop shows, computer games, action movies – the lure of violence surely is entertaining to plenty of people. Do we really need *those people* to come see our plays?

It's such a worrisome way of thinking about storytelling. I personally worry about the rising tide of violence and can't help but wonder if a few lessons in empathy aren't exactly what are called for in a contemporary culture, which is increasingly fragmented by ever-narrower views of identity. I think back to those groundlings, crowding the pit while the aristocracy lounged in the stalls above, and it seems a wonder that the classes came together to watch Shakespeare's timeless brilliance enact itself for everyone. The next time people seemed to unite in the theatre was in the nineteenth century, when everyone flocked to those much-maligned melodramas. Those crowded theatres seem to answer that sad question: *Can't we all get along?* Apparently the answer is, yes we can, if there's a really good show that entertains and informs and thrills people of different classes and genders and races all at once.

It sounds, in my head, like a dirty little secret. But it does harken back to our instigators, those mighty Greeks. Who is it for? Everyone, everyone.

Theresa Rebeck: Interview with Cindy Rosenthal, 21 May 2015, New York City

CR I think of you as someone that has always written women who are strong, who talk back. I think of you as an advocate for women – in how you write women characters and in the viewpoints you express in your essays and plays. Would you say you write for women – that women are your ideal spectators?

TR I have to say, I think I imagine gender-neutral spectators. I am interested in the way theatre creates community. I think strong storytelling is what people are yearning for – and with a strong story, well-drawn characters, and interesting language and wit and compassion, you can reach people across age groups, and class and gender and race. I'm interested in inviting in as many people as possible; I believe in accessibility. I don't see theatre as an elitist art form; I love the way it can speak to large numbers of people at once, the way it creates community.

CR Can you elaborate on that? Sometimes people see the word 'accessible' as a pejorative.

TR Yes, that is an issue right now. And I regret it. I kind of feel that after a play, I want everyone in the audience to say, 'That was fantastic; I want to see another play.' A lot of people have a lot of nervousness around theatre that people like; there's a worry that 'accessible' means pandering, or too much commercialized spectacle. I worry, on the other hand, about elusive, hyper-intellectual theatre that leaves the audience mystified and feeling like theatre is smarter than them, and no fun. I see no reason why theatre shouldn't embrace a kind of storytelling, which is entertaining and moving and emotionally and intellectually probing all at once.

For instance, last night I saw a play that's very successful right now and it's sort of mocking itself. And it just didn't quite work, finally. It felt like they got caught up in the 'this is so funny – let's make it even funnier' approach. And seriously, if they had taken a more emotionally invested attack on the material, it would have been just as funny. For me, the goal is to leave the comedy floating and simultaneously leave a lot of blood on the floor.

CR Between 2000 and 2009, who were the directors, designers, actors you most wanted to collaborate with?

TR I think I'm an actors' writer. Actors are hungry for plays that allow them to do what they've been trained to do and want to do – find largeness of soul and create something complicated and funny. I've worked a lot with Julie White, Kristine Neilsen. I adore her. She's a genius. Brian Dykstra, Hamish Linklater, Reg Rogers. Christopher Evan Welch. Chris was a thrilling actor who passed away recently. All of them are really funny, very good with language, emotionally complex.

In terms of designers, Alexander Dodge is a set designer who did *The Understudy*. He's a crazy genius. I've started directing – I just did *All My Sons* (Arthur Miller) at the Alley in Houston. He did the set for that, which was stunning. I trust him utterly. His sets really explain the universe of my plays. Directors? I've worked with Michael Mayer a lot, Rebecca Taichman. Adrienne Campbell-Holt is my favorite person to work with right now. She is serious, deft, beautifully supportive of the actors. Great with design.

CR Can you talk about *The Understudy*? Have you used the construct of 'the play within the play' in your work before?

TR I hadn't tried that before, and I haven't since.

CR Where did you get the idea?

TR Oh I don't – people ask me that, you know, where do you get your ideas? And I think well, no one knows where any of it comes from – we don't know.

CR But Kafka flew in –

TR I do get obsessed with writers. I was obsessed with Dickens for a period of time and I remain obsessed with him. And I was obsessed with Kafka for quite a while. I read his diaries. My husband and I went to Prague one year and took the Kafka tour, which was hilarious. I had a lot of Kafka in my brain. I have family from the Czech Republic. His terror of being disempowered by culture – he was sensing the onrush of totalitarianism and fascism in Europe. I sometimes feel the same terror of the commercialism and the corporate theocracy in America. We feel very small in systems that are very large that don't give a shit about us. So that was all in my head and then at some point a play emerged. A play within a play, I guess.

CR The lack of women in theatre – women are not doing much better in New York, in theatre, in terms of employment and presence, than in Hollywood, that's for sure.

TR It's a very dangerous pattern, excluding women from the storytelling voices of the culture. It does feel like there's a crisis in storytelling right now. It worries me – how did we get here? Things have been better. They were better in 1912.
　I think it could have gone even further, but women have started to stand up and say this is active discrimination. I think that finally it is starting to embarrass the power structure. I don't understand this idea – that you only let in one woman every ten years. How did that become acceptable to my male colleagues? It's startling and worrisome. When things get that unbalanced too much, pressure gets put on the one woman in the room and there's a nervousness around it that's extraordinarily unhealthy. I saw *Peter and the Starcatcher* – eleven boys and one girl. I confess I didn't enjoy it as much as other people did because I kept thinking, how long will it take before they kill her and eat her?
　I don't know. I think that when the numbers are so dysfunctional, it becomes clear that the best work isn't getting done. That's true in TV, film and the theatre. It's not just that so many women's voices are being excluded.

There's a kind of cronyism that creeps in and the system becomes about holding that cronyism in place.

CR Do you feel more hopeful now than in the decade we're concerned about in this volume – 2000–9?

TR There has been some movement but way too little. When it became clear that writers of color were being excluded from the conversation, everyone rightly stood up and said we cannot tolerate that. Many programs were put in place to support Hispanic and African American writers. So, when women said – we're half the human race, we're more than half the audience, instead of hearing – you know, the girls are right, we should be inviting them in, this is an exciting moment – they didn't do that. There was pushback.

CR Can you say how completing a PhD focused on Victorian melodrama has impacted your playwriting?

TR I became really fascinated by the question of elitism vs. populism in the theatre while I was working on my dissertation about nineteenth-century melodrama. Many of the plays of the nineteenth century are fascinating. The psychology and the language are somewhat depleted compared with what came next – but there's a great epic energy in the storytelling, and beautiful, weird expressionistic elements in the stagecraft. It was in many ways a golden age for the theatre; audiences weren't shrinking then as they are now; people went to the theatre every night of the week. People of all classes came together, and got different things out of it.

CR You've written about the phenomenon that many theatres are only interested in the brand-new play, the never-produced-anywhere-else play. What is that about?

TR I've asked some people who run the theatres that do new plays what that's about and several people actually told me it's about the Pulitzer. People think that there's always a possibility that a brand-new play could win a Pulitzer Prize. If that play ends up winning a Pulitzer, then the theatre where it is first produced gets to have its name on it. I thought that was pretty weird, but seriously I heard that from several people. There's also the feeling that it's easier to get funding for a first production of a new play. I think that grant writers and funders should start looking into ways to support the second and third productions of contemporary plays. That's where the play finds itself, usually.

CR Can you talk about *Omnium Gatherum*? I saw it at the Variety Arts Theatre in 2003. I was stunned by it – for me it was the first play that spoke intensely, appropriately, powerfully to the post 9/11 moment. And it was incredibly funny. How did that play – your first collaborative work – come about?

TR I live in New York, and I was here on 9/11 and I was on the phone with my friend Alexandra Gersten when it happened. Just after the first plane hit, the news media kept calling it 'an apparent accident'. I remember thinking – this is no accident! Alex's husband flew planes and he was watching as well, and he said there's no way that's an accident – the airspace around the towers is completely off limits to smaller planes. And no small plane would make a hole like that. Then the phones all went out, and we couldn't talk for days. By the time we did talk again, both of us were thinking about writing about this terrible crisis.

There were a lot of people who had a different reaction. I went to a meeting at New Dramatists and listened to a lot of people express the concern that theatre was irrelevant now. But Alex and I both were on a different track. I had never written a play with another person before, but there was a strong feeling as we were living through that time that you didn't want to be alone; you really did want to be with people. While we were struggling with how to respond, the natural response seemed to be – do this with someone. We needed to be in the room together, talking about it.

CR It is a play that is stylistically very different from other work you've done. Not real/realism but surreal/surrealism. And absurdism. I remember it terrified me too – not unlike the event itself.

TR There is Theresa Rebeck as a writer and Alexandra Gersten as a writer and then there was the two of us together. A different entity.

CR When you look back on the piece – do you think of it as reflecting a particular moment in time – that particular moment in time? Is it relevant to, resonant with today?

TR I just recently thought of it – and said to myself – we've got to get this piece revived. I think it is still frighteningly accurate. When we did it at the Actors Theatre of Louisville Humana Festival, it was the night George Bush declared war on Iraq. People were standing in the aisles sobbing. This is what we were talking about. Don't do this. We have to stop right now. I remember when Alex and I were writing it and the US was invading Afghanistan, there was no stopping that. It was going to happen. But the play does argue for a halt to reactivity and it's an important argument. I was just in London, while Parliament was voting to go drop bombs on Syria in response to the attack on Paris,[2] and everyone was making the same arguments, don't do this, don't keep the madness spinning forward. This is fifteen years later.

CR Can we talk about *Mauritius* for a moment? Where did the focus on stamp collecting come from?

TR I've always been fascinated and intrigued by valuable objects in general. I was interested, at one time, in writing a play about expensive bottles of wine. I'm dead curious about what it means to drink a glass of wine that costs tens of thousands of dollars. I may actually do that someday. So I had started thinking about objects that have crazy financial value attached to them.

I had been trolling around the Internet and came across these two very expensive stamps. I was thinking about them and became interested in the mind of the collector. I also became interested in how many different ways the stamps could be identified as valuable. Everyone in the play has a different angle on what the stamps mean.

CR What have you learned – working in Hollywood – that has had an impact on your playwriting?

TR I think there's a forward motion in writing for television that becomes a useful thing to know how to do. Sometimes they dial it up too hard in TV, but at the same time I'd have to say it's important to know how fast you can accomplish things if you need too; it's an interesting tool in your toolkit.

I also think it's important to write a lot and in television you write a lot. Film and theatre have a terribly different pace. There's something almost journalistic about television – like writing for a magazine or a newspaper.

There's also a serious need to finish things. A lot of writers have a neurosis about not wanting to finish things. I am the opposite. I am terribly anxious until I finish a draft. Then, of course, you can rewrite and I do; I rewrite a lot. But until I have a finished first draft I feel like I have nothing.

CR With your playwriting, do you feel as if the world you are reflecting is a New York City milieu – a US milieu – or something more global?

TR Oh, I don't know. My work is produced in a lot of countries now and that is obviously something I am grateful for – that my work reaches people on an international level.

CR Are you ever nervous about writing across racial lines? This is something that many people in the theatrical community are concerned about now.

TR Oh, I know that's true, that people are shredding that question. I feel that there is urgency behind the debate but I'm not sure I agree with the essence of the concern. I worry that we are all so focused on issues of individual identity that we've lost sight of the larger question, which is how does theatre create community?

A few years ago, I wrote a play that had a couple of African American characters in it and a lot of people said to me, how do you give yourself permission to write African American voices? In television you're never asked that question – they never ask you to justify how you write an African American, an Asian American, a Mexican American. At the same time the executives and the show runners have gotten strangely fixated on having women writers write the 'character stuff' and the 'female characters' while the male writers are on the 'harder stuff' like 'action'. It sounds idiotic to me when these issues come up in television around gender, because of course in the theatre we write both men and women and no one makes a fuss about it. When you think of it that way, it starts to sound weird, in general, that anyone would insinuate that a playwright can't possibly inhabit the consciousness of a person of another race. Tennessee Williams was never asked how he justified writing women.

Overall I would have to say that I identify as an American writer. I feel responsibility to write as an American.

CR Is there anything else you'd like to say about something that happened during the decade we are focusing on – the years between 2000 and 2009 – that had an impact on you and on your playwriting?

TR I grew up in Ohio with the understanding that I was equal to others in this country – I am a democrat with a little d. It is alarming to me that more and more we seem to be drifting away from that essential understanding, in America. What happened on Wall Street and the way the country was almost dismantled by people with tremendous money and privilege behaving like criminals? The rise of the power of the one percent? All of this is not what America was, when I was growing up.

In 2000, I was enormously disturbed when Bush the second stole the presidential election. I have relatives who are Republicans and were delighted when people in Florida were shut out of the system, during that process – one of my cousins was actually laughing at the little old ladies and the nonsense about the hanging chads. He was gloating that the election had been stolen! I'll never forget the fight we had. Because Republicans and Democrats can't be expected to agree about much, but one person one vote is not a liberal position – it is the basis of a democracy.

And then when Al Gore came out and told everyone not to flip out, it was so disheartening. I had friends all over the world who said to me, 'Why aren't you all marching? What your Supreme Court has done is equivalent to a coup!'

I think we were all just hoping that the country would stabilize after we got through all that, but I don't think we ever recovered. Everything just kept spinning out of control from that moment. I think the disastrous decision to invade Iraq, which was perpetrated by the Bush presidency, is the source of so much ongoing tragedy. It's hard to see where it will end.

But more and more our country is run as a monarchy, a corporate monarchy. That realization is deeply terrifying to me and is where much of my work comes from.

Sarah Ruhl: Interview with Cindy Rosenthal, 10 June 2015, New York City

CR Your plays are about the relational element in important ways – and are based on a deep emotional core. In other published interviews, you've said that you come to this emotional place differently from other playwrights. Would you like to comment further on that?

SR Yes. The other night, at Theatre for a New Audience, we were talking about how subtext has become a stand-in for the unsaid. There is a category of being and emotion that has to do with the unsaid, which is an older, more ancient concept than subtext. It has to do with restraint and empty space as opposed to secret, hidden meaning. The actors I really respond to are able to find emotion in those reservoirs but also by connecting immediately with the language, rather than providing a more innate psychological arc.

CR I appreciate that. It's not about creating a biographical backstory. It's about being there – in the moment, with the language – and letting it happen. You've talked about the kind of collaboration that happens between a playwright, the director and actors in a room, but you've also spoken about the aspect of a playwright's work that is not collaborative. Could you speak to that distinction in terms of the three plays we are focusing on for this volume – *Eurydice*, *The Clean House*, and *the vibrator play*?

I didn't agree at all, by the way, with Charles Isherwood's [*New York Times*'s critic] review of *The Oldest Boy*. I didn't feel that the piece was realistic or naturalistic at all – you took us on a very surprising, theatrical journey.

SR I don't read reviews because it makes me feel incapable of writing the next play. But I do get the lay of the land from other people – my mother and my husband – and I did hear that he described the play as naturalistic and I was so surprised. There was a puppet and it was about reincarnation and consciousness – and I thought, 'Well, if naturalism has been pushed so far that it includes a puppet in a living room – that's just great.'

CR In the decade that is the focus of our book, 2000–9, there were critics that associated your play *Eurydice* with 9/11 and assumed that the play is a response to 9/11. Does that hold true for you?

SR I have to think about whether that is possible – in terms of when I wrote it. Actually, I wrote it before 9/11. I wrote it in 2000. It took a while to finish. It was a play about loss, but it was more about a personal family loss. My father's death. It may have coincided with a larger cultural loss. But technically speaking, I didn't write it from that place.

Scott Bradley, the designer, dreamed that design. He dreamed that there was a wall of letters, and an

upside-down world. Those elements of the production
spoke to a sense of 9/11 – perhaps in an unconscious way.
Eurydice is a myth I've always been preoccupied with. This
kind of myth bears the weight of all of us.

CR Are there other designers, actors, directors who are 'your
people' in this way?

SR With *Eurydice* and *the vibrator play* I got to work with Les
Waters, who I love and I'm working with again now. Les
Waters commissioned *the vibrator play* on the day *Eurydice*
opened, before the reviews came out. What I love about Les
is that he's so deliberate and specific about language and
about silence and empty space. He told me once that he
learned from Caryl Churchill never to talk about a play. So
it's interesting that the collaboration is not about talking;
we don't cognitively dissect what we're doing – it's more
unspoken. Another thing I love about Les is that he is a
watcher of actors – I feel that actors respond to his gaze,
but often there is nothing said. Later on in the process he
gets specific. I love his visual sense. He also has a great
musical sense.
   I worked with Bill Rauch on *The Clean House*. I adore
Bill. His whole life is about relation, about a love for the
community, about engaging the audiences in a different way.
His work with the Cornerstone Theater is so important. I
worked with Jessica Thebus in Chicago – I've known her
my whole life – Jess did a beautiful production of *The Clean
House* at the Goodman. I've managed to work regionally
– I also worked with Blanka Zizka at the Wilma in
Philadelphia; at the Wilma they did all three of these plays.

CR You obviously have a very strong relationship with
regional theatres. Do you feel you are stretching regional
theatre audiences with your plays, or is the stretching
happening the other way around?

SR Sadly, I think it is the other way – New York has become
so economically conservative but the regional theatres are
stretching New York and New York is not even aware of

it. New play development that happens outside New York is much more radical and that's the only way you can bring radical theatre into New York. Well, not the only way. Places like Soho Rep are doing ground-breaking work all the time. But it's very hard to do challenging work in New York that hasn't already had a good review in the *New York Times*.

CR Do you travel a lot?

SR I used to – but I've really stopped now that I have three kids. My twins are five now and my big girl is nine. Motherhood happened right in the middle of that decade.

CR Would you consider your work autobiographical?

SR I think all artists work that way, to a degree. One reason I stopped writing poetry is because I didn't like the confessional mode. What appeals to me about playwriting is that you are always already yourself, but you can stretch in terms of gender, in terms of age, ethnicity. Sometimes I want to go back to poetry – I did make a little book of poetry for my husband for our anniversary, a little thin volume and I letter-pressed it and I had a hundred copies made. Part of the gift to him was giving it to other people because he thinks I'm way too secretive about my poetry.

CR Does your current project, the play based on letters between Elizabeth Bishop and Robert Lowell, feel like it is combining these two worlds for you?

SR Yes. I feel I am such a supplicant to Bishop. I think she is so amazing. The quality of restraint and the unsaid. Her work is so beautiful. The back and forth between Lowell who was so confessional and Bishop who was so private and so metaphorical really appealed to me. It was a way of listening in to their conversation.

CR *Melancholy Play* has recently been set to music. Can you talk about your interest in music? Is it connected to your interest in poetry?

SR I think it must be – the way that language is rhythmic and can do more things than reflect reality. So when language is musicalized, it does a completely different thing than just sit there on a page. I love working with composers. I loved working with Todd Almond.

CR Are you pleased with the new musical version of *The Melancholy Play* at Trinity Rep?

SR Yes. I love that company and their performances and that play is looking at emotion in a very specific way and music helps so much. Music can support you and leap over certain logical steps that people can get mired in otherwise as spectators.

CR Where did the idea to make the piano so integral to *the vibrator play* come from?

SR I think because in the nineteenth century you didn't have piped-in music – you had a piano and someone played it. There was something for me about the human range of an instrument and the way it could reach a number of people – and how for Mrs Daldry it was an expression of what she could not otherwise do or say.

CR Can we go back again to the decade that is the subject of our book? Were there any seismic events, in your personal life or elsewhere, that had a significant impact on you?

SR In 2000–9 I got married, I had a child, I moved to New York, and my plays started getting produced. It was a period of incredible movement and change from the solitude of writing alone to working with people a lot. I was enraged politically at the beginning of the 2000s. Just enraged. A lot of the time. I completed the third part of *Passion Play* at that time. I am really interested in politics but it doesn't always come out in the writing. *Passion Play* was one way to address culturally and politically what was going on. I felt like we were living under a presidency that was not earned; Bush was not elected by the popular vote – it was

a Supreme Court decision and his brother in the state of
Florida contributed to the outcome. I felt as if the war was a
trumped-up, Oedipal drama. I was just enraged.

I feel as if Barack Obama has restored some semblance
of decency to the country. I'm working on a piece now
with Mark Wing Davey who is a collaborator and dear
friend. He does a 'Joint Stock' process with NYU students.
He spends two weeks with the graduate acting students;
they do research, talk, improvise. We're working on a play
about the whipping boys in the courts of Charles I and II
– these whipping boys would be elevated to a dukedom or
earldom later on in life. I'm looking at that period and also
at Jeb and George Bush on the eve of the election in Florida
and Texas. I'm looking at sibling rivalry and monarchical
succession. It's been really interesting.

I wish it would write itself. It seems so easy when the
actors are doing all the work. Mark had used this model
with Caryl Churchill when they developed *Mad Forest*,
which was a response to the Romanian Revolution. It's a
wonderful model.

CR Are there people we haven't mentioned yet who you have
collaborated with, or those you would like to work with or
who you see as co-travelers?

SR I should mention Rebecca Taichman who I adore and work
with over and over. Someone I haven't worked with yet but
who I think is a co-traveler is Anne Washburn, especially in
terms of what she is doing with language. I love watching
Branden Jacobs-Jenkins's work – *An Octoroon* is really
extraordinary – the way he creates a sense of event, the
way he engages the audience, the way he deals with the
contemporary, with history, with the personal. You have
no idea what is going to happen and then a bunny walks
on stage and you are overjoyed. He redirects you into the
moment. That is something I try to do and that I also love
in fiction. It feels as if theatre was doing that in the 1960s
and 1970s but then there was the tyranny of realism for
a while. I think we're finally leaping out of that. And Lisa
Kron – with *Fun Home* – I admire her so much.

CR The other playwrights in our book are Chuck Mee, Theresa Rebeck and Lynn Nottage.

SR Chuck Mee is like a fairy godfather to me, a huge influence. He gave *Eurydice* to Les Waters. I'm friends with his children – his daughters have been in my plays; his ex-wife is one of my best friends. Funnily enough, Lynn, Theresa, and I were on the cover of *American Theatre* magazine during the decade we are discussing – I was pregnant with Anna and I don't think I knew I was pregnant. But I was really cranky about having my picture taken. I remember the photographer kept saying, 'It's women, so you should show more skin. Let's have your arms show.' I think this was 2005. I remember we were all on the cover because we were heavily produced that year.

CR You have won some significant awards. What have they meant to you? The MacArthur Grant, which you won in 2006 ...

SR The MacArthur Grant means everything – because, unlike the Pulitzer, they pay you money to do your work. It's amazing. It allowed me to have a babysitter so I could continue writing. It allowed me to say no to commercial projects when they came along. I had a responsibility to do the work that was important to me. I had been given this enormous gift.

CR All of the playwrights in this volume actually write about theatre – as theatre. Do you have any thoughts on why/ how you do that? You did it in *Stage Kiss*, which is more recent, outside the bounds of 2000–9.

SR I think the fun thing about writing about theatre when you are in theatre is that you are writing from and about your life. But it's also a wonderful metaphor – for the world of illusion and fantasy. So you can toggle back and forth between the texture of ordinariness where we all live and the images we are representing – it goes back to Plato's cave and connects to Shakespeare's plays. There is a reason why the metaphor of theatre has been used by philosophers all through history.

I'm working on a play now called *For Peter Pan on Her 70th Birthday*. It's for my mom. Peter Pan is interesting – an icon for the twenty-first century. The play is about five siblings in their seventies watching their father die. And they each take on a role from Peter Pan and fly up to Never Never Land.

CR Something that you write about – that I appreciate so much and that is important to many women – is 'help'.

SR I'm laughing because I just don't get it – I don't know how you write and have children and not have help. Some people do. But I don't know how I could with three kids. And yet I grew up with this very Midwestern sense that you should do everything yourself. That you shouldn't rely on other people. That conflict was really imperiling. When I had twins, I just gave over. I do think the phrase that Hillary Clinton quotes – 'It takes a village' – is true and we've gotten mired in the bizarre idea of the nuclear family that emerged in the 1950s and it threatens to make a woman choose between home and work in this obscene way. I don't know what to say about it.

CR Do you feel that the challenges – of managing your life as a mother and an artist – have changed the form of your playwriting? Did you turn to writing the '100 essays' – the collection of brief essays you published – during that period of your life for this reason?

SR In retrospect, I think I wrote the essays as a form of survival – to keep the writing alive when I couldn't write a play. When the kids were old enough, I began writing plays again and stopped writing in the essay form. I still write an essay every once in a while.

CR My co-editor Julia Listengarten told me she loved directing your play *Eurydice*. She describes your work as both abstract and visceral and feels that the imagery and poetry in your plays coalesce in unique ways. She also observed that it sometimes seems as if your plays are meant to be read, rather than staged. Do you have a response to that?

SR I purposely make my plays more readerly on the page than we tend to perceive plays. I don't think it means they are meant to be read rather than staged, but since I started writing in other forms, like poetry and essays, I wanted there to be the possibility of a private readership for the plays, as opposed to having just a public relationship to the work. And I appreciate how things look on a page. Plays are hard to read – they are sort of scrunched and stage directions are in capital letters or parentheses. So I tried to lay the plays out in a way that would make a reader feel a more private response to them.

CR Do dreams or dream imagery have an impact on your work?

SR Occasionally. Nilo Cruz was a teacher of mine and he said he needs to have a couch or bed near his desk so that he can easily fall asleep and wake up and write again. I love a nap. But I do think when you are really inside a play it does make you a little sleepy. And I do think when you are really inside a play it seems as if you didn't write it. Hopefully it feels as if the characters are writing you. Whether you call it the collective unconscious or God or the primordial sludge – whether dreaming it, sleeping it – you have to get out of the way of the sludge.

CR To me your plays feel very spiritual. Does your Buddhist practice have an impact on your playwriting?

SR It's interesting. I was raised Catholic. My first play was *Passion Play*, which is dealing with that inheritance. I didn't get confirmed because I had problems with the church. I was really interested in literature and art as a religious practice and not in institutional religion. When I wrote *The Oldest Boy*, I was not a Buddhist, I was just interested in Buddhism. I read so much during the course of researching

that play that after I wrote it I went to a teaching by this
amazing western woman – who had done a retreat in a cave
in the Himalayas for a few years – and she was offering
refuge at the end of the teaching and I thought – when will
I have another opportunity like this? So I took refuge with
her. But I am just at the very very beginning.

CR Does your father's passing always come forward when you
write about death? Is that the primary loss that figures, that
still comes up for you?

SR Yes. I think loss is like one of those clown cars in the
circus. When someone new dies, all the clowns come
out of the car. It's funny; after my friend David Adjmi, a
playwright, saw *The Oldest Boy*, he said – it's all about
your father. That was very insightful. My father's death
struck me at a time in my life when it was really hard going.
I was just becoming a grown-up. He left too early. I do feel
like I'm a different person now. There was a period in my
plays where I was not writing about death, where there was
no afterlife. *Stage Kiss* is one, *the vibrator play* is another.
Although a child has died in that play, off stage.

I think that theatre is a place of ghosts – I love Japanese
Noh Dramas and the notion that theatre is a structure that
reckons with ghosts. I think we are afraid of that structure
in our secular culture.

CR There is something uncanny about your plays, being a
spectator of them. The tears just come. They don't announce
themselves. They just start to flow – boom – they're there.
In the experience of your plays, tears hit like a wave that
you don't see coming.

SR As a playwright, the one thing you can't do with your
plays is come in as an audience member and experience
them that way.

CR I love the wit and the humour in *The Clean House* –
there's such a lovely quality to the humour in that play. Do
you like to tell jokes? Are you a good joke teller?

SR No. Not really. I grew up in a family that liked telling jokes. My father loved telling jokes and he was very witty. My mother is hilarious and has a great sense of the absurd and irony.

CR You know – in reading and seeing and experiencing your plays – I was certain you were Jewish. There is something very *haimisha* going on.

SR I think I was – in another life. If I had married a Jewish man I would have converted. But as it was – I married a half-Thai, half-Australian man instead.

NOTES

1 Introduction: Living in the 2000s

1. Hannah Fischer, *A Guide to U.S. Military Casualty Statistics: Operation New Dawn, Operation Iraqi Freedom, and Operation Enduring Freedom* (Washington, DC: Congressional Research Service, 2014), https://www.hsdl.org/?view&did=750720 (accessed 2 July 2015).
2. Thomas L. Friedman, *The World Is Flat: A Brief History of the Twenty-First Century*, expanded edn (New York: Picador/Farrar, Straus and Giroux, 2007).
3. Chris Gaither and Dawn C. Chmielewski, 'Fears of Dot-Com Crash, Version 2.0', *Los Angeles Times*, 14 July 2005, http://articles.latimes.com/2006/jul/16/business/fi-overheat16 (accessed 20 March 2015).
4. 'The Impact of the September 2008 Economic Collapse', PEW Charitable Trusts, 28 April 2010, http://www.pewtrusts.org/en/research-and-analysis/reports/2010/04/28/the-impact-of-the-september-2008-economic-collapse (accessed 20 March 2015).
5. National Center for Education Statistics, http://nces.ed.gov/pubs2013/2013309.pdf (accessed 12 February 2015).
6. Linda A. Jacobsen and Mark Mather, 'U.S. Economic and Social Trends Since 2000', *Population Bulletin* 65 (1) (2010), http://www.prb.org/Publications/Reports/2010/useconomicsocialtrends.aspx (accessed 12 February 2015).
7. Michael Planty and Jennifer L. Truman, 'Firearm Violence, 1993–2011', US Department of Justice (Bureau of Justice Statistics), May 2013, www.bjs.gov/content/pub/pdf/fv9311.pdf (accessed 25 February 2015).
8. 'Gender Inequality and Women in the US Labor Force', International Labour Organization, http://www.ilo.org/washington/

areas/gender-equality-in-the-workplace/WCMS_159496/lang--en/index.htm (accessed 27 February 2015).

9. 'Women's Employment During the Recovery', Department of Labor Special Reports, http://www.dol.gov/_sec/media/reports/femalelaborforce/ (accessed 27 February 2015).

10. Jacobsen and Mather, 'U.S. Economic and Social Trends Since 2000'.

11. Andrea Elliott, 'After 9/11, Arab-Americans Fear Police Acts, Study Finds', *New York Times*, 12 June 2006, http://www.nytimes.com/2006/06/12/us/12arabs.html?pagewanted=all&_r=0 (accessed 25 March 2015).

12. See Michael A. Turner, *Historical Dictionary of the United States Intelligence* (Lanham, MD: Rowman & Littlefield, 2014), 123.

13. *The National Security Strategy,* National Security Council, September 2002, http://georgewbush-whitehouse.archives.gov/nsc/nss/2002/index.html (accessed 3 July 2015).

14. 'President Discusses Beginning of Operation Iraqi Freedom', President's Radio Address, 22 March 2003, http://georgewbush-whitehouse.archives.gov/nsc/nss/2002/index.html (accessed 20 June 2015).

15. For more information on Tax Legislation, 2000–9, see http://www.taxpolicycenter.org/legislation/2000.cfm#health06 (accessed 20 June 2015).

16. See http://americasbesthistory.com/abhtimeline2000.html for more detailed information that includes events not directly related to US politics (accessed 20 June 2015).

17. 'National Marriage and Divorce Trends', Centers for Disease Control and Prevention, http://www.cdc.gov/nchs/nvss/marriage_divorce_tables.htm (accessed 5 February 2015).

18. 'NCHS Data Brief', Centers for Disease Control and Prevention, http://www.cdc.gov/nchs/data/databriefs/db136.htm (accessed 10 February 2015).

19. Elizabeth Arias, 'United States Life Tables, 2009', *National Vital Statistics Report* 62 (7) (2014), http://www.cdc.gov/nchs/data/nvsr/nvsr62/nvsr62_07.pdf (accessed 12 February 2015).

20. See Tim Footman, *The Noughties: A Decade that Changed the World, 2000–2009* (Richmond: Crimson, 2009), 97–110.

21. See 'Consumer Expenditures in 2008', US Department of Labor, http://www.bls.gov/opub/reports/cex/consumer_expenditures2008.pdf (accessed 4 January 2016).

22   Jacobsen and Mather, 'U.S. Economic and Social Trends Since 2000'.
23   Ibid.
24   See 'Addressing Prescription Drug Abuse in the United States', Centers for Disease Control and Prevention, http://www.cdc.gov/drugoverdose/pdf/hhs_prescription_drug_abuse_report_09.2013.pdf (accessed 20 June 2015).
25   See Megan Voeller, 'The Top Ten Phenomena in Visual Art in 2000–2009', *CL Tampa Bay*, 30 December 2009, http://cltampa.com/dailyloaf/archives/2009/12/30/the-top-10-phenomena-in-visual-art-in-2000-2009#.VN0dKShiFJB (accessed 2 July 2015).
26   Kinsey Lane Sullivan, '14 Incredible Works That Have Redefined Art in the 21st Century', *Arts.Mic*, 17 June 2014, http://mic.com/articles/90529/14-incredible-works-that-have-redefined-art-in-the-21st-century' (accessed 2 January 2016).
27   '10 Years of Primetime: The Rise of Reality and Sports Programming', Media and Entertainment (Nielsen), 21 September 2011, http://www.nielsen.com/us/en/insights/news/2011/10-years-of-primetime-the-rise-of-reality-and-sports-programming.html (accessed 1 July 2015).
28   'Internet Now Major Source of Campaign News', Pew Research Center, 31 October 2008, http://www.people-press.org/2008/10/31/internet-now-major-source-of-campaign-news/ (accessed 2 July 2015).
29   See *The Complete Guide to Social Media*, https://rucreativebloggingfa13.files.wordpress.com/2013/09/completeguidetosocialmedia.pdf (accessed 2 July 2015). See also Andreas M. Kaplan and Michael Haenlein, 'Users of the World, Unite! The Challenges and Opportunities of Social Media', *Business Horizons* 53 (1) (2010): 59–68.
30   Ibid.
31   Lev Grossman, 'You – Yes, You – Are TIME's Person of the Year', *Time*, 25 December 2006, http://content.time.com/time/magazine/article/0,9171,1570810,00.html (accessed 3 July 2015).

2 Theatre in the 2000s

1   Theatre Communication Group is the national organization of American theatre that was founded in 1961 to foster professional not-for-profit theatre in the US.

2   Ben Cameron, 'Mapping a New Landscape', *American Theatre*, January 2000, https://www.tcg.org/publications/at/2000/landscape.cfm (accessed 1 April 2015).

3   Celia Wren, 'Dissolving the Barriers', *American Theatre*, July/August 2011, http://www.tcg.org/publications/at/julyaugust11/fieldco.cfm (accessed 1 April 2015).

4   *The TriBeCa Playhouse Stage-Door Canteen* received the Special 2002 Drama Award.

5   Trav S. D., '9/11: America's Theatres Respond', *American Theatre*, November 2001, https://www.tcg.org/publications/at/2001/events.cfm (accessed 10 April 2015).

6   Stephen Holden, 'Reno: Rebel Without a Pause', *New York Times*, 2 May 2003, http://www.nytimes.com/2003/05/02/movies/film-in-review-reno-rebel-without-a-pause.html (accessed 10 April 2015).

7   Ibid.

8   Michael Billington, 'The Guys', *Guardian*, 16 May 2002, http://www.theguardian.com/stage/2002/aug/16/theatre.artsfeatures (accessed 10 April 2015).

9   Marvin Carlson, '9/11, Afghanistan, and Iraq: The Response of the New York Theatre', *Theatre Survey* 45 (1) (2004): 3–17.

10 Lawrence Van Gelder, '"Our Town," Mass Nudity and Other Bedfellows', *New York Times*, 14 March 2002, http://www.nytimes.com/2002/03/14/theater/theater-review-our-town-mass-nudity-and-other-bedfellows.html (accessed 12 April 2015).

11 Alisa Solomon, 'When We Dread Awaken', *Village Voice*, 12 November 2001, http://www.villagevoice.com/2002-11-12/theater/when-we-dread-awaken/ (accessed 12 April 2015).

12 Ben Brantley, 'Yes, He Survived Sept. 11, but What's in It for Him?' *New York Times*, 19 December 2002, http://www.nytimes.com/2002/12/19/theater/theater-review-yes-he-survived-sept-11-but-what-s-in-it-for-him.html (accessed 12 April 2015).

13 See James Harding, *The Ghosts of the Avant-Garde(s): Exorcising Experimental Theater and Performance* (Ann Arbor: University of Michigan Press, 2013), 186.

14 Lenora Inez Brown, 'The View from Here: 11 Artists Talk About the Challenge of Putting 9/11 on Stage', *American Theatre*, September 2002, http://www.tcg.org/publications/at/2002/view.cfm (accessed 12 April 2015).

15 Christopher Rawson, 'The Arts Respond: Theater Faces Brave New World with New Works, Classics', *Post-Gazette*, 8 September

2002, http://old.post-gazette.com/ae/20020908drama0908fnp5.asp (accessed 20 April 2015).
16   Ibid.
17   Brown, 'The View from Here'.
18   Ibid.
19   See Dorothy Chansky's chapter on Theresa Rebeck in this book.
20   Randy Gener, 'Who Will Speak for the Children? Peter Sellars's Children of Herakles Gives Theatrical Shelter to Refugee Kids Lost in the System', *American Theatre*, December 2002, http://www.tcg.org/publications/at/2002/children.cfm (assessed 30 June 2015).
21   Mark Kennedy, '10 Years After 9/11, Where Are the Iconic Plays?' Associated Press, 22 August 2011, http://news.yahoo.com/10-years-9-11-where-iconic-plays-173341106.html (accessed 20 April 2015).
22   Ibid.
23   Leo Benedictus, 'What to Say About ... Rupert Goold's Decade', *Guardian*, 12 September 2011, http://www.theguardian.com/culture/2011/sep/12/rupert-goold-decade-9-11 (accessed 12 April 2015).
24   http://www.antenna-theater.org/about/ (accessed 10 April 2015).
25   Ibid.
26   Ibid.
27   http://www.sojourntheatre.org/ (accessed 10 April 2015).
28   Ibid.
29   Michael Rohd and Shannon Scrofano, 'Seven Introductions: A Dialogue', in Megan Alrutz, Julia Listengarten and M. Van Duyn Wood (eds), *Playing with Theory in Theatre Practice* (Basingstone: Palgrave Macmillan, 2011), 287.
30   Ibid., 282.
31   Moisés Kaufman, 'Into the West: An Exploration in Form', *American Theatre*, December 2007, http://www.tcg.org/publications/at/2000/form.cfm (accessed 15 April 2015).
32   Moisés Kaufman, 'Anatomy of Experiment', *American Theatre*, July/August 2010, http://www.tcg.org/publications/at/julyaugust10/laramie.cfm (accessed 15 April 2015).
33   Ibid.
34   Eliza Bent, 'Bilingual Bicycles', *American Theatre*, July/August

2011, http://www.tcg.org/publications/at/julyaugust11/strategies. cfm (accessed 1 June 2015).

35 Ibid.
36 Claudia Orenstein, 'Agitational Performance, Now and Then', *Theater* 31 (3) (2001), http://www.notbored.org/yale.html (accessed 1 June 2015).
37 Eliza Bent, 'Monopolizing Metro: Some Artists Go Underground to Come Out on Top', *American Theatre*, April 2009, http://www.tcg.org/publications/at/apr09/strategies.cfm (accessed 15 June 2015).
38 David Pogue, 'The MP3 Experiment', *New York Times*, 28 May 2009, http://pogue.blogs.nytimes.com/2009/05/28/the-mp3-experiment/?_php=true&_type=blogs&_r=2 (accessed 15 June 2015).
39 Randy Gener, 'Electronic Campfires', *American Theatre*, December 2007, https://www.tcg.org/publications/at/dec08/builders.cfm (accessed 15 June 2015).
40 Ibid.
41 See Jennifer Parker-Starbuck, *Cyborg Theatre: Corporeal/Technological Intersections in Multimedia Performance* (Basingstoke: Palgrave, 2011).
42 Examples of these organizations included the National Alliance for Musical Theatre and New York Musical Theatre Festival.
43 Gerald Bordman and Richard Norton, *American Musical Theatre: A Chronicle*, 4th edn (Oxford: Oxford University Press, 2010), 831. Norton also points to a number of organizations such as Encores in New York and Reprise in LA that emerged to focus on preserving old musicals.
44 Ben Brantley, *Broadway Musicals: From the Pages of the New York Times* (New York: Harry N. Abrams, 2012), 314.
45 Bordman and Norton, *American Musical Theatre*, 854.
46 Ibid., 840.
47 Brantley, *Broadway Musicals*, 326.
48 Ibid., 341.
49 Ibid. Indeed, despite their use of popular music, some of these jukebox musicals did not last long; among productions that had short Broadway runs were *All Shook Up* (2005); *Lennon* (2005); *Ring of Fire* (2006), with Johnny Cash music; and *The Times They Are A-Changin'* (2006), which incorporated Bob Dylan songs and Twyla Tharp choreography.

50 Clive Barnes, http://criticometer.blogspot.com/2006/11/mary-poppins.html (accessed 18 June 2015).
51 Bordman and Norton, *American Musical Theatre*, viii.
52 Ibid.
53 Charles Isherwood, 'Sex and Rock? What Would the Kaiser Think?' *New York Times*, 11 December 2006, http://www.nytimes.com/2006/12/11/theater/reviews/11spri.html?pagewanted=all&_r=0 (accessed 17 March 2016).
54 Brantley, *Broadway Musicals*, 317.
55 Bordman and Norton, *American Musical Theatre*, 834.
56 Brantley, *Broadway Musicals*, 344.
57 David Patrick Stearns, 'The Smart Set: These Brainy New Composers May Be the Hope of the American Musical Theatre', *American Theatre*, February 2000, https://www.tcg.org/publications/at/2000/smart.cfm (accessed 18 June 2015).
58 Sheldon Patinkin, *'No Legs, No Jokes, No Chance': A History of the American Musical Theatre* (Chicago: Northwestern University Press, 2008), 525.
59 See Terry Berliner, 'A Nationwide Boom: The Not-for-Profit Musical Factory', *American Theatre*, April 2006, https://www.tcg.org/publications/at/Apr06/music3.cfm (accessed 27 June 2015).
60 Mark Blankenship, 'Breaking the Sound Barrier', *American Theatre*, February 2006, https://www.tcg.org/publications/at/Feb06/breaking.cfm (accessed 27 June 2015).
61 Ben Cameron, 'Do I Hear Waltz?' *American Theatre*, February 2000, https://www.tcg.org/publications/at/2000/waltz.cfm (accessed 29 June 2015).
62 Ibid.
63 Theatre for Young Audiences (TYA) is an umbrella term that includes Theatre in Education (TIE), youth theatre, theatre performed by performers of any age for young or family audiences, and Theatre for the Very Young (TVY).
64 http://assitej-usa.org/about/mission-history/ (accessed 29 June 2015).
65 'Applied theatre' refers to works performed with marginalized communities to approach issues of social or political injustice, most commonly through original devised work with the members of the community.
66 See Roger L. Bedard, *TYA Today* 17 (2) (2003).
67 Brian Guehring, 'Challenges, Strategies, and Mission: An

Interview with Leaders of Queer Youth Theatre', *TYA Today* 21 (1) (2007): 21.
68 Ibid.
69 Arts on the Horizon, the first American company to solely produce TVY work, opened in May 2011 in Alexandria, Virginia, with *Drumming with Dishes*.
70 See Megan Alrutz, 'Redefining "Young" Audiences: Theatre for the Early Years', *TYA Today* 23 (1) (2009): 4–9.
71 See Hans-Thies Lehmann's analysis of post-dramatic theatre in which the focus is on visual storytelling rooted in associative and sensory experiences. Hans-Thies Lehmann, *Postdramatic Theatre*, trans. Karen Jürs-Munby (New York: Routledge, 2006).
72 *AT25: An Eye on the Future*, https://www.tcg.org/publications/at/apr09/paulus.cfm (accessed 10 June 2015).
73 Ibid., https://www.tcg.org/publications/at/apr09/bither.cfm (accessed 17 March 2016).
74 Thomas Friedman, *The World Is Flat: A Brief History of the Twentieth Century*, expanded edn (New York: Picador/Farrar, Straus and Giroux, 2007), 8.
75 The NEA budget for 2000 was $97.6 million, a significant reduction from $162.5 million in 1995. The major cut was made in 1996, when the budget was reduced by 39 per cent. Toward the end of the decade, the NEA budget rebounded, reaching $155 million in 2009.
76 See Dean Adams, 'Puttin' the Profit in Nonprofit Broadway Theatre Companies', *Theatre Symposium* 22 (2014): 48–61.
77 Brantley, *Broadway Musicals*, 325.
78 Ibid.
79 Gretchen Van Lente, 'What's That Puppet Doing in My Play? Smitten by Puppet Love, 5 Playwrights Compare Notes on Writing for Objects Brought to Life', *American Theatre*, February 2006, https://www.tcg.org/publications/at/feb04/doing.cfm (accessed 29 June 2015).
80 Alex Ross, 'Taymor's Mythology', *New Yorker*, 25 October 2004, http://www.therestisnoise.com/2004/10/julie_taymors_e.html (accessed 29 June 2015).
81 In his staging of Berlioz's *Symphonie Fantastique* (1998), puppets performed inside a giant water tank.
82 Blankenship, 'Breaking the Sound Barrier'.

83 http://americanrepertorytheater.org/inside/articles/articles-vol-2-i3a-dreams-wood-sprite-introducing-martha-clarke (accessed 29 June 2015).
84 Ibid.
85 Gena Hamshaw, 'Rockafella and Kwikstep Hip-Hop to Success', *Columbia Spectator*, 22 October 2002, http://columbiaspectator.com/2002/10/24/rockafella-and-kwikstep-hip-hop-success (accessed 27 June 2015).
86 Randy Gener, 'Mad Dog: The Poetry of Moving Bodies', *American Theatre*, December 2004, https://www.tcg.org/publications/at/dec04/maddog.cfm (accessed 25 June 2015).
87 Ibid.
88 http://www.theatremovementbazaar.org/ (accessed 25 June 2015).
89 http://www.flaneurproductions.com/company.html (accessed 27 June 2015).
90 See Guillermo Gómez-Peña, 'The New Global Culture: Somewhere between Corporate Multiculturalism and the Mainstream Bizarre (a Border Perspective)', *TDR* 45 (1) (2001): 7–30.
91 http://siti.org/content/about-us (accessed 29 June 2015).
92 Gener, 'Who Will Speak for the Children'?
93 'Program Brings International Artists to U.S. Theatres', *American Theatre*, 17 (3) (2000): 66.
94 http://watermillcenter.org (accessed 27 June 2015).
95 http://publictheater.org/Programs--Events/Under-the-Radar-Festival (accessed 27 June 2015).
96 P.S. 122 – Performance Space 122 – was founded in 1979 in an abandoned public school building in the East Village and evolved into a major arts organization dedicated to fostering and promoting contemporary performance.
97 Steven Leigh Morris, 'Group Think: Shape-Shifting Ensembles are Surfacing on Major U.S. Stages, Trailing New Techniques and Changing the Playmaking Rules', *American Theatre*, March 2013, http://www.tcg.org/publications/at/issue/featuredstory.cfm?story=1&indexID=27 (accessed 30 June 2015).
98 Ibid.
99 http://www.playwrightshorizons.org/about/mission-and-history/ (accessed 30 June 2015).
100 Charles Isherwood, 'Explaining the Unbearable, If Only in Fragments', *New York Times*, 18 April 2008, http://www.nytimes.

com/2008/04/18/theater/reviews/18ear.html (accessed 30 June 2015).

101 http://www.lct.org/about/claire-tow-theater/ (accessed 6 July 2015).

102 See http://theoneill.org/summer-conferences/npc/artistic-director/ (accessed 30 June 2015).

103 http://wptheater.org/about/mission/ (accessed 30 June 2015).

104 Eliza Bent, 'Remix to Ignition: Hot, Fresh and Out of the Kitchen (Sink)! A Chicago Festival Give Playwrights of Color Under 40 New Avenues for Productions', *American Theatre*, February 2010, http://www.tcg.org/publications/at/feb10/strategies.cfm (accessed 30 June 2015).

105 http://nnpn.org/about/overview (accessed 30 June 2015).

106 http://nnpn.org/programs/national-showcase-of-new-plays (accessed 30 June 2015).

107 http://www.13p.org/ (accessed 30 June 2015).

108 https://www.tdf.org/press/88/TDFs-Outrageous-Fortune-The-Life-and-Times-of-the-New-American-Play-examines-the-collaboration-in-crisis-between-playwrights-and-those-who-produce-their-work (accessed 30 June 2015).

109 Patrick Healy, 'Playwrights' Nurturing Is the Focus of a Study', *New York Times*, 14 January 2010, http://www.nytimes.com/2010/01/14/theater/14playwrights.html (accessed 30 June 2015).

110 Marsha Norman in 'Not There Yet: What Will it Take to Achieve Equality for Women in the Theatre?' *American Theatre*, November 2009, http://www.tcg.org/publications/at/nov09/women.cfm (accessed 30 June 2015).

111 Ibid.

112 Penny Farfan and Lesley Ferris (eds), 'Introduction', in Penny Farfan and Lesley Ferris (eds), *Contemporary Women Playwrights into the Twenty-First Century* (Basingstoke: Palgrave Macmillan, 2013), 4.

113 Doug Wright, *I Am My Own Wife* (New York: Faber and Faber, 2004), xi.

114 Debbie Thomson, 'Digging the Fo'-Fathers: Suzan-Lori Parks; Histories', in Philip C. Kolin (ed.), *Contemporary African American Women Playwrights* (Abingdon, Oxon: Routledge, 2007), 173.

115 http://caridadsvich.com/about/ (accessed 7 July 2015).

116 Ben Brantley, 'Dreams of "Metamorphoses" Echo in a Larger Space', *New York Times*, 5 March 2002, http://www.nytimes.com/2002/03/05/theater/theater-review-dreams-of-metamorphoses-echo-in-a-larger-space.html (accessed 30 June 2015).

117 Stephen Bottoms, 'Christopher Shinn', in Martin Middeke, Peter Paul Schnierer, Christopher Innes and Matthew C. Roudané (eds), *The Methuen Drama Guide to Contemporary American Playwrights* (London and New York: Bloomsbury, 2014), 347.

118 Christopher Innes, 'Neil LaBute', in Middeke, Schnierer, Innes and Roudané (eds), *Methuen Drama Guide*, 143.

119 Ibid.

120 Charles Isherwood, 'Woman of 1,000 Faces Considers the Body', *New York Times*, 8 October 2009, http://www.nytimes.com/2009/10/08/theater/reviews/08easy.html?_r=0 (accessed 30 June 2015).

121 Ibid.

122 Elin Diamond, 'Deb Margolin, Robbie McCauley, Peggy Shaw: Affect and Performance', in Penny Farfan and Lesley Ferris (eds), *Contemporary Women Playwrights into the Twenty-First Century* (Basingstoke: Palgrave Macmillan, 2013), 272.

123 Sarah Hart, 'Looking Both Ways: Gina Gionfriddo, Rolin Jones and Adam Rapp on Traveling a Two-Way Street between Theatre and Screen', *American Theatre*, July/August 2008, https://www.tcg.org/publications/at/julyaugust08/looking.cfm (accessed 30 June 2015).

124 Ibid.

125 See Lillian Manzor on Caridad Svich in *Oxford Encyclopedia of Latinos and Latinas in the United States*, ed. Suzanne Oboler and Deena J. Gonzáles, Vol. 1 (Oxford: Oxford University Press, 2005), 186.

126 See Carlson, '9/11, Afghanistan, and Iraq: The Response of the New York Theatre'.

127 Christopher Wallenberg, 'In Katrina's Wake', *American Theatre*, May/June 2010, http://www.tcg.org/publications/at/mayjune10/katrina.cfm (accessed 30 June 2015).

128 Wendy Arons and Theresa J. May, 'Ecodramaturgy in/and Contemporary Women's Playwriting', in Farfan and Ferris (eds), *Contemporary Women Playwrights*, 181.

129 Ken Jaworowski, 'When Justice Makes You Gasp: "The Exonerated," Revived at the Culture Project', *New York Times*, 20 September 2012, http://www.nytimes.com/2012/09/20/theater/

reviews/the-exonerated-revived-at-the-culture-project.html?_r=0 (accessed 30 June 2015).

3 Charles Mee

1. Charles L. Mee, Jr, 'I Like to Take a Greek Play', *Theatre Journal* 59 (3) (2007): 361–3. Charles Mee's professional name has varied over the years. Earlier in his career, he went by Charles L. Mee, Jr and Charles L. Mee. His friends and colleagues know him as Chuck Mee.
2. www.charlesmee.org (accessed 29 June 2015). Unless otherwise indicated, all quotations in this chapter from Mee's plays are taken from his website. Individual plays on the site are not paginated.
3. For more on this patronage arrangement, see Jennifer Schlueter, 'Patronage and Playwriting: Richard B. and Jeanne Donovan Fisher's Support of Charles Mee', in Robert A. Schanke (ed.), *Angels in the American Theater: Patrons, Patronage, and Philanthropy* (Carbondale: Southern Illinois University Press, 2007), 88–103.
4. Charles L. Mee, Jr, Amanda Smith and Carol Martin, 'Martha Clarke's *Vienna: Lusthaus* Play Text and Photo Essay', *TDR: The Drama Review* 31 (3) (1987): 42–58.
5. Seldom produced since, *Bedtime Stories* and *The Rules* were titled *The Imperialists at the Club Cave Canem* and *The Constitutional Convention: A Sequel*, respectively, at the time of their original production.
6. Erin B. Mee, 'Shattered and Fucked Up and Full of Wreckage: The Words and Works of Charles L. Mee', Interview, *TDR: The Drama Review* 46 (3) (2002): 93.
7. http://www.charlesmee.org/orestes.shtml (accessed 29 June 2015). Tina Landau's memorable production of *Orestes 2.0* was produced by the landmark site-specific theatre company in New York known as En Garde Arts on a hulking industrial ruin at the Penn Yards pier on the Hudson River. For more on En Garde Arts, see James Schlatter, 'En Garde Arts: New York's New Public Theatre', *PAJ* 21 (2) (1999): 1–10.
8. Matt Wilder, 'Fantasizing About Chuck Mee', *TheatreForum* 5 (1994): 43.
9. The discussion of *Big Love* here is based in part on my earlier

writing in Scott T. Cummings, *Remaking American Theatre: Charles Mee, Anne Bogart and the SITI Company* (Cambridge: Cambridge University Press, 2006), 78–85. In some instances, a phrase or a sentence has been reused verbatim.

10 Adam Feldman, 'Big Love: Theater Review', *Time Out New York*, 23 February 2015, http://www.timeout.com/newyork/theater/big-love (accessed 7 July 2015).

11 Alvin Klein, '"Big Love": Not Just a Catchy Title', *New York Times*, 18 March 2001: Section 14CN-10.

12 Steven Winn, 'Fools Fall Hard in Charles L. Mee's Play "Big Love"', *San Francisco Chronicle*, 27 April 2001, C7.

13 Malcolm Johnson, 'A Modern Take on Ancient Conflicts', *The Hartford Courant*, 9 March 2001, D1.

14 At the time of its creation, it was known as the Saratoga International Theatre Institute, which eventually led to the SITI Company. By plan, Suzuki withdrew from working with the group after several years, but international collaboration remains at the core of SITI's mission.

15 For a detailed, step-by-step account of the development of *bobrauschenbergamerica*, see Cummings, *Remaking American Theatre*, 159–274.

16 Tim Youker, 'Reading Collage Drama as Documentary Drama: Trash Archives and *Dissensus* in Charles L. Mee's Lives of the Artists', *Modern Drama* 58 (2) (2015): 218.

17 Holly Johnson, 'Theater Review: "bobrauschenbergamerica" a Delightful, Dizzying Show at Portland Playhouse', http://www.oregonlive.com/performance/index.ssf/2009/04/theater_review_bobrauschenberg.html (accessed 18 July 2015).

18 Mee, 'Shattered and Fucked Up and full of Wreckage', 87.

19 Michael Bigelow Dixon, Interview with Charles L. Mee, '*Wintertime*: A Study Guide' (Minneapolis: Guthrie Theatre, 2003), 12.

20 Quoted in Cummings, *Remaking American Theatre*, 206. The jolt – what some would call aesthetic arrest – triggered by Bob the Pizza Boy prompted cultural critic John Rockwell to write a *New York Times* piece about other 'mesmerizing moments' and the experience of the sublime in theatre, opera, film and music: John Rockwell, 'Living for the Moments: When Contemplation Turns to Ecstasy', *New York Times*, 24 October 2003, E4.

21 Neil Genzlinger, 'A Collage of Sly Tricks in Honor of a Collagist', *New York Times*, 16 October 2003, E5.

22 Daniel Mufson, 'Love American Style', *Village Voice*, 21 October 2003, http://www.villagevoice.com/arts/love-american-style-7141047 (accessed 15 June 2015).
23 Martin Harries, 'Having Your Cage', *Hunter On-Line Theatre Review*, October 2003, http://www.hotreview.org/articles/havingyourcage.htm (accessed 1 June 2015).
24 Dixon, Interview with Charles L. Mee, 12.
25 Lawrence Christon, 'Review: "Wintertime"', *Variety*, 9–15 September 2002, 36.
26 Marilyn Stasio, 'Review: "Wintertime"', *Variety*, 8–14 March 2004, 46.
27 Ben Brantley, 'New Year's Revolutions: Doors Slam, Clothes Drop', *New York Times*, 3 March 2004, E3.
28 Charles L. Mee, *A Nearly Normal Life: A Memoir* (Boston: Little Brown, 1999), 40.
29 Dixon, Interview with Charles L. Mee, 11.
30 Les Waters, telephone interview with the author, 24 July 2000.
31 Anne Bogart, interview with the author, Saratoga Spring, New York, 18 June 2000.
32 Kim Weild, a director who graduated from the Columbia University MFA directing programme run by Anne Bogart, staged *Soot and Spit* at Arizona State University (ASU) in 2013. She also directed *Big Love* at ASU in 2010. Wield's 2010 MFA thesis production at Columbia was *Fêtes de la Nuit*, another Mee play written for but not produced by the SITI Company. It premiered in 2005 at the Berkeley Repertory Theatre where it was directed by Waters.
33 As of late 2015, Mee's 'Lives of the Artists' section also contained plays about Picasso, Matisse and Van Gogh that had yet to be produced.

4 Lynn Nottage

1 Randy Gener, 'Conjurer of Worlds', *American Theatre*, October 2005, 144.
2 Lynn Nottage, *Crumbs from the Table of Joy and Other Plays* (New York: Theatre Communications Group, 2004), ix.
3 Victoria Myers, 'Lynn Nottage: Theatre Artist, Nurturer, Hunter

and Gatherer', *The Interval*, the-interval.com (accessed 16 January 2016).

4 Steve Lickteig, 'Intimate Conversation', in programme for *Intimate Apparel* world premiere at Baltimore Center Stage, 21 February–30 March 2003, 6.

5 Randy Gener, 'In Defense of *Ruined*: Five Elements that Shape Lynn Nottage's Masterwork', *American Theatre*, October 2010, 118–19.

6 Nottage, *Crumbs from the Table of Joy*, 252.

7 Lenora Inez Brown, 'Dismantling the Box: An Interview with the Playwright', *American Theatre*, July–August 2001, 50.

8 'A Talk with the Playwright: Lynn Nottage', *Kentucky Educational Television*, n.d. (accessed 16 January 2016).

9 Lickteig, 'Intimate Conversation', 7.

10 Myers, 'Lynn Nottage'.

11 Lynn Nottage, 'Lives Rescued from Silence', *Los Angeles Times*, 13 April 2003, http://articles.latimes.com/2003/apr/13/entertainment/ca-nottage13 (accessed 16 January 2016).

12 Lickteig, 'Intimate Conversation', 6.

13 Whoriskey quoted in Gener, 'In Defense of *Ruined*', October 2005, 144.

14 Ibid.

15 Interestingly, Nottage's next play, *Fabulation, or the Re-Education of Undine*, is directly inspired by Edith Wharton; here Nottage follows the rise and fall of a social climber, who bears a resemblance to the central figure (also Undine) in Wharton's novel *The Custom of the Country*.

16 Margo Jefferson, 'Hungry Hearts, Avid Dreams in Crazy Quilt of Old New York', *New York Times*, 12 April 2004. Jefferson describes Nottage's 'Edith Wharton-esque' style in the following passage: 'Ms. Nottage has chosen to write a drama in the popular sweeping style of the 19th and early 20th centuries. Intricate plotting guides (or flings) the heroine across the boundaries of class and caste, worlds connected by romance, greed, ambition. Everyone is as much social type as individual: the virtuous single woman who must make her way in the world; the handsome, untrustworthy man; the good-hearted unglamorous gentleman; the "fallen" or decadent woman who means well by the heroine but is too selfish not to betray her.' http://www.nytimes.com/mem/theater/treview.html?res=990de6dc1138f931a25757c0a9629c8b63&_r=0 (accessed 16 January 2016).

17 Mike Giuliano, *Variety*, 10 March 2003, 41.
18 Justin Glanville, '*Apparel* Inaugurates Roundabout Space', *Associated Press*, 11 April 2004.
19 Gener, 'In Defense of *Ruined*', October 2005, 24.
20 Ibid., 144.
21 Ann M. Fox, 'Battles on the Body: Disability, Interpreting Dramatic Literature, and the Case of Lynn Nottage's *Ruined*', *Journal of Literary & Cultural Disability Studies* 5 (1) (2011): 4.
22 Lynn Nottage in Nilo Cruz, 'Nilo Cruz & Lynn Nottage', *The Dramatist*, March–April 2010, 23.
23 Ibid.
24 Lynn Nottage in Mervyn Rothstein, 'Lynn Nottage Brings Her *Intimate Apparel* to Center Stage', *Playbill* 21 (6) (31 March 2003): 35.
25 Lynn Nottage, *Intimate Apparel and Fabulation, or The Re-Education of Undine* (New York: Theatre Communications Group, 2006), 23.
26 Lickteig, 'Intimate Conversation', 7.
27 Lynn Nottage, 'The Best Performance I've Ever Seen', *Observer*, 2 May 2010, 31.
28 Davis is quoted in Simi Horowitz, 'Corsets as Metaphor', *Backstage*, 29 April 2004, 7.
29 Nottage in Rothstein, 'Lynn Nottage Brings Her *Intimate Apparel* to Center Stage'.
30 Jason Zinoman, 'Lynn Nottage Enters Her Flippant Period', *New York Times*, 13 June 2004, section 2, 3.
31 Nottage, *Intimate Apparel and Fabulation, or The Re-Education of Undine*, 94.
32 Zinoman, 'Lynn Nottage Enters Her Flippant Period', 6.
33 Ibid.
34 Ibid.
35 Michael Sommers, *Star-Ledger*, 14 June 2004.
36 Margaret Drabble said this about Undine in 'The Beautiful and the Damned', *Guardian*, 19 June 2004, http://www.theguardian.com/books/2004/jun/19/classics.edithwharton (accessed 16 January 2016).
37 Sommers, *Star-Ledger*.

38   Ben Brantley, 'A Mighty Diva's Humbling Fall to Rough Roots in the Projects', *New York Times*, 14 June 2004, http://www.nytimes.com/mem/theater/treview.html?res=9f03e7df1030f937a25755c0a9629c8b63 (accessed 16 January 2016).
39   Ibid.
40   Peter Marks, *Washington Post*, 6 July 2004, C1, C5.
41   Fiona Mountford, 'PR Fable Is Absolutely Fabulous', *Evening Standard*, 21 February 2006, https://www.questia.com/newspaper/1G1-142353941/pr-fable-is-absolutely-fabulous-theatre (accessed 12 October 2016).
42   Michael Billington, 'Fabulation', *Guardian*, 21 February 2006, https://www.theguardian.com/stage/2006/feb/21/theatre2 (accessed 12 October 2016).
43   Gener, 'In Defense of *Ruined*', 120.
44   Nottage, 'The Best Performance I've Ever Seen', 31.
45   Nottage in Gener, 'In Defense of *Ruined*', 119.
46   Lynn Nottage in Alexis Greene, 'Lynn Nottage', *Round Up* 8 (2007–8): 25.
47   Nottage in Gener, 'In Defense of *Ruined*', 119.
48   Nottage in Cruz, 'Nilo Cruz & Lynn Nottage', 24.
49   Ibid.
50   Jill Dolan, '*Ruined*, by Lynn Nottage', *Feminist Spectator*, 16 March 2009, http://feministspectator.princeton.edu/2009/03/16/ruined-by-lynn-nottage/ (accessed 16 January 2016).
51   Ben Brantley, 'War's Terrors, Through a Brothel Window', *New York Times*, 11 February 2009, http://www.nytimes.com/2009/02/11/theater/reviews/11bran.html?_r=0 (accessed 12 October 2016).
52   Fox, 'Battles on the Body', 12–13.
53   Brantley, 'War's Terrors, Through a Brothel Window'.
54   Lynn Nottage, *Ruined* (New York: Dramatists Play Service, 2010), 68.
55   Nottage in Greene, 'Lynn Nottage', 25.
56   Steven Oxman, *Variety*, 17 November 2008, http://variety.com/2008/legit/reviews/ruined-2-1200472158/ (accessed 12 October 2016).
57   Chris Jones, *Chicago Tribune*, 21 November 2008, http://articles.chicagotribune.com/2008-11-21/entertainment/0811190180_1_lynn-nottage-horrors-ruined (accessed 12 October 2016).

58   Kate Kellaway, *Observer*, 25 April 2010, 38.
59   Charles Isherwood, 'Bearing Witness to the Chaos of War', *New York Times*, 22 March 2009, section 2, 9.
60   Myers, 'Lynn Nottage: Theatre Artist'.
61   Lynn Nottage, Foreword, *The Penguin Arthur Miller* (New York: Penguin, 2015), xiii.
62   Susannah Clapp, *Observer*, 8 June 2014, 33.
63   Nottage, Foreword, *The Penguin Arthur Miller*, xvii.
64   Lynn Nottage, *One More River to Cross: A Verbatim Fugue* (New York: Dramatists Play Service, 2015).

5 Theresa Rebeck

1   Theresa Rebeck, 'How I Learned to Stop Worrying and Love Broadway', *Guardian*, 28 September 2007, http://theresarebeck.com/how-i-learned-to-stop-worrying-and-love-broadway/ (accessed 31 May 2015).
2   See Michael Buckley, 'Stage to Screens: A Chat with Theresa Rebeck', *Playbill*, 18 January 2004, http://www.playbill.com/news/article/stage-to-screens-a-chat-with-theresa-rebeck-remembering-uta-hagen-117404 (accessed 31 May 2015).
3   Ibid.
4   Leslie (Hoban) Blake, 'Rebeck on a Roll', *Encore*, September 1996.
5   Theresa Rebeck, 'Cracking Broadway', *New York Times*, 13 June 1999, section 2, 4.
6   Marshall Heyman, 'Back on Broadway, with Cincinnati Flavor', Heard and Scene, *Wall Street Journal*, 27 November 2012, A24.
7   Theresa Rebeck, *The Butterfly Collection*, in *Theresa Rebeck Complete Full-Length Plays Volume II: 1999–2007* (Hanover, NH: Smith and Kraus, 2007), 75.
8   Laura Hedlin, 'Touring the City's Seminars', Arts & Entertainment, *Wall Street Journal*, 1 December 2011, A30.
9   Robert Simonson, 'An Acute Interest in Bad Behavior', *New York Times*, 23 September 2007, section 2, 7.
10 Theresa Rebeck, 'Introduction', *Complete Plays 1989–1998* (Hanover, NH: Smith and Kraus, 1999), 3.

11 Kate Taylor, 'One Writes, the Other Acts. Sparks Fly', *New York Times*, 1 November 2009, section 2, 6.
12 Steve Parks, 'Rebeck Knits Up a Sad and Funny Yarn', *Newsday*, 13 May 1999, B11.
13 Stephen Holden, 'Knitters Undone by a Needler', *New York Times*, 2 July 1993, http://www.nytimes.com/1993/07/02/movies/review-theater-knitters-undone-by-a-needler.html (accessed 1 June 2015).
14 Richard Huff, '"Brooklyn Bridge"? I Was Shoved', *Daily News*, 26 June 1994, City Lights, 3.
15 Ibid.
16 Rebeck, 'Introduction', *Complete Plays 1989–1998*, 5.
17 Theresa Rebeck, *View of the Dome*, in *Complete Plays 1989–1998*, 273–4.
18 Ben Brantley, 'It's Politics, So Everyone Must Be Corrupt. Right?' *New York Times*, 1 October 1996, http://www.nytimes.com/1996/10/01/theater/it-s-politics-so-everyone-must-be-corrupt-right.html (accessed 3 June 2015).
19 Jesse McKinley, 'Please Pass the Salt (and the Terrorism)', *New York Times*, 21 September 2003, section 2, 5.
20 Ibid., 7.
21 Ibid.
22 Evangeline Morphos, 'Theresa Rebeck', *BOMB Magazine* 97 (Fall 2006): 42.
23 Parts of this section are drawn from Ann Folino White and Dorothy Chansky, 'The Dinner from Hell/The Chef from *Le Cordon Bleu*: *Omnium Gatherum* and Food as Status Symbol After 9/11', in Dorothy Chansky and Ann Folino White (eds), *Food and Theatre on the World Stage* (New York and London: Routledge, 2015), 136–49.
24 John Lahr, 'Cultural Gas', *New Yorker*, 6 October 2003, 136.
25 Quotes are from, respectively, Matthew Murray, review of *Omnium Gatherum*, 17 September 2004, www.talkinbroadway.com (accessed 2 June 2015); Mark Steyn, 'Recent Evasive Events', *New Criterion*, November 2003, 40; and Charles Isherwood, 'Haute Cuisine Sparks a Hot Debate', *Variety* 392 (7) (29 September 2003): 68.
26 Theresa Rebeck and Alexandra Gersten-Vassilaros, *Omnium Gatherum* (New York: Samuel French, Inc., 2003), 14. All quotes

are from this edition, which sets 'Bobby Flay' in Suzie's line. A household name, Flay signifies as relatable and his food as expensive but not outrageous American cuisine.

27 Zachary Pincus-Roth, 'Off B'way Trio Revisits History', *Variety* 392 (4) (8 September 2003): 62.

28 David Finkle, 'Omnium Gatherum', 25 September 2003, http://www.theatermania.com (accessed 2 June 2015).

29 Virginia Gerst, 'The Food's the Thing: Area Chefs Cater to a New Audience in Next Theatre Production', *Chicago Tribune*, 3 November 2004, 10; and Florence Fabricant, 'Food Takes Center Stage, with Chefs in the Wings', *New York Times*, 8 October 2003, http://www.nytimes.com/2003/10/08/dining/food-takes-center-stage-with-chefs-in-the-wings.html (accessed 2 June 2015).

30 Robert Simonson, '*Omnium Gatherum* No More at Variety Arts Theatre as 9/11 Play Closes Nov. 30', *Playbill*, November 2003. Available online: http://www.playbill.com/article/omnium-gatherum-no-more-at-variety-arts-theatre-as-9-11-play-closes-nov-30-com-116537 (accessed 12 October 2016).

31 Isherwood, 'Haute Cuisine Sparks a Hot Debate', and Steyn, 'Recent Evasive Events'; Ben Brantley, 'A Feisty Feast of Wicked Wit', *New York Times*, 26 September 2003, http://www.nytimes.com/mem/theater/treview.html?res=9d04eedd153df935a1575ac0a9659c8b63&_r=0 (accessed 13 June 2015).

32 In 'Readers Are Key Ingredient as Virtual Kitchen Heats Up', *New York Times* writer Bob Tedeschi reports that food and recipe websites are ordinary, ubiquitous and popular among women across classes and income levels (although obviously not among those lacking any access to the Internet). Tedeschi's article reports that 50 million people, or one-third of 'active Internet users in the United States', visited a food website during the month of May 2007. The article appeared in the *Times* on 25 June 2007.

33 Lahr, 'Cultural Gas'.

34 Peggy Phelan, *Unmarked* (New York: Routledge, 1993), 21.

35 Jeanne Colleran, *Theatre and War: Theatrical Responses Since 1991* (New York: Palgrave Macmillan, 2012), 7, 91. The other plays include Anne Nelson's *The Guys*; Neil LaBute's *The Mercy Seat*; John McGrath's *Hyperlynx*; Craig Wright's *Recent Tragic Events*; and Steven Berkoff's *Requiem for Ground Zero*.

36 Ibid., 103.

37 Ibid., 104.

38 Ibid., 103.
39 Theresa Rebeck, *Mauritius* (New York: Samuel French, Inc., 2008), 73. All quotes are from this edition.
40 Charles McNulty, 'All the Arts All the Time/Review of "Mauritius"', LATIMESBLOGS, 5 April 2009, http://latimesblogs. latimes.com/culturemonster/2009/04/review-maruitius-at-pasadena-playhouse.html (accessed 15 June 2015).
41 Robert Risko, 'Pay and Play', *New Yorker*, 15 October 2007, http://www.newyorker.com/magazine/2007/10/15/pay-and-play (accessed 15 June 2015).
42 McNulty, 'Review of "Mauritius"'.
43 Ben Brantley, 'Three Thugs and a Stamp Collection', *New York Times*, 5 October 2007, http://www.nytimes.com/2007/10/05/theater/reviews/05maur.html?_r=0 (accessed 15 June 2015).
44 Frank Rizzo, 'Review: "Mauritius"', *Variety*, 19 October 2006, http://variety.com/2006/legit/reviews/mauritius-2-1200512490/ (accessed 15 June 2015); Sandy MacDonald, 'Mauritius', *TheaterMania.com*, 19 October 2006, http://www.theatermania.com/new-york-city-theater/reviews/10-2006/mauritius_9274.html (accessed 15 June 2015).
45 Matthew Murray, 'Broadway Reviews: Mauritius', *Talkin' Broadway*, 4 October 2007, https://www.talkinbroadway.com/world/Mauritius.html (accessed 15 June 2015).
46 McNulty, 'Review of "Mauritius"'.
47 Beverly Creasey, 'What Happened in Boston, Willie' (Review of *Mauritius*), *The Theater Mirror*, 2006, http://www.theatermirror.com/BEVmhtcbca.htm (accessed 15 June 2015).
48 Theresa Rebeck, *The Understudy* (New York: Dramatists Play Service, Inc., 2010), 7. All page numbers are from this edition.
49 David Rooney, 'Review: "The Understudy"', *Variety*, 5 November 2009, http://variety.com/2009/legit/reviews/the-understudy-2-1200477578/ (accessed 29 June 2015).
50 Linda Winer, 'A Backup Waits for the Star to Fall in "The Understudy"', *Newsday*, 5 November 2009, http://www.newsday.com/entertainment/theater/a-backup-waits-for-the-star-to-fall-in-the-understudy-1.1568630 (accessed 4 July 2015).
51 Charles Isherwood, 'When a Star Takes a Turn Awaiting a Star Turn', *New York Times*, 6 November 2009, http://www.nytimes.com/2009/11/06/theater/reviews/06understudy.html?_r=0 (accessed 29 June 2015).

52 John Timpane, 'Theater No Trivial Pursuit to "The Understudy" Playwright Theresa Rebeck', *philly.com*, 4 January 2011, http://articles.philly.com/2011-01-04/news/26357888_1_kafka-theresa-rebeck-alexandra-gersten-vassilaros (accessed 29 June 2015).

53 Ted Otten, '"The Understudy" Now Playing at McCarter Theatre Center's Matthews Theatre', *Times of Trenton*, 17 October 2014, http://www.nj.com/timesentertainment/index.ssf/2014/10/the_understudy_now_playing_at.html (accessed 2 July 2015).

54 Ibid.

55 Amanda N. Gunther, 'Review: The Understudy at Everyman Theatre', 9 September 2014, http://www.theatrebloom.com/2014/09/review-the-understudy-at-everyman-theatre/ (accessed 2 July 2015).

56 Anita Gates, 'Out of Position in a Play Inside a Play', *New York Times*, 28 August 2011, Connecticut Section, 10.

57 Timpane, 'Theater No Trivial Pursuit'.

58 Rebeck, *The Understudy*, 28.

59 Quoted in Timpane.

60 Patricia Cohen, 'Charging Bias by Theaters, Female Playwrights to Hold Meeting', *New York Times*, 25 October 2008, C1, 8.

61 Melissa Silverstein, 'Text of Theresa Rebeck Laura Pels Keynote Address', womenandhollywood.com, 16 March 2010, http://womenandhollywood.com/2010/03/16/text-of-theresa-rebeck-laura-pels-keynote-address/ (accessed 4 July 2015).

62 Bruce Weber, 'Like Father (a Writer), Like Son (an Actor) and Neither Is Likeable', *New York Times*, 4 October 2000, http://www.nytimes.com/2000/10/04/theater/theater-review-like-father-a-writer-like-son-an-actor-and-neither-is-likable.html (accessed 4 July 2015).

63 Quoted in Silverstein.

64 Ibid.

65 Ibid.

66 See Jill Dolan, 'Making a Spectacle, Making a Difference', *Theatre Journal* 62 (2010): 561–5.

67 Melissa Silverstein, 'Women's Voices Milling from the Theatre – Does Anyone Care?' 7 February 2007, http://www.womensmediacenter.com/feature/entry/womens-voices-missing-from-the-theatredoes-anyone-care (accessed 4 July 2015).

68 Gordon Cox, 'Fest's "Scene" Stealer', *Variety*, 10 April 2006, 36.
69 Ben Brantley, 'All About Ego, Showbiz and a Little Black Dress', *New York Times*, 12 January 2007, http://www.nytimes.com/2007/01/12/theater/reviews/12scen.html?pagewanted=all (accessed 16 June 2015).
70 Morphos, 'Theresa Rebeck', 43.
71 Perhaps the best-known example is the television series *Breaking Bad* (originally aired 2008–13), in which a high school teacher turns to drug dealing when he learns he has cancer and fears he will be unable to provide for his wife and two children. Over the course of the series, he commits murder, betrays colleagues and lies endlessly (not to mention indulging in illegal activities) in the name of 'family'.
72 Morphos, 'Theresa Rebeck', 43.
73 Ibid.
74 Charles Isherwood, 'Sampling Newly Minted Plays by the Fest-Full', *New York Times*, 5 April 2006, E1.

6 Sarah Ruhl

1 Paula Vogel, 'Sarah Ruhl', *BOMB Magazine* 99, Spring 2007, http://bombmagazine.org/article/2902/sarah-ruhl (accessed 30 April 2015).
2 Ruhl has expressed her love of the anti-realism of the American musical in an interview published in Rosemarie Tichler and Barry Jay Kaplan, *The Playwright at Work* (Chicago: Northwestern University Press, 2012), 88.
3 Vogel, 'Sarah Ruhl'.
4 Sarah Ruhl, 'Six Small Thoughts on Fornes, the Problem of Intention, and Willfulness', *Theatre Topics* 11 (2) (2001): 194.
5 Ibid., 198.
6 Sarah Ruhl, *The Clean House*, in *The Clean House and Other Plays* (New York: Theatre Communications Group, 2006), 30.
7 Vogel, 'Sarah Ruhl'.
8 Alexis Greene, 'New Voices: Moira Buffini, Sarah Ruhl, and Rukhsana Ahmad', in Alexis Greene (ed.), *Women Writing Plays: Three Decades of the Susan Smith Blackburn Prize* (Austin: University of Texas Press, 2006), 219.

9   Wendy Weckwerth, 'More Invisible Terrains: Sarah Ruhl, Interviewed by Wendy Weckwerth', *Theater* 34 (2) (2004): 29.
10 The playwrights who comprised 13P were, in alphabetical order, Sheila Callaghan, Erin Courtney, Madeleine George, Rob Handel, Ann Marie Healy, Julia Jarcho, Young Jean Lee, Winter Miller, Sarah Ruhl, Kate Ryan, Lucy Thurber, Anne Washburn and Gary Winter. Rob Handel served as the company's managing director and fundraiser. '13P: Who We Are', http://13p.org/who (accessed 10 May 2015).
11 '13P: Mission', http://13p.org (accessed 10 May 2015). The group fulfilled its mission, produced its 13th and final play in the summer of 2012 and then 'immediately imploded'.
12 '13P: Sarah Ruhl (P#13)', http://13p.org/who/playwrights/p13 (accessed 10 May 2015).
13 Leslie Atkins Durham reminds us that when Ruhl began her writing career, only around 8 per cent of plays on Broadway were written by women, and in the regional theatre that number hovered between 20 per cent and 30 per cent. Leslie Atkins Durham, *Women's Voices on American Stages in the Early Twenty-First Century: Sarah Ruhl and Her Contemporaries* (New York: Palgrave Macmillan, 2013), 1. The recent compilation of a 'List' of underrecognized female playwrights by The Kilroys underscores the continued failure of the American theatre to extend equity to female and transgender writers. The list is available at http://thekilroys.org/list-2015/ (accessed 10 May 2015).
14 Greene, 'New Voices', 233.
15 Caridad Svich, 'In Conversation with Sarah Ruhl', *The Dramatist* 34 (2) (2002): 36.
16 Weckwerth, 'More Invisible Terrains', 30.
17 Ruhl, *Eurydice*, in *The Clean House and Other Plays* (New York: Theatre Communications Group, 2006), 344. Subsequent citations from this play will be indicated by page numbers in parentheses.
18 Durham, *Women's Voices*, 36.
19 Charles Isherwood, 'A Comic Impudence Softens a Tale of Loss', *New York Times*, 3 October 2006, E1. Available online: http://www.nytimes.com/2006/10/03/theater/reviews/03eury.html?_r=0 (accessed 12 October 2016).
20 Ibid.
21 Charles Isherwood, 'The Power of Memory to Triumph over Death', *New York Times*, 19 June 2007, E1. Available online:

http://www.nytimes.com/2007/06/19/theater/reviews/19seco.html (accessed 12 October 2016).

22 Anita Gates, 'Critic's Notebook: Love and Loss, in This Life and the Next', *New York Times*, 8 October 2006. Available online: http://query.nytimes.com/gst/fullpage.html?res=9504E5D91530F 93BA35753C1A9609C8B63 (accessed 12 October 2016); Louise Kennedy, 'A Season of Grief', *Boston Globe*, 24 December 2006, N1.

23 For a summary of critical responses to the play, see James Al-Shamma, *Sarah Ruhl: A Critical Study of the Plays* (Jefferson, NC: McFarland & Co., 2011), 13–14.

24 George W. Bush, 'Address to the Nation', http://www.presidentialrhetoric.com/speeches/09.20.01.html (accessed 1 May 2015). 'Keep shopping' was an interpretation adduced by Frank Pellegrini of *Time* magazine in 'The Bush Speech: How to Rally a Nation', *TIME Magazine*, 21 September 2001, http://content.time.com/time/nation/article/0,8599,175757,00.html (accessed 1 May 2015).

25 'At O'Hare, President Says "Get on Board"', news release, 27 September 2001, http://georgewbush-whitehouse.archives.gov/news/releases/2001/09/20010927-1.html (accessed 1 May 2015).

26 Isherwood, 'The Power of Memory'.

27 Gates, 'Critic's Notebook'.

28 Louise Kennedy, 'Dream World Travelers', *Boston Globe*, 19 September 2008, D4.

29 Svich, 'In Conversation', 36–7.

30 John Lahr, 'Surreal Life: The Plays of Sarah Ruhl', *New Yorker*, 17 March 2008, http://www.newyorker.com/magazine/2008/03/17/surreal-life (accessed 30 April 2015).

31 Durham, *Women's Voices*, 32.

32 Ibid., 39.

33 Núria Casado-Gual, 'Ancient Voices in Contemporary Theatrical Forms: The Case of "The Bacchae" by Kneehigh Theatre and "Eurydice" by Sarah Ruhl', *Journal of Dramatic Theory and Criticism* XXIX (1) (2014): 70.

34 Dinitia Smith, 'Playwright's Subjects: Greek Myth to Vibrators', *New York Times*, 14 October 2006, B7. Available online: http://www.nytimes.com/2006/10/14/theater/14ruhl.html (accessed 12 October 2016).

35 Ruhl, *The Clean House*, 63. Subsequent citations from this play will be indicated by page numbers in parentheses.
36 Frank Rizzo, 'Resident: *The Clean House*,' Variety 396.7 (4 October 2004–10 October 2004): 121.
37 Charles Isherwood, 'Always Ready with a Joke, If Not a Feather Duster', *New York Times*, 31 October 2006, E1. Available online: http://www.nytimes.com/2006/10/31/theater/reviews/31clea.html (accessed 12 October 2016).
38 Campbell Robertson, 'The Virtues of a Messy House', *New York Times*, 3 October 2004. Available online: http://query.nytimes.com/gst/fullpage.html?res=9403E4DF1238F930A35753C1A9629C8B63 (accessed 12 October 2016).
39 Smith, 'Playwright's Subjects'.
40 Rizzo, '*The Clean House*'.
41 Durham, *Women's Voices*, 55, 73.
42 Greene, 'New Voices', 230–1.
43 Weckwerth, 'More Invisible Terrains', 32.
44 Al-Shamma, *Sarah Ruhl*, 40.
45 Weckwerth, 'More Invisible Terrains', 32. Ruhl also shares her views on comedy in 'Joking Aside: A Conversation about Comedy with Christopher Durang, Gina Gionfriddo, Sarah Ruhl, and Wendy Wasserstein', in Greene (ed.), *Women Writing Plays*, 181–90.
46 Al-Shamma, *Sarah Ruhl*, 39.
47 Vogel, 'Sarah Ruhl'; Rachel P. Maines, *The Technology of Orgasm: 'Hysteria', the Vibrator, and Women's Sexual Satisfaction* (Baltimore: Johns Hopkins University Press, 1999).
48 Quotes are from Charles Isherwood, 'Beyond Electricity, Toward Female Emancipation', *New York Times*, 20 November 2009; John Lahr, 'Good Vibrations: Sarah Ruhl and "Finian's Rainbow" Score', *New Yorker*, 30 November 2009: C3. Available online: http://www.nytimes.com/2009/11/20/theater/reviews/20innextroom.html (accessed 12 October 2016); http://www.newyorker.com/magazine/2009/11/30/good-vibrations-2 (accessed 30 April 2015); and Peter Marks, '"In the Next Room": A Few Good Vibes Aren't Enough', *Washington Post*, 3 September 2010, C1.
49 Isherwood, 'Beyond Electricity'.
50 Lahr, 'Good Vibrations'.
51 Quotes are from Channing Gray, '2nd Story Play Overuses a

Single Comic Device', *Providence Journal*, 12 May 2011, D4; Marks, 'In the Next Room'; Cameron Woodhead, 'Shallow Drama Limps to Climax', *The Age* (Melbourne, Australia), 13 April 2011, 17; and Charles McNulty, 'Review of *In the Next Room*', *Los Angeles Times*, 2009, http://latimesblogs.latimes.com/culturemonster/2009/02/in-the-next-room.html (accessed 5 May 2015).

52 Situating *In the Next Room* within the tradition of the feminist history play from 1976 to 2010, Katherine Kelly observes that it 'offers itself as a provisional, sometimes ironical, and often open-ended commentary on the desire to know the past, to inherit a past, and the likelihood that such knowledge and inheritance will be imperfect'. Katherine E. Kelly, 'Making the Bones Sing: The Feminist History Play, 1976–2010', *Theatre Journal* 62 (4) (2010): 660.

53 This and subsequent quotes from the play are taken from Sarah Ruhl, *In the Next Room or the vibrator play* (New York: Theatre Communications Group, 2010).

54 Kelly, 'Making the Bones Sing', 658–9.

55 Patricia Cohen, 'From "Vibrator" to "Cougar Town," It's Still a Man's World', *New York Times*, 19 December 2009, C1. Available online: http://www.nytimes.com/2009/12/19/theater/19sex.html (accessed 12 October 2016).

56 Ibid.

57 Vogel, 'Sarah Ruhl'.

58 Private conversation with Rob Handel, 6 July 2015.

Afterword

1 Ben Brantley and Charles Isherwood, 'The Best Theater of 2015', *New York Times*, 8 December 2014, http://www.nytimes.com/2015/12/13/theater/best-broadway-off-broadway-2015.html (accessed 9 December 2015).

2 Ibid.

3 Ibid.

4 The world premiere of *Eclipsed* took place at Washington, DC's Woolly Mammoth Theatre Company in September 2009.

5 https://emosfestival.wordpress.com/faq/what-is-ecodrama/ (accessed 1 December 2015).

6   Gia Kourlas, 'Weaving Silk into Puppetry and Music: "The Rite of Spring," Basil Twist's Spin on Stravinsky', *New York Times*, 13 October 2014, http://www.nytimes.com/2014/10/14/arts/dance/the-rite-of-spring-basil-twists-spin-on-stravinsky.html (accessed 29 June 2015).

7   http://www.clydefitchreport.com/2010/06/how-anne-bogart-forged-a-new-american-document/ (accessed 29 November 2015).

8   Ibid.

9   Jonathan Mandell, interview with Erin Mee, 'Pool Play Q and A: Erin Mee on Immersive Theater, Art vs. Academia, Her Famous Father', http://newyorktheater.me/2014/01/28/pool-play-q-and-a-erin-mee-on-immersive-theater-art-vs-academia-her-famous-father/ (accessed 1 December 2015).

10 http://witnessrelocation.org/mission/ (accessed 30 November 2015).

11 http://www.charlesmee.org/plays.shtml#dance (accessed 30 November 2015).

12 Timothy J. Schaffer, 'Heaven on Earth' (review), *Theatre Journal* 63 (4) (2011): 634–7, https://muse.jhu.edu/login?auth=0&type=summary&url=/journals/theatre_journal/v063/63.4.schaffer.pdf (accessed 2 December 2015).

13 Jeremy M. Barker, 'Dan Safer on Interpreting Charles Mee', http://www.culturebot.org/2015/04/23668/dan-safer-on-interpreting-charles-mee/ (accessed 2 December 2015).

14 Todd Ziegler, 'Mee's *The Glory of the World* Celebrates Merton at Humana Festival', http://www.broadwayworld.com/louisville/article/BWW-Reviews-Mees-THE-GLORY-OF-THE-WORLD-Celebrates-Merton-at-Humana-Festival-20150411# (accessed 3 December 2015).

15 Diep Trap, 'Humana 2015: Charles Mee Toasts the Many Sides of Thomas Merton', *American Theatre*, March 2015, http://www.americantheatre.org/2015/03/27/humana-2015-charles-mee-toasts-the-many-sides-of-thomas-merton/ (accessed 3 December 2015).

16 Ben Brantley, 'A Black Actress Trying to Rise Above a Maid', *New York Times*, 9 May 2011, http://www.nytimes.com/2011/05/10/theater/reviews/by-the-way-meet-vera-stark-at-second-stage-review.html (accessed 5 December 2015).

17 Dwyer Murphy, interview with Lynn Nottage, 'History of Omission', *Guernica: A Magazine of Art and Politics*, 1 May 2013, https://www.guernicamag.com/interviews/history-of-omission/ (accessed 8 December 2015).

18 Nelson Pressley, 'Lynn Nottage: A Playwright Made for D.C. Audiences Rarely Sees Her Work Produced Here', *Washington Post*, 12 April 2014, https://www.washingtonpost.com/entertainment/theater_dance/lynn-nottage-a-playwright-made-for-dc-audiences-rarely-sees-her-work-produced-here/2014/04/10/b9663312-bc4e-11e3-96ae-f2c36d2b1245_story.html (accessed 9 December 2015).

19 Murphy, interview with Lynn Nottage.

20 Charles Isherwood, 'Lynn Nottage's "Sweat" Examines Lives Unraveling by the Industry's Demise', *New York Times*, 16 August 2015, http://www.nytimes.com/interactive/2015/07/29/theater/20150802-sweat.html (accessed 9 December 2015).

21 http://www.nytimes.com/2015/08/17/theater/review-lynn-nottages-sweat-examines-lives-unraveling-by-industrys-demise.html (accessed 9 December 2015).

22 Murphy, interview with Lynn Nottage.

23 http://www.playbill.com/article/lynn-nottage-will-pen-stage-adaptation-of-black-orpheus-george-c-wolfe-to-direct-com-323278 (accessed 9 December 2015).

24 Ben Brantley, 'Shredding Egos, One Semicolon at a Time', *New York Times*, 20 November 2011, http://www.nytimes.com/2011/11/21/theater/reviews/seminar-by-theresa-rebeck-with-alan-rickman-review.html (accessed 5 December 2015).

25 Ibid.

26 Claudia La Rocco, 'Sexism Onstage, with a Twist', *New York Times*, 23 December 2011, http://www.nytimes.com/2011/12/24/theater/women-playwrights-and-gender-stereotypes-on-broadway.html (accessed 5 December 2015).

27 Patrick Healy, 'Staging the Politics of Abortion', *New York Times*, 13 April 2011, http://www.nytimes.com/2011/04/14/theater/theresa-rebecks-play-o-beautiful-at-university-of-delaware.html (accessed 5 December 2015).

28 Ibid.

29 Charles Isherwood, 'Stage Kiss, a Sarah Ruhl Comedy, at Playwrights Horizons', *New York Times*, 2 March 2014, http://www.nytimes.com/2014/03/03/theater/stage-kiss-a-sarah-ruhl-comedy-at-playwrights-horizons.html (accessed 25 November 2015).

30 John Lahr, 'Mouth to Mouth: Sarah Ruhl on Attraction and Artifice', *New Yorker*, 30 May 2011, http://www.newyorker.com/magazine/2011/05/30/mouth-to-mouth (accessed 30 November 2015).

31   Ibid.
32   Charles Isherwood, 'A Stamp on the Outside, Intimacy on the Inside: "Dear Elizabeth," a Sarah Ruhl Play', *New York Times*, 10 December 2012, http://www.nytimes.com/2012/12/11/theater/reviews/dear-elizabeth-a-sarah-ruhl-play.html (accessed 1 December 2010).
33   Sarah Ruhl, *Dear Elizabeth: A Play in Letters* (New York: Faber and Faber, 2014), xvi.
34   Isherwood, 'A Stamp on the Outside, Intimacy on the Inside'.
35   Marilyn Stasio, 'Off-Broadway Review: "The Oldest Boy"', *Variety*, 3 November 2014, http://variety.com/2014/legit/reviews/oldest-boy-review-sarah-ruhl-off-broadway-1201346054/ (accessed 29 November 2015).
36   Sarah Ruhl, *100 Essays I Don't Have Time to Write: On Umbrellas and Sword Fight* (New York: Farrar, Straus and Giroux, 2015), 32.
37   Charles Isherwood, 'When Two Beautiful Lives Begin to Unravel', *New York Times*, 4 November 11, http://www.nytimes.com/2011/11/05/theater/reviews/belleville-at-yale-repertory-theater-review.html (accessed 14 December 2015).
38   Hilton Als, 'Real Gone Girl: Young Jean Lee; Identity Plays', *New Yorker*, 3 November 2014, http://www.newyorker.com/magazine/2014/11/03/real-gone-girl (accessed 14 December 2015).

Documents

1   This essay is published in this book for the first time.
2   Rebeck added this reference to the 13 November terror attacks in Paris while editing her interview in December 2015.

BIBLIOGRAPHY

Books on the 2000s

Amis, Martin. *The Second Plane: September 11, 2001–2007*. London: Jonathan Cape, 2008.

Anderson, Chris. *Free: The Future of a Radical Price*. New York: Hyperion, 2009.

Bennett, Jill. *Practical Aesthetics: Events, Affects and Art after 9/11*. London and New York: I.B. Tauris, 2012.

Butler, Judith. *Frames of War: When Is Life Grievable?* London and New York: Verso, 2009.

Footman, Tim. *The Noughties 2000–2009: A Decade that Changed the World*. Richmond: Crimson Publishing, 2009.

Friedman, Thomas L. *The World Is Flat: A Brief History of the Twenty-First Century*, expanded edn. Picador/Farrar, Straus and Giroux, 2007.

Friedman, Thomas L. *Hot, Flat and Crowded: Why We Need a Green Revolution – and How It Can Renew America*. New York: Picador/Farrar, Straus and Giroux, 2008.

Holtzman, David H. *Privacy Lost: How Technology Is Endangering Your Privacy*. Hoboken, NJ: Jossey-Bass, 2006.

Krugman, Paul. *The Return of Depression Economics and the Crisis of 2008*. New York: W. W. Norton, 2008.

McCabe, Aemmon and Terrence McNamee. *Decade*. London: Phaidon Press, 2010.

Nagel, Carol, ed. *American Decades: 2000–2009*. Farmington Hills, MI: Gale Publisher, 2011.

Persky, Stan. *Reading the 21st Century: Books of the Decade, 2000–2009*. Montreal: McGill Queen's University Press, 2012.

Books on American theatre in the 2000s

Arons, Wendy and Theresa J. May, eds. *Readings in Performance and Ecology*. Basingstoke: Palgrave Macmillan, 2012.

Bordman, Gerald and Richard Norton. *American Musical Theatre: A Chronicle*, 4th edn. Oxford: Oxford University Press, 2010.

Bowles, Norma and Daniel-Raymond Nadon. *Staging Social Justice: Collaborating to Create Activist Theatre*, Foreword by Bill Rauch. Carbondale: Southern Illinois University Press, 2013.

Brantley, Ben. *Broadway Musicals: From the Pages of the New York Times*. New York: Harry N. Abrams, 2012.

Cohen-Cruz, Jan. *Engaging Performance: Theatre as Call and Response*. London and New York: Routledge, 2010.

Durham, Leslie Atkins. *Women's Voices on American Stages in the Early Twenty-First Century: Sarah Ruhl and Her Contemporaries*. Basingstoke: Palgrave Macmillan, 2013.

Farfan, Penny and Lesley Ferris, eds. *Contemporary Women Playwrights into the Twenty-First Century*. Basingstoke: Palgrave Macmillan, 2013.

Kolin, Philip C., ed. *Contemporary African American Women Playwrights*. London: Routledge, 2007.

Middeke, Martin, Peter Paul Schnierer, Christopher Innes and Matthew C. Roudané, eds. *The Methuen Drama Guide to Contemporary American Playwrights*. London and New York: Bloomsbury, 2014.

Ozieblo, Barbara and Noelia Hernando-Real, eds. *Performing Gender Violence: Plays by Contemporary American Women Dramatists*. New York: Palgrave Macmillan, 2012.

Parker-Starbuck, Jennifer. *Cyborg Theatre: Corporeal/Technological Intersections in Multimedia Performance*. Basingstoke: Palgrave, 2011.

Patinkin, Sheldon. *'No Legs, No Jokes, No Chance': A History of the American Musical Theatre*. Chicago: Northwestern University Press, 2008.

Spencer, Jenny, ed. *Political and Protest Theatre after 9/11*. New York and London: Routledge, 2012.

Recommended books on American theatre

Aronson, Arnold. *American Avant-Garde Theatre: A History.* New York: Psychology Press, 2000.
Bean, Annemarie. *A Sourcebook of African-American Performance: Plays, People, Movements.* New York: Routledge, 1999.
Bigsby, Christopher. *A Critical Introduction to Twentieth-Century American Drama*, 3 vols. New York: Cambridge University Press, 1985.
Bigsby, Christopher. *Modern American Drama 1945–2000.* New York: Cambridge University Press, 2000.
Block, Geoffrey. *Enchanted Evenings: The Broadway Musical from* Show Boat *to Sondheim.* Oxford: Oxford University Press, 1997.
Brantley, Ben. *The New York Times Book of Broadway: On the Aisle for the Unforgettable Plays of the Last Century,* 1st edn. New York: St Martin's Press, 2001.
Brown-Guillory, Elizabeth. *Their Place on the Stage: Black Women Playwrights in America.* Westport, CT: Praeger, 1990.
Cohen-Cruz, Jan. *Local Acts: Community-Based Performances in the United States.* New Brunswick, NJ, and London: Rutgers University Press, 2005.
Craig, Carolyn Casey. *Women Pulitzer Playwrights: Biographical Profiles and Analyses of the Plays.* Jefferson, NC, and London: McFarland, 2004.
Elam, Harry J. and David Krasner. *African American Performance and Theater History: A Critical Reader.* New York: Oxford University Press, 2001.
Greenfield, Thomas A. *Broadway: An Encyclopedia of Theater and American Culture*, 2 vols. Santa Barbara, CA: Greenwood, 2010.
Harvell, Tony A. *Latin American Dramatists since 1945: A Bio-Bibliographical Guide.* Westport, CT: Praeger, 2003.
Hill, Errol G. and James V. Hatch. *A History of African American Theatre.* Cambridge: Cambridge University Press, 2006.
Houchin, John H. *Censorship of the American Theatre in the Twentieth Century.* Cambridge: Cambridge University Press, 2009.
Kolin, Philip K. and Colby H. Kullman. *Speaking on Stage: Interviews with Contemporary American Playwrights.* Tuscaloosa: University of Alabama Press, 1996.
Krasner, David. *American Drama 1945–2000: An Introduction.* Malden, MA: Blackwell, 2006.

Krasner, David. *A Companion to 20th Century American Drama.* Malden, MA: Blackwell, 2007.
Kuftinec, Sonja. *Staging America: Cornerstone and Community-Based Theater.* Carbondale: Southern Illinois University, 2005.
Leonard, Robert H. and Ann Kilkelly. *Performing Communities: Grassroots Ensemble Theatres Deeply Rooted in Eight U.S. Communities.* Oakland, CA: New Village Press, 2006.
Marsh-Lockett, Carol P., ed. *Black Women Playwrights: Visions on the American Stage.* New York: Psychology Press, 1999.
Most, Andrea. *Theatrical Liberalism: Jews and Popular Entertainment in America.* New York: New York University Press, 2013.
Murphy, Brenda. *The Cambridge Companion to American Women Playwrights.* New York: Cambridge University Press, 1999.
Osborne, Elizabeth A. *Staging the People: Community and Identity in the Federal Theatre Project.* Basingstoke: Palgrave Macmillan, 2011.
Robinson, Marc. *The Other American Drama.* Baltimore, MD: Johns Hopkins University Press, 1997.
Roudané, Matthew Charles. *American Drama since 1960: A Critical History.* New York and London: Twayne Publishers, Prentice Hall International, 1996.
Saxon, Theresa. *American Theatre: History, Context, Form.* Edinburgh: Edinburgh University Press, 2011.
Shailor, Jonathan. *Performing New Lives: Prison Theatre.* London: Jessica Kingsley Publishers, 2011.
Shiach, Don. *American Drama 1900–1990.* Cambridge: Cambridge University Press, 2000.
Stanlake, Christy. *Native American Drama: A Critical Perspective.* Cambridge: Cambridge University Press, 2010.
Williams, Dana A. *Contemporary African American Female Playwrights: An Annotated Biography.* Westport, CT: Greenwood, 1998.
Wilmer, S. E. *Theatre, Society and the Nation: Staging American Identities.* Cambridge: Cambridge University Press, 2008.
Wilmeth, Don B. *The Cambridge Guide to American Theatre.* Cambridge: Cambridge University Press, 2007.
Wilmeth, Don B. and Christopher Bigsby. *The Cambridge History of American Theatre*, 3 vols. Cambridge: Cambridge University Press, 2006.
Young, Harvey. *The Cambridge Companion to African American Theatre.* Cambridge: Cambridge University Press, 2012.

The playwrights

Charles Mee

Plays

Mee, Charles. www.charlesmee.org (accessed 17 March 2016).
Mee, Charles. *History Plays*. Baltimore, MD: Johns Hopkins University Press, 1998.

Recommended books and articles

Berchild, Christopher. 'This Geometry of Memory: SITI and Charles Mee's *Hotel Cassiopeia*', *TheatreForum* 31 (2007): 11–18.
Bryant-Berteil, Sarah. '*The Trojan Women a Love Story*: A Postmodern Semiotics of Tragedy', *Theatre Review International* 25 (1) (2000): 40–52.
Campbell, Peter A. 'Remaking the Chorus: Charles Mee Jr.'s *Orestes 2.0*', *Comparative Drama* 45 (2) (2011): 65–79.
Cummings, Scott T. 'Love Among the Ruins', *American Theatre* 18 (10) (2000): 18–22.
Cummings, Scott T. *Remaking American Theatre: Charles Mee, Anne Bogart and the SITI Company*. Cambridge: Cambridge University Press, 2006.
Hartigan, Karelisa. 'Greek Tragedy Transformed: A. R. Gurney and Charles Mee Rewrite Greek Drama', in *Dramatic Revisions of Myths, Fairy Tales and Legends: Essays on Recent Plays*, ed. Verna A. Foster, 39–49. Jefferson, NC: McFarland, 2012.
Kozinn, Sarah. 'An Invitation to Pillage: Witness Relocation's *Heaven on Earth*', *Drama Review* 56 (2) (2012): 184–90.
Mee, Charles L. *A Nearly Normal Life: A Memoir*. Boston: Little Brown, 1999.
Mee, Erin B. 'Shattered and Fucked Up and Full of Wreckage: The Words and Works of Charles L. Mee', interview, *Drama Review* 46 (3) (2002): 83–104.
Reilly, Kara. 'The Collage Reality (Re)Made: The Postmodern Dramaturgy of Charles L. Mee', *American Drama* 14 (2) (2005): 56–69.
Schlueter, Jennifer. 'Staging Versailles: Charles Mee and the Re-Presentation of History', *Journal of American Drama and Theatre* 17 (3) (2005): 5–23.

Solomon, Alisa. 'Charles L. Mee, Jr.: The Theatre of History', *Performing Arts Journal* 11 (1) (1989): 67–77.
Youker, Timothy. 'Reading Collage Drama as Documentary Drama: Trash Archives and *Dissensus* in Charles L. Mee's Lives of the Artists', *Modern Drama* 58 (2) (2015): 218–37.

Lynn Nottage

Plays

Nottage, Lynn. *Crumbs from the Table of Joy and Other Plays*. New York: Theatre Communications Group, 2003.
Nottage, Lynn. *Intimate Apparel and Fabulation*. New York: Theatre Communications Group, 2006.
Nottage, Lynn. *Ruined*. New York: Theatre Communications Group, 2009.
Nottage, Lynn. *By the Way, Meet Vera Stark*. New York: Theatre Communications Group, 2013.
Nottage, Lynn. *One More River to Cross: A Verbatim Fugue*. New York: Dramatists Play Service, 2015.

Recommended books and articles

Brown, Lenora Inez. 'Dismantling the Box: An Interview with the Playwright', *American Theatre* 18 (6) (2001): 50.
Buckner, Jocelyn L. *A Critical Companion to Lynn Nottage*. London: Routledge, 2016.
Carpenter, Faedra Chatard. 'The Innovation of Inclusion: Dramaturgy in the Mythos of a "Post-Racial Era"', *Review: The Journal of Dramaturgy* 21 (1) (2011): 16–21.
Cruz, Nilo. 'Nilo Cruz & Lynn Nottage', *The Dramatist* (March–April 2010): 20–8.
Dolan, Jill. '*Ruined*, by Lynn Nottage', *Feminist Spectator*, 16 March 2009, http://feministspectator.princeton.edu/2009/03/16/ruined-by-lynn-nottage/ (accessed 17 March 2016).
Fox, Ann M. 'Battles on the Body: Disability, Interpreting Dramatic Literature, and the Case of Lynn Nottage's *Ruined*', *Journal of Literary and Cultural Disability Studies* 5 (1) (2011): 1–15.
Friedman, Sharon. 'The Gendered Terrain in Contemporary Theatre of War by Women', *Theatre Journal* 62 (4) (2010): 593–610.
Katrak, Ketu H. '"Stripping Women of Their Wombs": Active Witnessing

of Performances of Violence', *Theatre Research International* 39 (1) (2014): 31–46.
Myers, Victoria. 'Lynn Nottage: Theatre Artist, Nurturer, Hunter and Gatherer', *The Interval*, the-interval.com (accessed 17 March 2016).
Narbona-Carrión, María Dolores. 'The Role of Female Bonding on the Stage of Violence', in *Performing Gender Violence: Plays by Contemporary American Women Dramatists*, ed. Barbara Ozieblo and Noelia Hernando-Real, 61–78. New York: Palgrave Macmillan, 2012.
Nottage, Lynn. 'Lives Rescued from Silence', *Los Angeles Times*, 13 April 2003, http://articles.latimes.com/2003/apr/13/entertainment/ca-nottage13 (accessed 17 March 2016).
Ozieblo, Barbara. '"Pornography of Violence": Strategies of Representation in Plays by Naomi Wallace, Stefanie Zadravec, and Lynn Nottage', *Journal of American Drama and Theatre* 23 (1) (2011): 67–79.
Shannon, Sandra G. 'An Interview with Lynn Nottage', in *Contemporary African American Women Playwrights*, ed. Philip C. Kolin, 194–201. London: Routledge, 2007a.
Shannon, Sandra G. 'An Intimate Look at the Plays of Lynn Nottage', in *Contemporary African American Women Playwrights*, ed. Philip C. Kolin, 185–93. London: Routledge, 2007b.
Shannon, Sandra G. 'Women Playwrights Who Cross Cultural Borders', in *The Cambridge Companion to African American Theatre*, ed. Harvey Young, 2015–229. Cambridge: Cambridge University Press, 2013.
Yonhee, Chun. 'Territory, Gender, and Body Politics: Lynn Nottage's *Ruined*', *Journal of Modern British and American Drama* 26 (4) (2013): 179–206.
Zygmonski, Aimee. '"Slaves? With Lines?": Trickster Aesthetic and Satirical Strategies in Two Plays by Lynn Nottage', in *Post-Soul Satire: Black Identity after Civil Rights*, ed. Derek C. Maus and James Donahue, 201–13. Jackson: University Press of Mississippi, 2014.

Theresa Rebeck

Plays

Rebeck, Theresa. *Complete Plays 1989–1998*. Hanover, NH: Smith and Kraus, 1999.
Rebeck, Theresa. *Theresa Rebeck Complete Full-Length Plays Volume II: 1999–2007*. Hanover, NH: Smith and Kraus, 2007.
Rebeck, Theresa. *Mauritius*. New York: Samuel French, Inc., 2008.

Rebeck, Theresa. *The Understudy*. New York: Dramatists Play Service, Inc., 2010.
Rebeck, Theresa. *O Beautiful*. Hanover, NH: Smith & Kraus, 2011.
Rebeck, Theresa. *Seminar*. New York: Samuel French, 2012.
Rebeck, Theresa. *Dead Accounts*. New York: Samuel French, 2015.
Rebeck, Theresa and Alexandra Gersten-Vassilaros. *Omnium Gatherum*. New York: Samuel French, Inc., 2003.

Recommended books and articles

Colleran, Jeanne. 'From the Ruins of 9/11: Grief and Terror', in *Theatre and War: Theatrical Responses since 1991*, by Jeanne Colleran, 87–104. New York: Palgrave Macmillan, 2012.
Dolan, Jill. 'Making a Spectacle, Making a Difference', *Theatre Journal* 62 (4) (2010): 561–5.
Hart, Sarah. 'A Date with Theresa Rebeck: An Evening with Her Plays May Make You Laugh or Shudder (or Both) – or See the Human Condition with Fresh Eyes', *American Theatre* 22 (October 2005), http://www.tcg.org/publications/at/Oct05/rebeck.cfm (accessed 10 September 2015).
Kalb, Jonathan. 'American Playwrights on Beckett', *PAJ: A Journal of Performance & Art* 29 (85) (2007): 1–20.
Kurahashi, Yuko. 'A Comparative Analysis of Three Plays on Disasters: *Omnium Gatherum*, *Carried Away on the Crest of a Wave*, and *Radio 311*', in *Text and Presentation 2014*, ed. Graley Herren, 192–208. Jefferson, NC: McFarland, 2014.
McKinley, Jesse. 'Please Pass the Salt (and the Terrorism)', *New York Times*, 21 September 2003, section 2, 5.
Morphos, Evangline. 'Theresa Rebeck', *BOMB Magazine* 97 (Fall 2006): 40–5.
Rebeck, Theresa. *Free Fire Zone: A Playwright's Adventures on the Creative Battlefields of Film, TV, and Theater*. Hanover, NH: Smith and Kraus, 2006.
White, Ann Folino and Dorothy Chansky. 'The Dinner from Hell/The Chef from *le Cordon Bleu*: *Omnium Gatherum* and Food as Status Symbol After 9/11', in *Food and Theatre on the World Stage*, ed. Dorothy Chansky and Ann Folino White, 136–49. New York and London: Routledge, 2015.

Sarah Ruhl

Plays

Ruhl, Sarah. *The Clean House*, in *The Clean House and Other Plays*, 1–116. New York: Theatre Communications Group, 2006a.
Ruhl, Sarah. *Eurydice*, in *The Clean House and Other Plays*, 325–411. New York: Theatre Communications Group, 2006b.
Ruhl, Sarah. *Late: a cowboy song*, in *The Clearn House and Other Plays*, 117–220. New York: Theatre Communications Group, 2006.
Ruhl, Sarah. *Dead Man's Cell Phone*. New York: Theatre Communications Group, 2008.
Ruhl, Sarah. *In the Next Room or the vibrator play*. New York: Theatre Communications Group, 2010.
Ruhl, Sarah. *Passion Play*. New York: Theatre Communications Group, 2011.
Ruhl, Sarah. *Dear Elizabeth: A Play in Letters from Elizabeth Bishop to Robert Lowell and Back Again*. New York: Faber & Faber, 2014a.
Ruhl, Sarah. *Melancholy Play: A Contemporary Farce*. New York: Samuel French, 2014b.
Ruhl, Sarah. *Stage Kiss*. New York: Theatre Communications Group, 2014c.
Ruhl, Sarah, Anton P. Chekhov and Virginia Woolf. *Chekhov's Three Sisters and Woolf's Orlando: Two Renderings for the Stage*. New York: Theatre Communications Group, 2013.

Recommended books and articles

Al-Shamma, James. *Sarah Ruhl: A Critical Study of the Plays*. Jefferson, NC: McFarland, 2011.
Al-Shamma, James. 'Worshiping the Black Sun: Melancholy in Eugene O'Neill and Sarah Ruhl', *Eugene O'Neill Review* 1 (2014): 61–78.
Brodie, Meghan. 'Casting as Queer Dramaturgy: A Case Study of Sarah Ruhl's Adaptation of Virginia Woolf's *Orlando*', *Theatre Topics* 24 (3) (2014): 167–74.
Butler, Thomas. 'Sarah Ruhl's *Dear Elizabeth* and the Mourning of Friends', *Journal of Dramatic Theory and Criticism* 28 (2) (2014): 67–84.
Durham, Leslie Atkins. *Women's Voices on American Stages in the Early Twenty-First Century: Sarah Ruhl and Her Contemporaries*. New York: Palgrave Macmillan, 2013.
Holzapfel, Amy Strahler. 'Auditory Traces: The Medium of the Telephone in Ariana Reines's *Telephone* and Sarah Ruhl's *Dead Man's*

Cell Phone', *Contemporary Theatre Review* 21 (2) (May 2011): 112–25, 253.
Kelly, Katherine E. 'Making the Bones Sing: The Feminist History Play, 1976–2010', *Theatre Journal* 62 (4) (2010): 645–60.
Lahr, John. 'Surreal Life: The Plays of Sarah Ruhl', *New Yorker*, 17 March 2008, http://www.newyorker.com/magazine/2008/03/17/surreal-life (accessed 30 April 2015).
Odendahl-James, Jules. 'Women's Voices on American Stages in the Early Twenty-First Century: Sarah Ruhl and Her Contemporaries', *Theatre Survey* 56 (3) (2015): 435–7.
Svich, Caridad. 'In Conversation with Sarah Ruhl', *The Dramatist* 34 (2) (2002): 36–9.
Tichler, Rosemarie and Barry Jay Kaplan. 'Sarah Ruhl', in *The Playwright at Work*, by Rosemarie Tichler and Barry Jay Kaplan, 74–91. Chicago: Northwestern University Press, 2012.
Vogel, Paula. 'Sarah Ruhl', *BOMB Magazine* 99 (Spring 2007), http://bombmagazine.org/article/2902/sarah-ruhl (accessed 30 April 2015).
Weckwerth, Wendy. 'More Invisible Terrains: Sarah Ruhl, Interviewed by Wendy Weckwerth', *Theater* 34 (2) (2004): 28–35.

Web resources

General

American Theater Web: http://www.americantheaterweb.com.
American Theatre Magazine: http://www.americantheatre.org/.
Digital Librarian: Performing Arts: http://www.digital-librarian.com/performing.html.
Theatre Communications Group: http://www.tcg.org/.
Theatre Reviews Limited: www.theatrereviews.com/.
Theatre Reviews Websites: www.theatremonkey.com/linksreviews.htm.

New York theatre

Broadway Database: Off-Off-Broadway: http://www.broadwayworld.com/off-off-broadway/.
Broadway League: https://www.broadwayleague.com/.
Internet Broadway Database: http://www.ibdb.com/.
New York Times: www.nytimes.com/pages/theater/.
Off-Off-Broadway Review: http://www.oobr.com/.

Playbill New York City Theatre Database: http://www.playbillvault.com/index.html.

Regional/resident/university theatre

American Alliance for Theatre and Education: http://www.aate.com/.
American Association of Community Theatre: http://www.aact.org/.
American Theatre for Higher Education: http://www.athe.org.
DC Theatre Scene: http://dctheatrescene.com/.
LA Theatre Review: http://www.latheatrereview.com/.
University/Resident Theatre Association: http://urta.com/.

INDEX

9/11, 2–4, 24, 28, 43–9, 85, 148, 214–16, 228, 233–4
  Omnium Gatherum, 137, 141, 142–8, 154, 156, 228–9
  post-9/11 culture, 11–12, 29, 35, 45–6, 49, 54, 78, 143, 168
abortion, 47, 60, 133, 159, 192–3
Acheson, Matt, 195
actors, theatre, 67, 126, 141, 153, 175, 185, 192, 199, 201, 225, 232–3
  Davis, Viola, 117–18, 120–1, 127, 214, 215
  double casting, 123–4, 176
  Rickman, Alan, 159, 192
  Understudy, The, 142, 152–5, 225–6
  White, Julie, 139, 153–4, 225
  see also names of specific actors
Actors Theatre of Louisville, 78, 87, 143, 189
  Humana Festival of New American Plays, 48, 80, 87, 94, 98, 100, 104, 111, 157, 189, 198, 229
Adjmi, David, 241
Afghanistan, 3–4, 13–16, 49, 61, 78, 88, 145
African Americans, 8, 10–11, 23–4, 113–14, 121, 135, 189–90, 231
  By the Way, Meet Vera Stark, 189–90
  Davis, Viola, 117–18, 120–1, 127, 214, 215
  Fabulation, or The Re-Education of Undine, 79, 114, 121–6, 130, 133, 190, 212–14
  Intimate Apparel, 113, 114, 116–21, 124–6, 130, 133–4, 211–15
  Obama, Barack, 6–7, 10, 12, 13, 16, 38, 132–3, 214–15, 237
  Rice, Condolezza, 10, 114, 124–5
Akalaitis, Joanne, 200
Akhtar, Ayad, 196
Albee, Edward, 83
American Conservatory Theater, 79
American Repertory Theater, 68, 71, 73, 75, 110
Andersen, Lemon, 77
Antenna Theater, 50–1
Arena Stage, 46, 191
art, 74, 91, 100, 102, 103–4, 110–11, 114, 208, 221
  bobrauschenbergamerica, 98–105, 203, 204
  Cornell, Joseph, 91, 110, 203
  installations, art, 27, 51, 74, 110–11, 190, 203, 217
  Rauschenberg, Robert, 91, 99–100, 103–5, 203

INDEX

surrealism, 56–73, 110, 168, 221, 229
Asian Americans, 8, 11, 84, 231
Atlantic Theater Company, 60
Auburn, David, 83
audiences, 41–2, 50–6, 58, 64–7, 79, 206, 209, 220–1
Austin, Lyn, 200, 203
avant-garde theatre, 68–9, 73–4, 77
Avignon Festival, 197, 205
awards, 26, 10, 23–5
  Tony Awards, 62, 64, 83–5
  see also Pulitzer Prize for Drama

Baker, Annie, 79, 185, 195
Bausch, Pina, 73, 109, 201, 207
Bear, Jessie, 205–6
Bell, Jonathan, 47
Berkeley Repertory Theatre, 75, 94, 167, 178, 194, 256 n.32
Big Love, 94–8, 105, 106, 108, 111, 198, 202
Biguenet, John, 89
Bilodeau, Chantal, 186
Blacks *see* African Americans
blogs, 21, 22, 31, 33, 131, 196, 208
blues, 60, 130, 214
bobrauschenbergamerica, 98–105, 203, 204
Bock, Adam, 80
Bogart, Anne, 92, 163
  collaboration with Charles Mee, 94, 98–9, 104, 109–11, 187, 198–204
  SITI Company, 50, 75, 77, 98–9, 105, 110–11, 187, 200
Bourne, Matthew, 59
Bradley, Scott, 233
Brantley, Ben, 59, 61, 62, 70, 85, 107–8

Nottage reviews, 125–6, 141–2, 190
Rebeck reviews, 145, 150, 151, 192
Brecht, Bertolt, 60, 61, 91–2, 127–9, 131, 180, 209–10, 217
Broadway, 43, 57–72, 75, 138, 142, 149, 151, 165, 185–7, 192
Brooks, Laurie, 65
Builders Association, 56
bullying, 9, 33, 159, 192, 193
Bush, George W., 8, 15, 44, 52, 229
  economic policies, 16, 20, 27, 30
  elections, U.S. presidential, 12, 14, 26, 245–6, 251
  Iraq War, 4, 29, 243, 246
  War on Terror, 4, 13, 26, 28, 38
Butz Norbert Leo, 192
By the Way, Meet Vera Stark, 189–90

Cabnet, Evan, 192
Cage, John, 74, 92, 103
Cameron, Ben, 41–2, 63–4
Campbell-Holt, Adrienne, 225
capitalism, 88, 126, 147–8
Cardenio, 110, 206–7
Castellucci, Romeo, 203
celebrity culture, 30–1, 86, 153
Cherry Lane Theatre, 80
Chicanos, 46, 53–4, 65, 73
children, 47, 60, 64–7, 127–8, 210, 216
  Children's Theatre Company, 64, 66
  Childsplay, 64–5
  Coterie Theatre, 64–5
  Imagination Stage, 64, 66–7

INDEX

Kennedy Center Theater for Young Audiences, 65
Seattle Children's Company, 66–7
see also teenagers
Children's Theatre Company, 64, 66
Childsplay, 64–5
Cho, Julia, 80, 164
Chong, Ping, 68, 77
choreographers, 58, 70, 73, 110–11, 187–9
  Bausch, Pina, 73, 109, 201, 207
  Bourne, Matthew, 59
  Clarke, Martha, 72–3, 92, 93, 201
  Cunningham, Merce, 103
  Dionisio, Gabriel, 73
  Garcia, Anita, 73
  Harris, Rennie, 73
  Safer, Dan, 111, 118–19, 202
  Stroman, Susan, 58, 70
  Tharp, Twyla, 70
Churchill, Caryl, 45, 180, 234, 237
Clarke, Martha, 72–3, 92, 93, 201
classes, economic, 13, 54, 61–2, 122–4, 139–41, 193, 202–3, 216–17, 223, 227
Clean House, The, 161, 163, 171–7, 179
Fabulation, or The Re-Education of Undine, 79, 114, 121–6, 130, 133, 190, 212–14
Intimate Apparel, 113, 114, 116–21, 124–6, 130, 133–4, 211–15
Clean House, The, 161, 163, 171–7, 179
climate change, 1, 11, 21, 24, 186
Coates, George, 56
COIL Festival, 77

collaborations, artistic, 48–50, 52, 54, 56, 62, 68, 71, 79
  Bogart, Anne, 94, 98–9, 104, 109–11, 187, 198–204
  Gersten-Vassilaros, Alexandra, 48–9, 137, 143, 228–9
  Greenblatt, Stephen, 110, 206–7
  Mee, Charles, 92, 94, 98–9, 104–5, 109–11, 187–9, 198–204, 206–7
  Nottage, Lynn, 114, 117, 126, 127, 132, 190–1, 209–10
  Rebeck, Theresa, 48–9, 137, 143, 228–9
  Ruhl, Sarah, 163, 167, 178, 189, 194, 234, 238
  Waters, Les, 92, 94, 98, 105, 109–11, 163, 167, 178, 189, 194, 234, 238
  Whoriskey, Kate, 114, 117, 126, 127, 132, 190–1, 209–10
collages, 91, 100
  bobrauschenbergamerica, 98–105, 203, 204
  plays, 69, 91–2, 99, 110, 188, 203
collectives, theatre, 50–6, 68–9, 77, 81, 164–5, 186
  Antenna Theater, 50–1
  Culture Clash, 46, 48, 54, 78
  Imaginists Theatre Collective, 53–4
  Improv Everywhere, 55
  Lookingglass Theatre Company, 50, 85
  Redmoon Theater, 74
  Sojourn Theatre, 50–1
  Surveillance Camera Players, 54–5
  See also ensemble theatre; experimental theatre
comedians, 22–3, 32, 172
comedy *see* humour

community-based theatre, 50, 54, 218
composers, 60–2, 72, 79–80, 130, 185, 236
  Cage, John, 74, 92, 103
  Gordon, Ricky Ian, 62
  Guettel, Adam, 62
  Hollmann, Mark, 61
  Jones, Elton, 27, 61
  LaChiusa, Michael John, 62
  Sondheim, Stephen, 43
  Tesori, Jeanine, 62
Congo, 114, 116, 127–32, 189, 209–11
Ruined, 80, 83, 114, 116, 127–33, 208–16
Connecticut Repertory Theatre, 63, 193
Cooney, Doug, 65
Cornell, Joseph, 91, 110, 203
Corthron, Kia, 89
Coterie Theatre, 64–5
crime, 9, 10, 192
  drugs, 9, 21–2, 39, 182, 190
  hate crimes, 10–11, 47, 190
  see also rape; sexual abuse
critics *see* reviews, theatre
Cruz, Nilo, 83, 129, 240
Culture Clash, 46, 48, 54, 78
  Montoya, Richard, 46, 48
Cunningham, Merce, 103

Daily Life Everlasting, 111, 188, 202
Daldry, Stephen, 61
dance, 59, 62, 70–4, 7, 94, 101, 104–5, 109, 130–1, 187–9
  see also choreographers
dance-theatre, 48, 70, 72–4, 93, 105, 111–12, 200, 203, 207–8
Davis, Viola, 117–18, 120–1, 127, 214, 215

Dead Accounts, 159, 191–2
Dead Man's Cell Phone, 161, 163
deaf, the, 65, 67, 111, 185
Deaf West Theater, 185
Dear Elizabeth, 199
death, 84–6, 89, 169, 174–6, 241
Delbono, Pippo, 203, 205
design, theatre, 63, 124, 144, 225, 233–4
designers, theatre
  Acheson, Matt, 195
  Bradley, Scott, 233
  Dodge, Alexander, 225
  McLane, Derek, 124, 132
  Rockwell, David, 144
  Saunders, Matt, 68
  Schuette, James, 100
  Spangler, Walt, 124
  Steinmeyer, Jim, 59
  Twist, Basil, 71–2, 187
  see also Taymor, Julie
Dickens, Charles, 122, 158, 160, 221, 222, 226
digital media, 2, 22, 25, 31–8, 50–2, 56, 87, 196 *see also* social media; technology
Dionisio, Gabriel, 73
directors, 75, 92, 94, 109–10, 162–4, 184, 188
  Landau, Tina, 62, 63, 92, 94, 110, 111
  Papp, Joe, 93, 199–200
  Sullivan, Dan, 113, 118, 215
  Whoriskey, Kate, 114, 117, 126, 127, 132, 190–1, 209–10
  Woodruff, Robert, 92, 94, 200–1
  see also names of specific directors
disabilities, 65, 67, 119, 130–1
  deaf, 65, 67, 111, 185

Disney stage adaptations, 57, 59, 222
diversity, 54, 65, 67, 75, 78, 134, 165, 185, 188, 218
documentaries, 86, 89, 141, 180, 190
Dodge, Alexander, 225
Doyle, John, 75
drugs, 9, 21–2, 39, 182, 190

economy, 4–7, 18, 21, 27, 54, 61, 62, 65
  Bush, George W., 16, 20, 27, 30
  capitalism, 88, 126, 147–8
  Clean House, The, 161, 163, 171–7, 179
  effect on theatre, 57, 69, 81–2, 87, 186, 234–5
  Fabulation, or The Re-Education of Undine, 79, 114, 121–6, 130, 133, 190, 212–14
  frauds, 5–6, 9, 61
  Intimate Apparel, 113, 114, 116–21, 124–6, 130, 133–4, 211–15
  legislation, 6–7, 13, 16
  Sweat, 190–1, 203, 216–18
  unemployment, 1, 6, 11, 20, 190–1
Edinburgh Festival, 44
Ehn, Erik, 71, 211
elections, U.S. presidential, 12, 15–16, 21, 32, 132, 214–15, 231–2, 237
  2000, 12, 14, 26, 245–6, 251
ensembles, theatre, 50, 53–4, 73–4, 77–8, 92, 186, 188
  SITI Company, 50, 75, 77, 98–9, 105, 110–11, 187, 200
  see also collectives, theatre; experimental theatre

Ensler, Eve, 49, 83, 86, 180
environment, 11–12, 27, 88–9, 186
  climate change, 1, 11, 21, 24, 186
  Hurricane Katrina, 1, 11, 26–7, 86, 88–9
Eterniday, 111, 188
ethnicity, 10–11, 83–4, 196
  Asian Americans, 8, 11, 84, 231
  Chicanos, 46, 53–4, 65, 73
  Hispanics, 8, 10–11, 47, 76, 227
  Lationa/os, 65, 84, 122, 132, 231
  see also African Americans
Eugene O'Neill Theater Center, 76, 79–80
Euripides, 75, 92, 94, 201, 202
Eurydice, 162–71, 174, 176–7, 183, 233–4, 240
Eustis, Oskar, 71, 79
experimental theatre, 50–1, 69, 72–4, 77, 84, 111
  Builders Association, 56
  Flaneur Productions, 74
  Mabou Mines, 50, 68–9, 72, 77
  mad dog, 73–4
  Performance Works, 56
  Pig Iron Theatre Company, 74, 78
  Rude Mechanicals, 50, 95
  SITI Company, 50, 75, 77, 98–9, 105, 110–11, 187, 200
  Tectonic Theater Project, 50, 52–3
  Theatre Movement Bazaar, 74
  Witness Relocation, 111, 188
  Wooster Group, 50, 56, 68–9
  see also collectives, theatre; ensembles, theatre

Eyre, Richard, 59
Eyring, Teresa, 186

Fabulation, or The Re-Education of Undine, 79, 114, 121–6, 130, 133, 190, 212–14
Facebook, 27, 34, 36
fashion, 21, 27, 30–1, 32
feminism, 81, 87, 155–6, 165, 213–14
  Clean House, The, 161, 163, 171–7, 179
  Eurydice, 162–71, 174, 176–7, 183, 233–4, 240
  In the Next Room or the vibrator play, 161, 177–83, 233–4, 236, 241
  Spike Heels, 139–40, 158, 229–30
festivals, 44, 49, 61, 76–8, 80–1, 186–8, 197, 205
  Avignon Festival, 197, 205
  COIL Festival, 77
  Edinburgh Festival, 44
  Humana Festival of New American Plays, 48, 80, 87, 94, 98, 100, 104, 111, 157, 189, 198, 229
  Ignition Festival, 80
  New York International Fringe Festival, 61, 77
  Next Wave Festival, 76
  Under the Radar Festival, 77–8, 188
film, 10, 23–5, 29, 31, 44, 47, 57–8, 87, 221
Fisher, Jeanne Donovan, 198
Fisher, Richard, 92, 198
Flamboyán Theater, 45
Flaneur Productions, 74
Flea Theater, 44, 49
Foreman, Richard, 56

Fornes, Maria Irene, 162–4, 170, 180
frauds, 5–6, 9, 61
Frayn, Michael, 85

Garcia, Anita, 73
gender bias, 9–10, 81–4, 156, 165, 180–2, 192–3
gender identity, 10, 54, 59–60, 82, 184–5, 196
  lesbians, 10, 17, 26, 86, 106, 180
  see also LGBTQ; sexual identity
Gerber, Tony, 119, 127, 190
Gersten-Vassilaros, Alexandra, 48–9, 137, 143, 228–9
  Omnium Gatherum, 137, 141, 142–8, 154, 156, 228–9
Gilman, Rebecca, 80, 83
Gionfriddo, Gina, 87, 196
globalism, 1–2, 4, 7, 11, 13, 27, 29, 31, 42
Glory of the World, 111, 189
Gold, Sam, 192
Gómez-Peña, Guillermo, 74
González, José Cruz, 65, 84, 164
Goodman Theatre, 80, 83, 94, 127, 190, 193–4, 234
Goold, Rupert, 49, 191
Gordon, Ricky Ian, 62
Gore, Al, 12, 14, 24, 232
grants, 69, 159, 197, 206, 222, 228
Greek plays, 45, 49, 75, 91–2, 94, 162, 201, 207, 223
  Big Love, 94–8, 106, 108, 111, 198, 202
  Euripides, 75, 92, 94, 201, 202
  Eurydice, 162–71, 174, 176–7, 183, 233–4, 240
  Iphigenia 2.0, 110, 202, 208
  Orestes 2.0, 94, 99, 102–3, 200–1, 208
Greenberg, Richard, 83

Greenblatt, Stephen, 110, 206–7
grief, 46, 166, 168–9, 171, 174–6
   see also death; loss
Grote, Jason, 80
Guettel, Adam, 62
Guggenheim Foundation, 116, 127, 211
Guirgis, Stephen Adly, 196
Guirira, Danai, 185–6

Hamburger, Annie, 203–4
Harris, Rennie, 73
hate crimes, 10–11, 47, 190
Heaven on Earth, 111, 188
Herzog, Amy, 195
hip-hop, 25, 60, 63, 72–3, 77, 214
Hispanics, 8, 10–11, 47, 76, 227
Hollmann, Mark, 61
Holmes, Katie, 30, 192
homosexuals *see* gender bias; gender identity; lesbians; LGBTQ; sexual identity
Horovitz, Israel, 47, 160
Houghton, Jim, 205
housing, 6–7, 16, 19–20, 65, 100
Hove, Ivo van, 109, 185
Hudes, Quiara Alegría, 60, 196
Humana Festival of New American Plays, 48, 80, 87, 94, 98, 100, 104, 111, 157, 189, 198, 229
humour, 46, 174–6, 194
   comedians, 22–3, 32, 172
   Fabulation, or The Re-Education of Undine, 79, 114, 121–6, 130, 133, 190, 212–14
   musical comedy, 57–8, 61, 201
   romantic comedies, 62, 110, 206–7
   satire, 46, 54, 61–2, 143, 146, 185, 192
   Wintertime, 105–8, 199, 202–4

Hunter, Samuel D., 196
Hurricane Katrina, 1, 11, 26–7, 86, 88–9

Ignition Festival, 80
Imagination Stage, 64, 66–7
Imaginists Theatre Collective, 53–4
immersive theatre, 49–50, 66–7, 74–5, 188
Improv Everywhere, 55
In the Next Room or the vibrator play, 161, 177–83, 233–4, 236, 241
installations, art, 27, 51, 74, 110–11, 190, 203, 217
interactive theatre, 50–6, 66, 67, 74, 75, 190
Internet, the *see* World Wide Web
Intimate Apparel, 113, 114, 116–21, 124–6, 130, 133–4, 211–15
Iphigenia 2.0, 110, 202, 208
iPods, 19, 25, 32, 36, 55–6
Iraq, 3–4, 12–16, 21, 24, 49, 61, 145, 208, 229, 232
Isherwood, Charles, 60, 133, 145, 167–9, 173, 179, 191, 194, 233

Jacobs-Jenkins, Branden, 196, 237
Jones, Elton, 27, 61
Jones, Rolin, 87
Joseph, Rajiv, 196
Jucha, Brian, 48
jukebox musical, 57, 58–9, 248 n.48
Jules, Jenny, 126

Kafka, Franz, 124, 152–5, 225–6
Kane, Honour, 48
Kaufman, Moisés, 52–3, 107
Kennedy Center Theater for Young Audiences, 65

Kling, Kevin, 67
Kotis, Greg, 61
Kron, Lisa, 86, 237
Kushner, Tony, 45, 49, 62, 164

La MaMa, 44, 79, 111, 186–7, 188, 202
LaBute, Neil, 46–7, 86
LaChiusa, Michael John, 62
Lahr, John, 143, 147, 170, 178–9, 194
Landau, Tina, 62, 63, 92, 94, 110, 111
language, 53–4, 65, 84, 118–19, 140, 195–6, 210–11, 227
  Ruhl, Sarah, 162, 166, 169, 175, 194, 227, 232–3
Lationa/os, 65, 84, 122, 132, 231
Lauwers, Jan, 109
Lee, Young Jean, 81–2, 19
legislation, 6–7, 8, 10, 12–14, 16, 38
Lepage, Robert, 44
lesbians, 10, 17, 26, 86, 106, 180
Letts, Tracy, 84–5, 223
Lewis, E. M., 89
LGBTQ (lesbian, gay, bisexual, transgender and queer), 10, 31, 52–3, 65–6, 82–3
  lesbians, 10, 17, 26, 86, 106, 180
  marriage, same-sex, 8, 10, 17
Lincoln Center Theater, 53, 62, 63, 69, 75–7, 111, 172, 195
Lindsay-Abaire, David, 84
Linklater, Hamish, 225
Lookingglass Theatre Company, 50, 85
Lopez, Matthew, 196
loss, 46, 47, 84–5, 89, 166–9, 171, 174–6, 233–4, 241

Mabou Mines, 50, 68–9, 72, 77

Mac, Taylor, 185
MacArthur Foundation, 116, 161, 219, 238
mad dog, 73–4
Magic Theatre, 80, 105
magical realism, 162–4, 173, 175–6, 178, 183
  Clean House, The, 161, 163, 171–7, 179
  Eurydice, 162–71, 174, 176–7, 183, 233–4, 240
mainstream theatre, 68–78, 105, 183, 186, 193
Malpede, Karen, 186
Manhattan Theatre Club, 80, 127, 137
Margolin, Deb, 86–7
Mark Taper Forum, 80, 159, 192, 200
marriage, 8, 10, 17, 84, 95, 98, 130–1, 178, 181–2
  weddings, 32, 96–8, 117, 166, 171
Matlin, Marlee, 65
Mauritius, 137, 142, 148–51, 153, 157, 229–30
May, Theresa, 186
Mayer, Michael, 225
McBurney, Simon, 75
McCarter Theatre, 43, 105, 153, 158
McCauley, Robbie, 86–7
McLane, Derek, 124, 132
mediated culture, 55, 56, 87, 88
medical issues, 3, 19, 38–9, 60–1, 86–7, 107, 192
Mee, Charles
  Big Love, 94–8, 106, 108, 111, 198, 202
  bobrauschenbergamerica, 98–105, 203, 204
  Cardenio, 110, 206–7
  collaboration with Anne

Bogart, 94, 98–9, 104, 109–11, 187, 198–204
 collaboration with Dan Safer, 111, 118–19, 202
 collaboration with Les Waters, 92, 94, 98, 105, 109–11, 189
 collaboration with Stephen Greenblatt, 110, 206–7
 Daily Life Everlasting, 111, 188, 202
 Eterniday, 111, 188
 family, 188, 199, 205–6
 Fisher, Jeanne Donovan, 198
 Fisher, Richard, 92, 198
 Glory of the World, 111, 189
 Greek plays, 94, 110, 201, 207
 Greenblatt, Stephen, 110, 206–7
 Heaven on Earth, 111, 188
 Hotel Cassiopeia, 110, 203
 Iphigenia 2.0, 110, 202, 208
 Orestes 2.0, 94, 99, 102–3, 200–1, 208
 Pool Party, 188
 Shakespeare, 94, 106, 110, 201, 206–7
 Trojan Women, 94, 202
 Wintertime, 105–8, 199, 202–4
Mee, Erin N., 188, 205–6
Melancholy Play, 161, 165, 235–6
melodrama, 117–18, 158, 221–3, 227
Miller, Arthur, 49, 134, 185, 222–3, 225
Miranda, Lin-Manuel, 60, 185
monologues, 44, 47, 93, 96, 99, 101–2, 133, 154, 172, 176, 216
Montello, Joe, 58
Moraga, Cherríe, 164
motherhood, 116, 127–9, 213, 235–9

multiculturalism, 42, 65, 74, 76–77, 119, 121, 187, 218
multimedia, 27, 33, 47, 69–71, 77, 89, 190
Murray, Bill, 44
music, 22, 26, 63, 72, 129–30
 blues, 60, 130, 214
 composers, 61–2, 72, 79–80, 130, 236
 hip-hop, 25, 60, 63, 72–3, 77, 214
 musicians, 25–7, 30, 61
 rock and roll, 25–6, 51, 60
 YouTube, 25, 34, 36, 55
musical comedy, 57–8, 61, 201
musical theatre, 57–63, 72, 79–80
 jukebox musical, 57, 58–9, 248 n.48
 musicians, 25–7, 30, 61
MySpace, 23, 34, 36

national security, 3–4, 12–13, 47, 158
naturalism, 162, 194, 233
Neilsen, Kristine, 225
Nelson, Anne, 44
new play development, 78–81, 93, 157, 227–8, 235
 Humana Festival of New American Plays, 48, 80, 87, 94, 98, 100, 104, 111, 157, 189, 198, 229
New Victory Theater, 73
New York International Fringe Festival, 61, 77
New York Theatre Workshop, 45
newspapers, 2, 31–3, 85, 98, 126, 230 *see also* reviewers, theatre
Next Wave Festival, 76
Nixon, Richard, 93, 204
Norman, Marsha, 81–2
Norris, Bruce, 196

not-for-profit theatres, 63, 69, 81
  Theatre Communication
    Group (TCG), 41, 76, 186,
    245 n.1
Nottage, Lynn
  By The Way, Meet Vera Stark,
    189–90
  *Fabulation, or The
    Re-Education of Undine*,
    79, 114, 121–6, 130, 133,
    190, 212–14
  Intimate Apparel, 113, 114,
    116–21, 124–6, 130,
    133–4, 211–15
  Pulitzer Prize for Drama, 80,
    116, 127, 131–2
  Ruined, 80, 83, 114, 116,
    127–33, 208–16
  Sweat, 190–1, 203, 216–18
  Whoriskey, Kate, 114, 117, 126,
    127, 132, 190–1, 209–10

O Beautiful, 159, 191–3
Obama, Barack, 6–7, 10, 12, 13,
  16, 38, 132–3, 214–15, 237
O'Brian, Jack, 57, 192
Off-Broadway theatre, 44, 46, 60,
  63, 71, 73, 185, 193
  Atlantic Theater Company, 60
  Cherry Lane Theatre, 80
  Magic Theatre, 80, 105
  Manhattan Theatre Club, 80,
    127, 137
  New Victory Theater, 73
  Playwrights Horizons, 46,
    78–9, 83, 122, 155–6, 185
  Second Stage Theatre, 63, 85,
    86, 105, 107, 139–41, 157,
    167, 190
  Signature Theatre Company,
    110, 185
  Vineyard Theatre, 44, 58, 63,
    79

Oldest Boy, The, 195, 233, 240–1
Omnium Gatherum, 137, 141,
  142–8, 154, 156, 228–9
Orestes 2.0, 94, 99, 102–3,
  200–1, 208
organizations, theatre, 43, 53, 57,
  64–6, 69, 77–8, 88, 186
  Theatre Communication
    Group (TCG), 41, 76, 186,
    245 n.1

Parks, Suzan-Lori, 83, 135, 196
performance art, 44, 72–4, 77,
  86–7, 201
performance artists
  Gómez-Peña, Guillermo, 74
  Kron, Lisa, 86, 237
  Margolin, Deb, 86–7
  McCauley, Robbie, 86–7
  Reno, 44
  Shaw, Peggy, 86–7
  Smith, Anna Deavere, 86
  Torres-Tama, José, 89
Performance Works, 56
Pig Iron Theatre Company, 74, 78
Platel, Alain, 109, 197, 203
Playwrights, 47–9, 64–5, 71, 80–9
  Churchill, Caryl, 45, 180, 234,
    237
  emerging, 47, 60, 75, 78–81,
    164, 183–4
  Gersten-Vassilaros, Alexandra,
    48–9, 137, 143
  Miller, Arthur, 49, 134, 185,
    222–3, 225
  see also Nottage, Lynn; Mee,
    Charles; Rebeck, Theresa;
    Ruhl, Sarah; *and names of
    specific playwrights*
Playwrights Horizons, 46, 78–9,
  83, 122, 155–6, 185
politics, 2, 12, 14–15, 141–2,
  146–7, 232, 239

Gore, Al, 12, 14, 24, 232
Obama, Barack, 6–7, 10, 12, 13, 16, 38, 132–3, 214–15, 237
Tea Party, 2, 13, 16, 193
see also Bush, George W.; elections, U.S. presidential
Poor Behavior, 139, 159, 191–2
popular culture, 72–3
celebrity culture, 30–1, 86, 153
comedians, 22–3, 32, 172
fashion, 21, 27, 30–1, 32
see also music; social media
presidents, U.S., 142
Nixon, Richard, 93, 204
Obama, Barack, 6–7, 10, 12, 13, 16, 38, 132–3, 214–15, 237
see also Bush, George W.; elections, U.S. presidential
P.S. 122, 77, 251 n.95
Public Theater, 49, 62, 63, 69, 77, 79, 84, 86, 143, 186, 188, 199
Pulitzer Prize for Drama, 61, 84–5, 127
Nottage, Lynn, 80, 116, 127, 131–2
Rebeck, Theresa, 137, 138, 142, 227–8
Ruhl, Sarah, 161, 173, 179
puppetry, 54, 58, 66, 68–9, 70–2, 74–5, 185–7, 195
Taymor, Julie, 59, 70–2, 187
Twist, Basil, 71–2, 187

race, 8, 10–11, 59–60, 83–4, 115, 189, 191, 217
Asian Americans, 8, 11, 84, 231
see also African Americans; ethnicity; racism
racism, 10–11, 41, 46, 60, 65, 126, 189–90, 196, 230–1

radio, 32–3, 50–1, 74
rape, 97, 182–3, 193
Ruined, 80, 83, 114, 116, 127–33, 208–16
Rapp, Adam, 87
Rauschenberg, Robert, 91, 99–100, 103–5, 203
realism, 131, 150–1, 162, 195–6, 237–8
Rebeck, Theresa
Ben Brantley reviews, 145, 150, 151, 192
Dead Accounts, 159, 191–2
Gersten-Vassilaros, Alexandra, 48–9, 137, 143, 228–9
Mauritius, 137, 142, 148–51, 153, 157
O Beautiful, 159, 191–3
Omnium Gatherum, 137, 141, 142–8, 154, 156, 228–9
Poor Behavior, 139, 159, 191–2
Pulitzer Prize for Drama, 137, 138, 142, 227–8
Seminar, 159, 191–3
Spike Heels, 139–40, 158, 229–30
television work, 137–9, 141, 159, 191, 230–1
Understudy, The, 142, 152–5, 225–6
Zealot, 159, 191–2
Redmoon Theater, 74
regional theatres, 64–4, 70–1, 77, 79–80, 95, 105, 164–5, 183, 193, 234–5, 283
American Conservatory Theater, 79
American Repertory Theater, 68, 71, 73, 75, 110
Arena Stage, 46, 191
Berkeley Repertory Theatre, 75, 94, 167, 178, 194, 256 n.32

Connecticut Repertory
 Theatre, 63, 193
Goodman Theatre, 80, 83, 94,
 127, 190, 193–4, 234
Mark Taper Forum, 80, 159,
 192, 200
McCarter Theatre, 43, 105,
 153, 158
San Jose Repertory Theatre,
 105, 114
Steppenwolf Theatre, 63,
 71–2, 79–80, 143
Wilma Theater, 95, 105, 234
Woolly Mammoth, 46, 79–80,
 95, 269 n.4
Yale Repertory Theatre, 80,
 161, 167–8, 172, 194
see also Actors Theatre of
 Louisville
religion, 2, 11, 28, 85, 121, 142,
 193, 240–2
reviews, theatre, 44–5, 98, 126,
 145, 149–54, 173, 219–21,
 233
 Isherwood, Charles, 60, 133,
  145, 167–9, 173, 179, 191,
  194, 233
 Variety, 107, 118, 132, 151,
  157, 173
 see also Brantley, Ben
revivals, 57, 75, 89, 140–1, 154,
 185
Rice, Condolezza, 10, 114, 124–5
Rickman, Alan, 159, 192
Rimmer, David, 44–5
Rivera, José, 164
Robbins, Tim, 44
rock and roll, 25–6, 51, 60
Rockwell, David, 144
Rogers, Reg, 225
romantic comedies, 62, 110,
 206–7
 Wintertime, 105–8, 199, 202–4

Roundabout Theatre, 43, 69, 113,
 120, 192
Rude Mechanicals, 50, 95
Ruhl, Sarah
 Clean House, The, 161, 163,
  171–7, 179
 collaboration with Les Waters,
  163, 167, 178, 189, 194,
  234, 238
 Dead Man's Cell Phone, 161,
  163
 Dear Elizabeth, 199
 Eurydice, 162–71, 174, 176–7,
  183, 233–4, 240
 *In the Next Room or the
  vibrator play*, 161, 177–83,
  233–4, 236, 241
 language, 162, 166, 169, 175,
  194, 227, 232–3
 Melancholy Play, 161, 165,
  235–6
 Oldest Boy, The, 195, 233,
  240–1
 Pulitzer Prize for Drama, 161,
  173, 179
 Stage Kiss, 193–4, 238–9, 241
Ruined, 80, 83, 114, 116,
 127–33, 208–16
Russell, Mark, 77, 251 n.95

Saar, David, 65
Safer, Dan, 111, 118–19, 202
San Jose Repertory Theatre, 105,
 114
Sanchez, Edwin, 47
Sarandon, Susan, 44
satire, 46, 54, 61–2, 143, 146,
 185, 192
Saunders, Matt, 68
Schreiber, Liev, 46
Schuette, James, 100
Schwartz, Jenny, 79
Seattle Children's Company, 66–7

Second Stage Theatre, 63, 85, 86, 105, 107, 139–41, 157, 167, 190
Sellars, Peter, 49, 75, 221
Seminar, 159, 191–3
sexual abuse, 85, 97, 99, 139–42, 182–3, 193
  Ruined, 80, 83, 114, 116, 127–33, 208–16
sexual identity, 10, 21, 31, 41, 54, 59–60, 65, 82–3
  lesbians, 10, 17, 26, 86, 106, 180
sexuality, 58, 59–60, 65, 130, 192–4
  In the Next Room or the vibrator play, 161, 177–83, 233–4, 236, 241
Shakespeare, 43, 73, 78, 92, 221–3
  Mee, Charles, 94, 106, 110, 201, 206–7
Shanley, John Patrick, 85
Shaw, Peggy, 86–7
Shawn, Wallace, 199
Sherman, Marc, 47
Shinn, Christopher, 44, 49, 85
Signature Theatre Company, 110, 185
  Houghton, Jim, 205
site-specific work, 27, 50–6, 74, 186, 203–4
SITI Company, 50, 75, 77, 98–9, 105, 110–11, 187, 200
  See also Bogart, Anne
Smith, Anna Deavere, 86
social media
  blogs, 21, 22, 31, 33, 131, 196, 208
  Facebook, 27, 34, 36
  MySpace, 23, 34, 36
  Twitter, 21, 29, 33, 34, 37, 53
Sojourn Theatre, 50–1
Son, Diana, 84

Sondheim, Stephen, 43
Spangler, Walt, 124
Spike Heels, 139–40, 158, 229–30
stage directions, 117, 163, 164, 176, 188–9, 240
Stage Kiss, 193–4, 238–9, 241
Steinmeyer, Jim, 59
Steppenwolf Theatre, 63, 71–2, 79–80, 143
stereotypes, 23, 31, 46, 54, 61, 83, 86, 148, 189
storytelling, 67, 70, 72, 78, 87, 164, 183, 185, 223, 224, 226–7
suicide, 60, 107, 192
Sullivan, Dan, 113, 118, 215
surrealism, 56, 73, 110, 168, 221, 229
Surveillance Camera Players, 54–5
Svich, Caridad, 48, 80, 83–4, 88, 166, 170
Sweat, 190–1, 203, 216–18

Taichman, Rebecca, 195, 225, 237
Taymor, Julie, 59, 70–2, 187
Tea Party, 2, 13, 16, 193
technology, 4–5, 19, 22, 23, 27, 34–8, 196
  iPods, 19, 25, 32, 36, 55–6
  video games, 23, 34, 35, 37, 51, 53
  see also social media
Tectonic Theater Project, 50, 52–3
teenagers, 17, 60, 65, 159, 192, 193
television, 2, 26, 31–2, 87, 159, 226, 264–5 n.71
  Rebeck, Theresa, 137–9, 139, 141, 159, 191, 230–1
terrorism, 1–4, 14–16, 146
  national security, 3–4, 12–13, 47, 158
Tesori, Jeanine, 62

Theatre Communication Group
(TCG), 41, 76, 186, 245 n.1
Theatre Movement Bazaar, 74
Thebus, Jessica, 193–4, 234
Thompson, Judith, 83
Tony Awards, 62, 64, 83–5
Torres-Tama, José, 89
torture, 15, 49, 83, 127
  Ruined, 80, 83, 114, 116,
    127–33, 208–16
  Trojan Women, 94, 202
Twist, Basil, 71–2, 187
Twitter, 21, 29, 33, 34, 37, 53

Under the Radar Festival, 77–8,
  188
Understudy, The, 142, 152–5,
  225–6
unemployment, 1, 6, 11, 20,
  190–1
university theatre, 85, 105, 114,
  139, 159, 179, 181, 193, 283
  Yale Repertory Theatre, 80,
    161, 167–8, 172, 194

Variety, 107, 118, 132, 151, 157,
  173
video games, 23, 34, 35, 37, 51, 53
Vietnam, 49, 93, 198, 204, 208
Vineyard Theatre, 44, 58, 63, 79
violence, 9, 13, 24, 45, 96–8,
  103, 106, 158, 237 *see also*
  sexual abuse; terrorism; war
Vogel, Paula, 71, 79, 161–5, 183

Waltz, Sasha, 109
war
  Afghanistan, 3–4, 13–16, 49,
    61, 78, 88, 145
  Iraq, 3–4, 12–16, 21, 24, 49,
    61, 145, 208, 229, 232
  Vietnam, 49, 93, 198, 204, 208
  War on Terror, 4, 13, 26, 28, 38
Washburn, Anne, 81, 237

Waters, Les, 75
  collaboration with Charles Mee,
    92, 94, 98, 105, 109–11, 189
  collaboration with Sarah Ruhl,
    163, 167, 178, 189, 194,
    234, 238
Weaver, Sigourney, 44
weddings, 32, 96–8, 117, 166, 171
Weems, Marianne, 56
Weidman, John, 70
Welch, Christopher Evan, 225
Wharton, Edith, 118, 125, 275
  n.15, 257–58 n.16 *see
  also Fabulation, or The
  Re-Education of Undine*
White, Julie, 139, 153–4, 225
Whitman, Walt, 103, 122, 187
Whoriskey, Kate, 114, 117, 126,
  127, 132, 190–1, 209–10
Wilma Theater, 94, 105, 234
Wilson, Robert, 73, 76, 158, 221,
  Wintertime, 105–8, 199, 202–4
Witness Relocation, 111, 188
Wolfe, George C., 62, 191
Women's Project Theater, 80, 194
Woodruff, Robert, 92, 94, 200–1
Woolly Mammoth, 46, 79–80, 95,
  269 n.4
Wooster Group, 50, 56, 68–9
workshops, 52, 63, 93, 99, 139,
  143, 158, 160, 220
World Wide Web, 34–5, 48, 282–3
YouTube, 25, 34, 36, 55
  see also social media
Wright, Craig, 46
Wright, Doug, 79, 82

Yale Repertory Theatre, 80, 161,
  167–8, 172, 194
YouTube, 25, 34, 36, 55

Zealot, 159, 191–2
Zimmerman, Mary, 85
Zizka, Blanka, 234